Qualitative Methods in Social Research

Qualitative Methods in Social Research

Kristin G. Esterberg

University of Massachusetts–Lowell

Boston   Burr Ridge, IL   Dubuque, IA   Madison, WI   New York
San Francisco   St. Louis   Bangkok   Bogotá   Caracas   Kuala Lumpur
Lisbon   London   Madrid   Mexico City   Milan   Montreal   New Delhi
Santiago   Seoul   Singapore   Sydney   Taipei   Toronto

McGraw-Hill Higher Education

A Division of The McGraw-Hill Companies

9 10 QSR QSR 0 9

Library of Congress Cataloging-in-Publication Data

Esterberg, Kristin G.
    Qualitative methods in social research / Kristin G. Esterberg.
        p.   cm.
    Includes bibliographical references and index.
    ISBN 0-7674-1560-4
    1. Social sciences—Research—Methodology. 2. Qualitative research.   I. Title.

H62 .E747 2001
300′.7′2—dc21

                                                                        2001032991

Sponsoring editor, Serina Beauparlant; production editor, Holly Paulsen; manuscript editor, Tom Briggs; design manager, Violeta Diaz; art editor, Rennie Evans; text designer, Glenda King; cover designer, Laurie Anderson; manufacturing manager, Randy Hurst. The text was set in 10/13 Berling by TBH Typecast, and printed on 50# Williamsburg Offset by R. R. Donnelley & Sons Company.

Credits

Page 186 reprinted from *Journal of Aging Studies*, vol. 13, Brittina Becker, "Narratives of Pain in Later Life and Conventions of Storytelling," pp. 73–87. Copyright © 1999 Elsevier Science. With permission from Elsevier Science.
Page 187 from Philip Smith, *Qualitative Inquiry* 5: 244–261. Copyright © 1999 by Sage Publications. Reprinted by permission of Sage Publications, Inc.
Page 208 from Theresa Montini, *Gender and Society*, pp. 9–23. Copyright © 1996 by Sage Publications. Reprinted by permission of Sage Publications, Inc.
Pages 221–233 ASA Code of Ethics. Used with permission of the American Sociological Association.

www.mhhe.com

Contents

CHAPTER 10   Writing About Research   199

Preface

Over the past year, I've had more than a few conversations that begin something like this: "What are you working on these days?" someone asks. "A book," I answer. "What's it about?" they ask. "Qualitative research methods," I respond. "Oh." End of conversation.

This book is aimed at those people who end the conversation there.

Those of us who are involved in qualitative research tend to find it endlessly engaging. I like teaching qualitative research methods perhaps more than any other subject. At the beginning of the semester, my students usually don't understand my attitude. They think I'm just a little odd but tend to be tolerant of my peculiarities. At least I'm enthusiastic. By the end of the semester, I usually have scored a few converts, who decide that investigating the social world is one of the most interesting things they could do.

This odd clash between my enthusiasm for the subject and students' preconceived notions about methods classes has pushed me to develop more creative strategies for teaching than I might otherwise have done. This book, then, is the product of that mismatch. I wrote this book because I was frustrated with the available texts on qualitative methods. I wanted to provide a broad overview of qualitative methodologies, including newer, more innovative approaches to textual analysis, and I wanted to do so in a way that would provide a more theoretically informed approach. Other texts focused exclusively on ethnography and observation, took too much of a "cookbook" approach to methods, or didn't discuss the current debates over qualitative methodologies. Much as I love to read cookbooks, I didn't want to write one. Still other texts, including a number of excellent texts for graduate students and professionals, tend to be written at too high a level for most undergraduate students.

This introductory text differs from others in that it takes a theoretically informed approach to qualitative research methods. It begins with a discussion of the debates surrounding positivism and encourages students to consider the challenges that postmodern, feminist, and other critical approaches have posed. Yet the text emphasizes practical skills as well. Throughout, the text encourages students to become more thoughtful observers of social life and encourages them to make informed choices about methodological questions. I believe that students are capable of making their own choices about methodological issues and that they can (and do) become invested in these issues. My experience is that students care about questions of representation, objectivity, and subjectivity, and they are willing to tackle difficult subjects if they anticipate a payoff.

This text is accessible to a broad range of students. Because most students are not intrinsically motivated by the subject, I try to engage them from the beginning using a variety of examples and approaches. Despite their initial hesitation, most students come to enjoy qualitative research methods because they get to *do* stuff. I teach methods using a hands-on approach, and I have found that students enjoy going out into the field and studying topics that interest them. In the book, I try to balance theoretical concerns with more practical issues, and I offer many vivid and concrete examples based on actual sociological research.

The text includes many examples of research, including excerpts from field notes, and of coding and data analysis conducted by both students and professional researchers. My aim is to show students a range of examples to which they can legitimately aspire. Because research methods are best learned through practice, the text includes a number of exercises, including suggestions for student collaboration, at the end of each chapter. Questions for thought encourage students to consider where they stand on both the theoretical and practical issues involved in conducting qualitative research, and suggestions for further reading provide additional resources.

ACKNOWLEDGMENTS

A number of people have helped make this book a much different—and better—book than I could have managed on my own. Thanks, first, to Serina Beauparlant, an extraordinary editor. Serina is a grueling taskmaster and supportive friend. I'm thankful to have worked with her on this book. Kazuyo Masuda and Sue Bergmeier generously read portions of the manuscript and provided tactful comments. Several years ago I had the opportunity to conduct collaborative research with Kazuyo Masuda and Ken Erickson; I'm thankful for the use of their field notes, which appear in this text. Heidi Elsinger, research assistant on the mothers project, has been helpful in numerous ways.

A number of reviewers have provided helpful commentary. They include Linda Grant, University of Georgia; Christy M. Ponticelli, University of South Florida; Kathryn J. Fox, University of Vermont; Dan E. Miller, University of Dayton; Jean H. Thoresen, Eastern Connecticut State University; Phyllis L. Baker, University of Northern Iowa; Judith K. Little, Humboldt State University; Cheryl Childers, Washburn University; Lynn Schlesinger, Plattsburgh State University of New York; Jane E. Prather, California State University, Northridge; Linda L. Shaw, California State University, San Marcos; Kathleen Slobin, North Dakota State University; Trudy A. Salsberry, Kansas State University; Amy L. Best, San Jose State University; and John P. Bartkowski, Mississippi State University.

In acknowledgment sections, authors often thank their families for letting them slide on their share of the household work. Sue Bergmeier and Katherine Ren Peng Bergmeier insisted that I be fully engaged and present in our family life. My life and work are much richer because of it.

Finally, thanks to my students, at both the University of Missouri–Kansas City and the University of Massachusetts at Lowell. My Kansas City students generously served as "guinea pigs," allowing me to initially develop my ideas about teaching qualitative methodologies. My students at Lowell continually push me to be a better teacher. I thank them all.

1

What Is Social Research?
Some Practical and Theoretical Concerns

WHAT IS SOCIAL RESEARCH?

What is social research? How does it differ from, say, journalism, or philosophy, or fiction, or any other way of knowing about the world? How does qualitative research, which this textbook focuses on, differ from quantitative research? What do social researchers do?

Sociologists answer these questions in many ways. These answers often reflect deep philosophical differences about the nature of social reality and the ways in which one should study it. Sociologists who prefer quantitative methodologies tend to argue that, unless researchers use something called *"the"* scientific method and follow the same kinds of rules that natural scientists (such as chemists) use, it isn't really social science research. Other sociologists believe that social science research is fundamentally different from the natural sciences. They argue that social research is primarily a matter of interpretation. In their eyes, the most important goal of social research is to investigate and illuminate how humans construct social reality.

I argue in this book that there are many different ways to do social research, with many different aims. What all these methods share is the goal of learning something about the social world, however that world is construed. While social scientists may disagree, sometimes heatedly, about the nature of social reality and the best ways to study it, they all agree on the importance of understanding the social world. Although I was trained in a quantitative tradition, modeled after the natural sciences, I have come to adopt an interpretive approach in my own research and writing. Yet I continue to appreciate the diversity of approaches that social scientists take in their work. In this text, I hope you will learn to make your own judgments about the social world and the best methods for studying it.

This text focuses on qualitative methods for social research. Although some have argued that the distinction between qualitative and quantitative methods is an artificial one (Jayaratne and Stewart 1991), there are some important differences. Most obviously, *quantitative research* involves enumerating things—that is, using numbers to describe relatively large groups of people. (This doesn't mean that qualitative researchers never count or use numbers; rather, it means that quantifying is not their main strategy.) Quantitative researchers might be interested, for example, in studying the effects of race and gender on people's earnings or the statistically significant differences between men's and women's earnings. But if there are only a small number of cases, quantitative research is of little use. Quantitative research is not particularly useful in revealing the meanings people ascribe to particular events or activities; nor is it well suited to understanding complicated social processes in context.

In contrast, *qualitative research* involves the scrutiny of social phenomena (Gubrium and Holstein 1997, pp. 11–14). Sociologists Jaber Gubrium and James Holstein argue that qualitative researchers look beyond ordinary, everyday ways of seeing social life and try to understand it in novel ways. Take, for example, the simple social act of talking on the telephone. When you answer the phone, chances are you don't think about the social rules for telephone talking. You merely pick up the phone and say, "Hello." You probably don't think about how you'll know who is on the other end; you simply expect the person to tell you. You might be frustrated if someone you don't know very well says, "It's me," and expects you to guess. A qualitative researcher might be interested in exploring this phenomenon further. In fact, sociologists who actually have done so have identified social rules for talking on the telephone. There are rules for determining whose turn it is to talk, for signaling that it's the other person's turn, and for determining how long silences can last before people become uncomfortable. (You might want to test this out the next time you're on the phone: How long can you remain silent before the other person speaks up?)

Instead of trying to extract abstract categories from social phenomena, as quantitative scholars do, qualitative researchers try to understand social processes *in context*. In addition, qualitative researchers pay attention to the subjective nature of human life—not only the subjective experiences of those they are studying but also the subjectivity of the researchers themselves. In other words, qualitative researchers try to understand the meanings of social events for those who are involved in them. They also try to understand the researchers' own perspectives: How do researchers' own points of view affect how they conduct their work?

Because qualitative research consists of words, many people, especially beginning researchers, think that it is easier than quantitative research, especially since there are no mathematical formulas to remember, no statistics to puzzle over. But this isn't actually so. Qualitative research can actually be more difficult, because it involves complex issues of interpretation. Gathering data typically takes longer in qualitative research, and the researcher has to develop his or her analytical skills and apply them to texts. Learning to think sociologically in qualitative research involves not only developing a set of discrete methodological skills (such as interviewing or doing participant observation) but also learning how to move back and forth between theory and evidence. It involves learning the art of interpretation. But moving from people's everyday speech or activities to a sociological analysis is a very difficult skill to learn.

Consider some of the difficulties. Let's imagine that you have been observing children on a playground for several months. You have visited several times a week for an hour at a time, and you have tried to take accurate and detailed notes about what you have seen. You have observed children doing many things: playing hopscotch and soccer and four-square, chasing one another, talking, arguing, yelling, crying. You have many pages of notes that document, in detail, a slice of children's playground life. How do you then make sense of it all? How do you begin to identify larger social patterns? How do you move from your notes and observations to a sociological analysis? That's what this book aims to help you with.

WHY DO RESEARCH?

People conduct research for many reasons. Some do it because it's fun—they enjoy the challenge of gathering data and trying to make sense of it. Doing research is a process of exploration, a way of finding out things that they're interested in. Other people conduct research because they have to, perhaps as part of their degree requirement or their work. Many people have jobs that require some type of research skills. Social workers, for example, may need to do social research to find out if a particular program or policy is effective. They might want to know if welfare-to-work initiatives that aim to move poor women into the labor force actually work. Do they actually help poor women move out of poverty? Others, like community organizers, social policy makers, or teachers, may need to read reports compiled by professional researchers. Teachers may need to know, for example, if whole-language reading strategies work better than phonics for some children. Even if they do not want to do the research themselves, they need to know what others have found. They also need to know how to evaluate research, rather than simply accept it at face value. If several studies suggest that whole-language reading strategies work better and several others recommend phonics-based approaches, the teachers need to know how to reconcile what seem to be conflicting results.

Some researchers are motivated by a sense of social justice. They want to right what they see as social wrongs, and they want to use social research to aid in that effort. For example, Ronnie Steinberg has conducted research on pay inequities in order to help close the gap between men's and women's pay. She describes herself as a feminist social scientist who does advocacy work on behalf of women (1996, p. 225). Others are motivated by a deep curiosity about the social world. Although basic research, which is aimed at creating knowledge for its own sake, may not have an immediate, practical purpose, it helps us to understand social life. For example, sociologist Jack Katz (1996) analyzed how families interacted in a Paris fun house in order to understand the social construction of humor. Although this research may not have an immediate application, knowing more about how people construct humor may—or may not—ultimately have some practical use. Like Katz, many social scientists conduct research because it's a way of learning about things that interest them.

DEVELOPING A SOCIOLOGICAL IMAGINATION

We shouldn't think of social research methods as merely a set of cookbook procedures for obtaining information. Whether qualitative or quantitative, social research methods are intertwined with theoretical concerns. When you try to understand the social world, you are developing what C. Wright Mills (1959) called a *sociological imagination*: the ability to see individual issues within a larger social context. Developing this sociological imagination involves theorizing. Sometimes, students groan or their eyes glaze over when I mention theory. People often think that theory is necessarily boring or arcane and clearly not useful in the "real" social world. But the ability to theorize is a highly useful skill. Life would be very confusing without the ability to theorize. In fact, you theorize all the time—you just don't think about what you're doing in that way.

Any time you try to understand the world around you, you are theorizing. You have theories for why your professors act the way they do and what will happen if you turn in an assignment late. You have theories for why some people get paid more than others and why some people go on to college and others do not. You may not formally frame those kinds of explanations, but they are theories nonetheless. What I mean by *theory* is not merely the abstractions you might encounter in a social theory class. You may have learned about Marx's theory of historical materialism or Durkheim's theory of social integration in your theory class. If so, you may have found the language used by these theorists laborious, perhaps difficult to understand. These are examples of theories that provide grand, overarching explanations of social phenomena. Although these types of explanation are certainly theory, they are not the only kind. Another way to think about theory is as a story about some event or some piece of the social world. A theory helps provide an explanation for a whole class of events. Some theories are highly abstract and difficult to understand; others are not. If you think about theories in this way, you can see that you use them all the time.

For example, let's say your parents immigrated to the United States before you were born. They have ways of doing things that they brought from their home country and ways of doing things they learned here. Because you were born in the United States, however, you feel clearly American. Yet you also have strong ties to your ethnic community. Sometimes, your parents seem too strict; other times, they seem just right. You probably have developed theories about why they act the way they do. One way of explaining your parents would be to theorize about why, *individually*, they act the way they do. You might see your mother as very strict in comparison with some of your friends' mothers, and maybe that is simply part of her personality. Or you might think about whether your family shares some commonalities with other immigrant families. In that case, you might want to theorize about how the experience of immigration affects family life. This would be an attempt to explain a whole class of families.

THE RESEARCH PROCESS: MOVING BETWEEN THEORY AND DATA

Before you can begin to conduct social research, you need to consider the relationship between theories and the empirical world. The empirical world is the world of the senses: the world you can see, hear, smell, touch, and (less frequently considered in the social sciences) taste. Traditional social research draws on the model of a natural scientist conducting research in a laboratory. In this tradition, often called the "scientific method," the main goal of

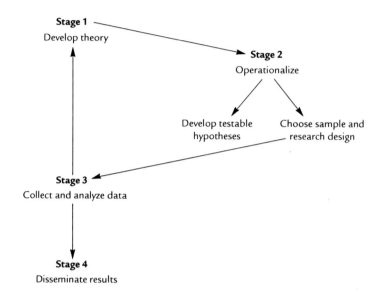

FIGURE 1.1   A Deductive Approach to Research

social research is theory construction and, most importantly, theory testing. Conventional social research uses *deductive reasoning*. That is, you begin with a theory and then deduce logical extensions of it, called hypotheses, that you can test.

The process of deductive reasoning is usually described as having several stages. The first stage involves developing a theory, usually based on the body of research that other scholars have already conducted. The second stage involves operationalizing the theory—that is, putting it in a testable form—by developing hypotheses and choosing a representative sample and a research design. The third stage involves actually carrying out the research: collecting data and conducting analyses. If the results of the test confirm the hypotheses, then the theory is considered more plausible. If not, the theory needs to be reconsidered and further research conducted. The final stage involves writing the results up and disseminating them either in a journal or book or in an oral presentation at a professional conference. Figure 1.1 summarizes the deductive reasoning process.

For example, Phyllis Moen wanted to investigate what factors might affect mothers' well-being. One theory suggested that when mothers work outside the home they experience role strain from being pulled in too many conflicting directions, and thus report greater stress (stage 1). Moen decided to test this hypothesis by measuring psychological distress among a sample of Swedish parents (stage 2). She found that the mothers reported much

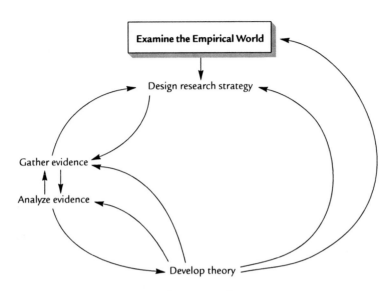

FIGURE 1.2   An Inductive Approach to Research

less distress in 1981 than they had in earlier periods, even though they were *more* likely to work outside the home in the later time period. Thus, she concluded that role strain isn't useful in understanding the effect of women's paid employment on their well-being (stage 3). She published this research in her 1989 book *Working Parents* (stage 4).

In qualitative research, investigators typically are less concerned with this kind of theory testing. Qualitative research often uses *inductive reasoning*. That is, rather than beginning with a particular theory and then looking at the empirical world to see if the theory is supported by "facts," you begin by examining the social world and, in that process, develop a theory consistent with what you are seeing. This approach, illustrated in Figure 1.2, is often called a "grounded approach" (Strauss and Corbin 1990).

For example, Susan Walzer (1998) also was interested in studying mothers' well-being, but in a very different way. She wanted to understand the process by which women and men become mothers and fathers—that is, how couples negotiate transitions to parenthood. Instead of beginning with a theory to test, however, she selected a sample of 50 new parents to interview in depth. As she analyzed the interviews, she realized that the experiences of the women seemed similar, as did the men's experiences. Based on her observations, she began to think about the different cultural meanings of parenthood for men and for women. The theories she developed to try to explain this gender differentiation arose from the empirical evidence she gathered.

There is a long history of grounded research within sociology. In the 1920s and for decades after, the University of Chicago served as a center of qualitative field research. Sociologists there saw the urban setting as a "social laboratory" for social scientists and social reformers (Park 1967). The Chicago School, as it was called, trained students to go out into the world and study the people and settings they encountered. Researchers trained in the Chicago School investigated, among other topics, Italian Americans living in an urban slum (Gans 1962), medical students (Becker, Geer, Hughes, and Strauss 1961), and marijuana smokers (Becker 1963). These scholars were encouraged to see how their empirical research could be "integrated with" social theory (Shaffir and Stebbins 1991, p. 9). At the same time, prominent anthropologists like Margaret Mead, Franz Boas, and Bronislaw Malinowski were developing procedures for fieldwork within the field of anthropology. This kind of research—intensively studying a specific social group by observing the group in its natural setting—is known as ethnography and sometimes as participant observation. Researchers who do this work are called ethnographers.

Women scholars were active in the early years of Chicago School sociology—and even earlier. Harriet Martineau, for example, was one of the founders of sociology (one whose role has been little discussed until recently). Her book *Society in America*, published in 1837, is considered by some to be one of the earliest examples of ethnographic research (Deegan 1991; Reinharz 1992). Later, in the period 1890–1920, a number of women scholars such as Jane Addams, Edith Abbott, and Sophonisba Breckenridge actively engaged in qualitative research. These women, many of whom were involved in applying the tools of sociology to the pressing problems of the day, had an impact on the development of sociology within the United States. In fact, Mary Jo Deegan, who has studied extensively the role of women in the history of sociology, argues that women scholars in the settlement movement both predated and actively shaped the contours of the more famous male scholars of the Chicago School (Deegan 1991).*

Sometimes, researchers move back and forth between inductive and deductive reasoning. Another way to think about the research process is as an ongoing dialogue between theoretical concerns and empirical evi-

---

*The settlement houses, established during the late nineteenth and early twentieth centuries, were centers of moral reform and progressive activism. Women involved with the settlement house movement were involved in a number of activities aimed at social improvement, including work on labor legislation (such as that establishing the 8-hour workday for women and children), housing, and public health and sanitation. The most famous was Hull-House in Chicago, established by Jane Addams in 1889. At Hull-House, women activists and scholars lived and supported each other. Some of the most important early women sociologists were associated with Hull-House and the settlement movement (Deegan 1991).

dence. If theories are stories about the way the world (or some portion of it) works, then they are always in a state of revision, and there are always other, alternative stories that could be told. In this sense, we are never really done theorizing, and we can rarely reject theories out of hand. Instead, we need to think about the multiple stories that might be told. At the same time, the process of telling stories alerts us to different features of the social world.

Michael Burawoy describes a process he calls "theory reconstruction" (Burawoy et al. 1991). He argues that one of the goals of research is to extend and improve existing theories based on an awareness of features of the empirical world that aren't explainable by current theories. When we do research we find things that, based on our theories, we didn't expect to find. But instead of interpreting these puzzles as a failure of the theories (and a need to reject them), he argues, we should use these "failures" to improve our theories.

Whatever you think about the relationship between theory and data, social research still entails some kind of movement between theoretical and empirical concerns. Different ways of thinking about the research process involve different *paradigms*, or worldviews. Rather than have your worldview remain implicit, or understood, it is much better to make it explicit. The choices researchers make about paradigms shape the research strategies they think they should use. These are partisan choices, and they reflect the training, sensibilities, and beliefs of researchers. That's why, as researchers, you need to think reflexively—that is, to think about who you are and what your beliefs about the social world are—in order to make these decisions.

As basic worldviews, paradigms represent beliefs about the nature of reality and the ways in which we create knowledge. Scientific paradigms attempt to answer a number of questions about social research:

- What is the purpose of social research?
- Should social research aim to improve the social world or merely comment on it?
- What is the nature of social reality?
- Is there an objectively "knowable" world out there, or is all knowledge subjective?
- What constitutes a good explanation or theory?
- How does one evaluate any particular theory?

Paradigms are not provable. That is, you cannot prove that one paradigm is essentially better than another. They are, essentially, matters of faith. But paradigms shape the methodological choices you make and the relationships you see between theory and data.

In this chapter, I'll discuss five different research traditions. The first one, called positivism, has been the dominant tradition in sociology since World War II, especially in quantitative research. A number of new traditions, in addition to the earlier tradition of field research developed by the Chicago School, have developed in opposition to this way of doing research. I'll discuss four alternatives: naturalism, social constructionism, feminism and critical approaches, and postmodernism. What's most important is not that you remember the labels, but that you see how they point you toward different directions in your research.

POSITIVISM: TRADITIONAL APPROACHES TO SOCIAL RESEARCH

Traditional approaches to social research are based on a paradigm known as *positivism*. In this tradition, the goal of social research is to discover a set of causal laws that can be used to predict general patterns of human behavior. Prediction is closely related to social control. If you can predict people's behavior, then you can also find ways to control it. Early positivists like Auguste Comte believed that sociology could become a "positive" science of society. By discovering the laws that governed social behavior, sociologists could develop policies that would improve, or even perfect, society.

The paradigm of positivism assumes that the social world is inherently knowable and that we can all agree on the nature of social reality. The social world thus has a regular order that social scientists can discover. Knowledge is created by deductive logic: finding ways to operationalize and then test social theories. Explanations in the form of causal reasoning are taken as "true" when they have no logical contradictions and are consistent with observed facts (empirical evidence). In this tradition, there is a sharp break between scientific ways of knowing and other ways of knowing (such as religion, intuition, or magic).

For example, suppose you have a theory that groups of oppressed people will protest when social conditions are at their worst. You go out and measure the social conditions (such as unfair laws, a lack of jobs and housing, and high arrest rates) of different groups of people. And you have good measures of protests—riots, demonstrations, and the like. What you find is that people seem to protest most not when social conditions are at rock bottom, as your theory predicted, but when things are improving. In this case, the empirical evidence (the measures of protests and social conditions) logically contradicts your theory. In the positivist tradition, you would have to reject your theory and come up with a new one. (This is, in fact, what many social researchers did.)

Social scientists who work within this tradition argue that social research must be value-free and objective. Social researchers must somehow free themselves from the social and cultural values that govern other kinds of human activity. They must transcend personal biases, prejudices, and values and remain neutral toward their object of study.

CHALLENGES TO TRADITIONAL WAYS OF DOING SOCIAL SCIENCE

There have been many challenges to the positivist tradition, on many grounds. For one thing, studying humans is different from studying other aspects of the natural world because human behavior isn't mechanistic. Humans have the capacity to reflect on their actions. In fact, when you study people, chances are they're going to change their behavior—even subtly—just because you are focusing on them. Molecules or atoms and other aspects of the physical world don't, by and large, do this. And unlike many features of the physical world, human behavior is very context sensitive. Thus, if you bring people into an experimental laboratory to study them, their behavior will be different from what it would be if you observe them in their homes or workplaces or other natural settings.

In addition, human reality is multifaceted. Humans can express themselves through art and literature and other forms of self-expression in addition to more goal-directed forms of behavior. Thus, some social scientists argue, it doesn't make sense to study humans using the same methodologies that physicists or chemists might.

Furthermore, in social research, humans are the researchers as well as the objects of study, which means that pure objectivity is impossible. We have a vested interest in what we study. As Dorothy Smith argues, "In the social sciences the pursuit of objectivity makes it possible for people to be paid to pursue a knowledge to which they are otherwise indifferent" (1987, p. 88). We are *not* indifferent to what we study! In fact, if we look at the ways in which social researchers have developed their theories and framed their research projects, we can see that these reflect the interests and priorities of the researchers. And because most researchers and theorists have come from the upper social classes, it's no surprise that much social research reflects the views of those people who have more power in society.

Theorists like Nancy Hartsock (1987), Sandra Harding (1986), and Patricia Hill Collins (1990) have argued that, if researchers begin their investigation from the perspective of dispossessed groups, they will end up with a very different perspective than if they begin from the perspective of the wealthy and powerful. So, for example, if you begin from the standpoint of poor women, you probably wouldn't develop theories of welfare rooted in the assumption that poor women are "lazy" or don't want to work. Rather, you probably would begin with an entirely different understanding of the problem of welfare. For example, you might begin by looking at the realities of poor women's lives, such as the low wages available or the difficulty in gaining decent child care or health care.

Challengers to traditional ways of doing social science argue that all knowledge is created within human interaction. Who we are shapes the kinds of theories we create and the kinds of explanations we offer. Instead of assuming that objectivity is possible, then, we need to be reflexive: We need to develop an understanding of how our positions shape the research topics we choose and the methods we use to study the social world. Literally, what we see is shaped by who we are. Laura Ellingson (1998) discusses these issues in her research on cancer survivors. A survivor of bone cancer herself, she argues that her experiences gave her crucial insights into the worlds of cancer survivors and clinic staff. Not only did she have a more thorough "technical understanding" of the clinical setting than other researchers who did not share her background, she also had an increased empathy for the patients she was studying. "Although no one can fully understand another's experience," she argues, "I come closer to putting myself in the place of another than one who has never known life threatening illness" (1998, p. 497). Because of her experiences, the research process itself was not without pain. For example, when she observed a patient ask her clinician about an endoscopy, she experienced nausea and gagged, remembering her own endoscopy years earlier. The way in which Ellingson wrote up her research reflects her position. She interspersed her report with memories of her own cancer treatment.

"YOU ARE HERE": LOCATING THE SELF IN SOCIAL RESEARCH

"You are here." Have you ever seen a map at, say, a mall or a tourist attraction, that labels where you are in relation to other places of interest? Studying these maps, you can figure out where you are and how to get to where you want to go. You need to do something similar in social research. Before you begin your research project, you have to consider where you stand on a number of important issues:

- What are your own biases and preconceptions?
- What are your own investments in particular issues and in particular ways of seeing the world?
- What do you already think you know, and how do you know it?

Instead of thinking of yourself as a neutral, disinterested observer, think about the connections that you bring to what you plan to study. We'll consider four research traditions that encourage you to ask these kinds of questions: naturalism, social constructionism, feminist and critical approaches, and postmodernism.

NATURALISM

One of the most influential approaches in qualitative research, especially as conducted by many anthropologists and other field researchers, has been *naturalism*. The goal of naturalistic forms of inquiry is to present the lives and perspectives of those being studied as faithfully as possible. Naturalistic research is often conducted in a particular geographic place (Gubrium and Holstein 1997). One of the best-known examples of this is *Tally's Corner*, a study of urban Black men whose lives centered around a particular street corner (Liebow 1967). Elliot Liebow wanted to understand the social lives of these men on their own terms. So, rather than begin with a concept like "delinquency," Liebow began by hanging out with the men to understand, as best he could, their experience.

The classic naturalist image is that of the field researcher who goes out into distant social worlds (either literally or figuratively) to study the people within them. In naturalistic inquiry, the researcher attempts to observe as carefully and accurately as possible and to present the stories of those being studied in their own voices. As Norman Denzin notes, this research is grounded in the "behaviors, languages, definitions, attitudes, and feelings of those studied" (1989, p. 71). To accomplish this, the researcher has to develop close, personal, and empathic relationships with those being studied; she or he has to become fully engaged with their world.

Although there are a few similarities between naturalistic and positivist research (the assumption, for example, that there is a "real world" out there that the researcher can document), there are many more differences. In naturalistic inquiry, the goal is not to abstract a few concepts and to determine the causal relationships among them, but to understand the social world of those being studied. The social context is crucial in naturalistic research. Typically, naturalistic researchers immerse themselves in their field settings, often living among those being studied for long periods of time. Rather than relying on impersonal methods (such as surveys or questionnaires), naturalistic observers rely on their own powers of observation or on in-depth personal interviews to collect data.

Although naturalism remains an important method within qualitative research, it is being supplanted by other paradigms. Critics have identified several problems with naturalism (Denzin and Lincoln 1998). For one thing, this tradition assumes that researchers can accurately portray the concerns and issues of those being studied. But the way in which they produce their social research privileges the researchers' accounts. Once they have collected their data, they still must present the final story. Because researchers have the final say, as it were, their account carries more weight than the accounts of those being researched. Researchers get to choose what to present and what to leave out and how to portray those being studied. The people who have been made the objects of study might disagree with the conclusions, but because they are not writing the final report, their disagreements may not be aired.

Critics also argue that it is impossible for naturalistic researchers to produce objective accounts. Rather, naturalistic reports are always filtered through researchers' perspectives. Also, when observing, researchers cannot attend to everything at once. For example, try to observe and write down everything that is going on in a classroom for just 10 or 15 minutes. You probably will not be able to see or hear everything or to understand all of what you see, and you certainly cannot write down everything. Therefore, you have to pick and choose among what you think is important. So it is with naturalistic research. The naturalistic observer selects what she or he thinks is important and, in this way, creates his or her own version of reality.

More fundamentally, the naturalistic perspective assumes that there's a social world "out there" that can be faithfully studied and reproduced. Other critics, such as those we will consider next, argue that *all* social life is constructed. Everyday life, in this view, is created through social interaction, and the activity of "conducting research" is no different. Thus, we need to pay attention to the researcher and to the social process of research, as well as to those researched.

SOCIAL CONSTRUCTIONIST
AND INTERPRETIVE APPROACHES

Social constructionist and interpretive approaches are enormously varied. What they share, however, is the notion that all social reality is constructed, or created, by social actors. These approaches ask us to focus on interaction: How do humans act toward one another and the objects in their worlds? What meanings do they attach to them?

Interpretive approaches in social research are closely related to a theoretical tradition called *symbolic interactionism*, which rests on three premises (Blumer 1969, p. 2). The first is that humans act toward things based on the meanings those things have for them. For example, a European American might look at a bundle of bamboo or wood sticks and think of them as kindling or as merely sticks, without a particular use or purpose. But someone from China or someone who has traveled throughout Asia might look at that same bundle of sticks and see pairs of chopsticks. And to my daughter Katherine, that same bundle of sticks might become a group of imaginary friends, or dolls, who are playing together. Each of us acts toward the sticks (starting a fire with them, using them to eat with, playing with them) on the basis of the meanings they hold for us.

The second premise is that the meanings of things arise out of social interaction. For example, in Chinese culture, the notion that bamboo sticks are eating utensils called chopsticks (or, more accurately, *kuài zi*) is constructed through group life. The sticks have a special name that all can recognize. Children learn to eat with chopsticks at a very early age, and chopsticks are offered in restaurants and households as appropriate eating utensils. If someone hands you a pair of chopsticks, it is understood that they are to be used to eat with, not to build a fire with or plant with or for some other use.

The third premise is that meanings are created (and changed) through a process of interpretation. There is nothing in the bamboo or wood itself that tells us whether the sticks are dolls or eating utensils or fuel or any other thing. We understand their uses—that is, we create their meanings—through a process of interpretation. Thus, when chopsticks are placed beside a bowl at mealtime, we interpret that they are intended as eating utensils. While waiting for her food to arrive, however, my daughter may interpret them as toys. And if, in interaction with my daughter, I interpret the sticks as eating utensils, I may become annoyed and ask that she stop playing with them. But if I interpret them as toys, I can play along with her. Because humans are social creatures, however, our interpretations of reality are not just individual creations. Although my daughter might prefer to see chopsticks as dolls or toys, hers is an idiosyncratic reading.* Creating and interpreting reality are essentially social processes.

What are the implications of this process of interpretation for qualitative research? First, this interpretive tradition assumes that researchers need to begin by examining the empirical world. That is, rather than begin with a theory or preconceived notion of the way the world works, researchers should begin by immersing themselves in the world inhabited by those they wish to study. This initial approach is similar to that of the naturalistic perspective. But instead of seeking to go "inside the worlds of their subjects," the researchers' emphasis is on understanding how individuals construct and interpret social reality (Gubrium and Holstein 1997, p. 38). There is no social reality apart from how individuals construct it, and so the main research task is to interpret those constructions. The focus is on how given realities are produced.

For interpretive scholars like Clifford Geertz, interpreting social reality is a lot like doing clinical work. Given a particular set of symptoms, these scholars ask, What could they mean? How can they be interpreted? Like a clinician, an interpretive researcher doesn't predict (as is the goal of the positivist researcher); rather, she or he diagnoses. How do you tell if a piece of interpretive research is good research? It must ring true, or at least seem plausible, to the participants themselves, and it must help to explain the "symptoms."

Because researchers, too, are human, the research process itself can be seen as a social production. The meanings of research are negotiated between and among researchers and research subjects, as well as among other social researchers. Researchers begin with the constructions social actors use to define what happens to them, but they do not stop there. As Clifford Geertz (1973) reminds us, researchers never truly capture the viewpoints of others. Researchers' writings are always interpretations of what they *think* their research subjects are doing. But their insights are always limited, because they cannot know for certain what is really going on. In this regard, interpretive writing is akin to fiction, in that it is fashioned from a researcher's interpretation, or best guess, of what is going on. But it is not wholly fiction because it is rooted in social actors' actual lives; it is not simply made up.**

---

*Or, at least, it is partially so. I am indebted to an anonymous reviewer who suggested that the use of chopsticks as dolls isn't really idiosyncratic. Rather, it can be understood within the social construction of childhood as a distinct period of life organized in particular ways—for example, characterized by "play" instead of "work."

**More recently, interpretive scholars have begun to examine the boundaries between fiction and social research. We will discuss these efforts shortly.

The next tradition we'll consider is feminism and critical research. In some respects, the division between various traditions is not clear-cut. There are some researchers, for example, who think of themselves as feminist and as constructionist. Nonetheless, the distinction helps highlight some important differences in the aims of social research.

FEMINIST AND OTHER CRITICAL APPROACHES

Critical Social Research

Feminist and critical researchers are a diverse group comprising many researchers who might not be happy to be lumped together in this way. Generally, critical social research, including feminist research, seeks insight into the social world in order to help people change oppressive conditions. In this context, criticism doesn't merely mean judging negatively; it also means, as feminist scholar Joyce Nielsen notes, exposing existing belief structures that "restrict or limit human freedom" (1990, p. 9). Whereas the goal of positivist research, described earlier, is to "predict and control" and the goal of interpretive research is to understand and interpret, the goal of critical social research is to work toward human emancipation.

For example, feminist researcher Pierrette Hondagneu-Sotelo (1996) studied immigrant women who did housecleaning in private households. But she wasn't interested only in how these women organized their work lives. She also wanted to find ways to act as an advocate to improve the women's working conditions, which typically included isolation, low pay, and opportunities for exploitation. With this in mind, she and her colleagues developed a set of novelas, or booklets that resemble comic books, that explain domestic workers' rights and some strategies for increasing their pay and decreasing the possibility of exploitation.

Like Hondagneu-Sotelo, critical researchers pay close attention to the underlying mechanisms that account for unequal social relations. They want to examine the nature of inequality and work toward the empowerment of those with less power. Thus, they want to understand not only people's subjective feelings and experiences but also the material world and power relations within it. Because oppression is reproduced most easily when people view oppressive conditions as natural or inevitable (Kincheloe and McLaren 1998, p. 263), many critical researchers focus on how oppressive conditions are constructed and maintained over time. In doing so, many critical researchers hope to uncover myths that maintain oppression (for example, myths about welfare mothers or immigrant domestic workers). Critical researchers also hope to communicate their findings to people—especially the people they study—so that they can use them to fight oppression.

How can you tell if an explanation is true or false in critical social science? As a first step, it is important to know if the descriptions are plausible to those being researched. At the same time, "good" critical research teaches people about their own experiences, gives them insight into their place in the social world, and helps them transform the world. Because of the nature of oppression, those in less powerful positions may not always be able to see clearly the ways in which their reality is shaped and limited by what Dorothy Smith (1987) calls the "relations of ruling." Critical social science is action-oriented; thus, values are involved. Critical researchers argue that social research is, itself, a moral and political activity. Scientific activity is never neutral, and it can be used as a source of social control. Thus, researchers must not only be aware of their own values but also embrace a set of carefully considered values.

Feminist Research

A feminist approach in sociology emerged in the late 1960s and early 1970s out of an interaction between feminist activists and sociologists (Laslett and Thorne 1997). Since that time, a vibrant body of research and theory and a network of scholars has developed. Feminist approaches to social science are extraordinarily diverse. Although some feminist scholars may take a more liberal approach and others a more radical one, what they share is a sense that social science as traditionally conducted does not fully take into account the presence of women in social life and the range of women's concerns. When feminist scholars looked at traditional sociological topics like work and occupations, and organizations, and at existing theory, they found that women's perspectives were not included. Apart from a few areas such as sociology of the family, women were essentially missing in sociological theory and research.

Feminist scholars have been among the most important critics of traditional ways of doing social science. Not all feminist social research is qualitative, and not all feminist scholars agree with one another on issues of theory and method. Still, feminist critiques have played an important role in transforming social research methodologies.

Understanding the distinction between methodology and method might be useful in highlighting the depth of the challenge feminist scholars posed. *Methods* are the actual tools or techniques that scholars might use, such as conducting a survey or interview. *Methodology* refers to the "theory and analysis of how research should proceed" (Harding 1987, p. 2). Feminist scholars have called for a transformation not so much in the concrete methods that social scientists might use but in the methodologies. And this makes sense. Researchers from a variety of paradigms might use very similar techniques when observing or asking questions. But how they think about these techniques and how they analyze the evidence they have amassed may differ radically.

Some of the earliest feminist scholars challenged social scientists to include women as subjects in their research. They also encouraged social researchers to study the contributions of earlier women social scientists whose work had been ignored or forgotten, like Harriet Martineau and Jane Addams. Increasingly, feminist scholars have argued that the very theories and methodologies social scientists have used are fundamentally flawed. Scholars such as Dorothy Smith and Patricia Hill Collins recommend a fundamental reshaping of the social research process. In an early influential statement, for example, Ann Oakley (1981) argued that the pretense of objectivity in interviews actually prohibits a deeper understanding of women's lives. In her interview studies of new mothers, she found that sharing her own experiences of mothering facilitated a much richer understanding of the women.

Dorothy Smith has argued for a fundamental transformation of sociology, urging that we create a sociology *for* women. Such a sociology would begin from the standpoint of women and be rooted in women's experiences of daily life. But it would not end there. The purpose of such a sociology would be to locate women's experiences in a broader network of ruling relations, which includes a complicated set of social practices and social institutions such as government, the military, business, and the media (Smith 1987, p. 3). It would seek to understand how women's lives are shaped by forces outside of their control. Yet, in looking at these larger-level forces, such a sociology must not lose sight of women's real and subjective experiences. Smith argues, "The development of a feminist method in sociology has to go beyond our interviewing practices and our research relationships to explore methods of thinking that will organize our inquiry and write our sociological texts so as to preserve the presence of actual subjects while exploring and explicating the relations in which our everyday worlds are embedded" (1987, p. 111).

Just as feminist scholarship challenged traditional methods, so has it come under challenge. In its earliest formulations, feminist scholarship often focused on the experiences of White, middle-class, and heterosexual women. The resulting theories and accounts thus did not necessarily reflect the experiences of women in all their diversity. Women of color, lesbians, disabled women, and others have challenged feminist scholars to be more inclusive in their scholarship (see, for example, Cannon, Higginbotham, and Leung 1991). Recent scholarship focusing on the intersections of race, class, gender, and sexuality has expanded and transformed this earlier feminist research.

What are the implications of feminist critiques of social research? Shulamit Reinharz (1992) argues that feminism is a perspective, not a method. In her survey of feminist methodologies, she identified a number of themes that characterize feminist research, including a critical stance toward traditional methodologies and theories, the goal of creating social change, the desire to represent human diversity, and the attempt to think about the relationship between researcher and those being researched. At the very least, feminist scholars argue, the experiences of women in all their diversity are important and must be included in designing and carrying out research. At their most expansive, feminist scholars argue that traditional methodologies themselves must be transformed.

POSTMODERNISM

The final research tradition we'll consider is *postmodernism.* Some scholars believe that social conditions have changed so dramatically that we have entered a new, postmodern era in which previous ways of knowing are no longer useful (see, for example, Gergen 1991). As traditional bases of authority have been undermined, they say, a variety of competing perspectives have replaced established ways of knowing. Although those who have been influenced by postmodernism may not agree on much, they tend to agree that there is not one reality, but instead a number of different realities and ways of knowing, all equally valid.

Some argue that the postmodern world is, increasingly, a world made up of texts and images characterized by a *hyperreality,* "a term used to describe an information society socially saturated with ever-increasing forms of representation: filmic, photographic, electronic, and so on" (Kincheloe and McLaren 1998, p. 269). As people are exposed to this rapidly growing number and variety of images and types of information, there is the erosion of what some call "master narratives," or single theories as all-encompassing explanations. There can no longer be one coherent, objective theory to explain social phenomena, but rather multiple stories, positions, and representations.

Postmodernism poses a crisis for previously accepted ways of knowing (and, hence, for qualitative research) that centers on two issues (Denzin and Lincoln 1998). First, postmodernists question whether "qualitative researchers can directly capture lived experience" (1998, p. 21). If there is no one objective reality, then a researcher cannot, of course, capture that reality in a study. If the self is fragmented, as scholars like Kenneth Gergen (1991) argue, then how can a researcher be fully reflexive (see also Gergen and Gergen 2000)? How can a researcher maintain a unified stance toward the subjects of his or her research?

The second issue revolves around what has been called the "legitimation crisis" (Lincoln and Denzin 2000). This crisis arose when anthropologists and other social scientists criticized the authority of the written text—that is, the idea that texts can be considered "accurate, true, and complete" (Lincoln and Denzin 2000, p. 1051). In the postmodern perspective, texts are always partial, limited, and rooted within a particular viewpoint. If all knowledge is limited and socially constructed, then how do we evaluate and interpret social research? If there is no one reality, but merely a variety of perspectives, then traditional criteria for evaluating and interpreting social research simply are not relevant.

Not surprisingly, scholars who have been influenced by postmodernism are not a unified group. There are substantial debates about what postmodernism is and what its implications are for doing qualitative research. For example, if there is no single reality or truth to be told, then there is no one "right" way of doing research or interpreting data. Rather, there are multiple stories, from multiple perspectives, that might be told. Qualitative research accounts are always incomplete and uncertain, because all knowledge is provisional. This has led some researchers to experiment with new forms of research—what George Marcus called "messy texts" (1998). So, for example, some researchers have experimented with the boundaries between qualitative research and fiction (Krieger 1991) and poetry (Richardson 1992). In her study of unmarried mothers, Laurel Richardson (1992) decided to write a poem, using the respondent's own words, to portray the life story of one of her informants, named Louisa May. She felt that by doing so she could portray Louisa May's life much more faithfully than if she had produced a simple transcript. In addition, if all knowledge is created by someone, then it is important to understand who that someone might be. Even if the self is, ultimately, fragmented and unknowable, it is important to consider the ways in which researchers are situated in particular, local settings.

MAKING CLAIMS ABOUT PARADIGMS

By now, you might be wondering why you've been reading what seems to be a philosophical discussion. Why should you care about paradigms? Why does a book about research methods have to be phrased so abstractly? I argue that if you don't think about them explicitly you will still be operating within the constraints of a paradigm. You just won't be doing it consciously, as a result of choices that *you* make. Throughout the rest of the book, I will try to show you how the choices you make about research traditions influence the research strategies that are available to you. For now, I urge you to think about which tradition(s) seem to make the most sense to you and which ones seem most plausible. This is a first step toward creating your own research project.

QUESTIONS FOR THOUGHT

1. Think about the different traditions you have just read about. Which ones seem more reasonable to you? Why? Do any seem less plausible to you? Why?

2. Have any readings in sociology particularly interested you? If so, which ones? What kinds of perspectives did they take? Why were the readings so compelling?

3. Think about who you are. What kind of family do you come from? Where do you live? What kinds of experiences have been most important to you in shaping your values? Now, think about someone who seems very different from you. If you are relatively young, you might think about someone who is older. If you live in a city, you might think about someone who lives on a farm. Or, if you are gay or lesbian, you might think about someone who is heterosexual. Now consider a social issue that you see as important. How might you go about researching it? How might someone who is very different from you think about the same subject?

EXERCISES

1. Try this one with a friend. Go to a public place—a library, shopping mall, cafeteria, or similar place—to observe. Observe for about 20 minutes. While you are doing so, take careful notes on everything you think is

important. After you have finished, read each other's notes. Did you both notice the same things? What differences do you see? Why do you think you saw things differently? How did your personal experiences give you somewhat different perspectives?

2. Every day for a week, read a national newspaper, such as the *New York Times*. As you go through the paper, look for stories that report the results of social research. How can you tell that social research is being reported? Can you think of any ways that the research being reported might be useful?

3. Try to find several qualitative research reports in the library. (You might browse, for example, through journals like *Journal of Contemporary Ethnography, Gender & Society, Symbolic Interaction,* or *Qualitative Inquiry.*) If your library provides access to a computer database that lets you print out whole articles, like Infotrac or EBSCOhost, you might search any topic that interests you. Or you can search using terms like "qualitative research" or "qualitative methods" or "qualitative study." These will yield too many citations for you to look at each one, but you can browse through to find ones that interest you. Alternatively, you might try to find writings by some of the researchers mentioned in this chapter. Once you've located several qualitative research reports, see if you can find descriptions of the researchers themselves. Do they give any personal information about themselves? Do they describe how they became interested in the topic? How do you think researchers' personal lives affect the choices they make?

4. Go back to the research reports that you found in Exercise 3. What kind of reasoning did the researchers use—inductive or deductive? How can you tell?

SUGGESTIONS FOR FURTHER READING

Examples of Qualitative Research

Becker, Howard; Blanche Geer; Everett Hughes; and Anselm Strauss. *Boys in White: Student Culture in Medical School.* New Brunswick, NJ: Transaction, [1961] 1977. A classic Chicago School study of the socialization of medical students.

Burawoy, Michael, et al. *Ethnography Unbound: Power and Resistance in the Modern Metropolis.* Berkeley: University of California Press, 1991. A collection of short ethnographies written by graduate students at the University of California, Berkeley, each of which uses the process of theory reconstruction.

Kondo, Dorinne. *Crafting Selves: Power, Gender, and Discourses of Identity in a Japanese Workplace*. Chicago: University of Chicago Press, 1990. An innovative study, influenced by postmodernism, of self and identity in a Japanese workplace.

Liebow, Elliott. *Tally's Corner*. Boston: Little, Brown, 1967. A classic field study of urban Black men.

Stacey, Judith. *Brave New Families: Stories of Domestic Upheaval in Late Twentieth Century America*. New York: Basic Books, 1991. A feminist analysis of postmodern family life.

Stack, Carol. *All Our Kin: Strategies for Survival in a Black Community*. New York: Harper, 1974. An important study of family and kinship in an urban Black community.

Whyte, William Foote. *Street Corner Society*, 4th ed. Chicago: University of Chicago Press, [1943] 1993. A study of Italian Americans in Boston's North End; one of the most widely read and influential field studies.

Resources on Research Paradigms

Lincoln, Yvonna S., and Egon G. Guba. "Paradigmatic Controversies, Contradictions, and Emerging Confluences." Pp. 163–188 in *Handbook of Qualitative Research*, 2nd ed., edited by Norman K. Denzin and Yvonna S. Lincoln. Thousand Oaks, CA: Sage, 2000. An overview of research paradigms and the controversies surrounding them.

DeVault, Marjorie L. *Liberating Method: Feminism and Social Research*. Philadelphia: Temple University Press, 1999. A look at research from a feminist perspective.

General Resources on Qualitative Research

Denzin, Norman K., and Yvonna S. Lincoln (eds.). *Handbook of Qualitative Research*, 2nd ed. Thousand Oaks, CA: Sage, 2000. A comprehensive guide.

2

Strategies for Beginning Research

GETTING STARTED: WHERE TO BEGIN?

Getting started is often one of the hardest tasks for beginning researchers. How do you know if you have a good idea for a research project? How can you tell if the research project is doable? Just as important, how can you tell if the research is worth doing? Even experienced researchers sometimes have trouble finding a topic, beginning a new research project, figuring out how to start, choosing a research strategy, or developing a general research plan.

The first step in any research project is deciding on a general topic and then refining the topic. Suppose you are interested in homelessness or in students' alcohol use. Homelessness in general would be far too big a topic—even for someone doing a Ph.D. dissertation—so you would have to find a way to make your research more manageable. You could focus on just one aspect of homelessness, such as the experiences of workers in homeless shelters or the effects of homelessness on children. To narrow down the topic of student alcohol use, you could focus on the role of alcohol at student parties or the effects of alcohol consumption on academic achievement. You also need to think about the different approaches you could take to your research, as reflected in the paradigms discussed in Chapter 1. But what do you do if you don't know what general topic interests you? How do you begin then?

GENERATING IDEAS

How do you generate useful, interesting ideas? It's hard to give sound advice on finding good research topics, for several reasons. One problem is that we don't usually think about where good ideas come from. They seem somehow serendipitous, a stroke of magnificent luck. Suppose you are walking down the street and suddenly notice that most of the streetlights are out on one block but functioning on the next. You also notice that the trash seems to be picked up on that block but not on the first one. This leads you to wonder about how different neighborhoods gain access to city services. Or suppose you read an article in the newspaper or see a program on TV that sparks your curiosity about how homeless people survive in the winter in cold climates. Or maybe you have a long-standing interest in sports or young children, and so research ideas seem to come naturally. These are all legitimate ways to identify a research topic. If you don't have any interests at all, you'll find it difficult to find an interesting research topic. But most of us are interested in at least *something*.

Often, qualitative researchers begin where they are. That is, they look at their own lives to see if they can find anything interesting to study, an unusual angle or puzzling event or phenomenon. Then they try to refine the topic into a more manageable—and researchable—form.

For example, Carol Freedman, a graduate student raising a young child, needed to do a research project for a course on research methods. She had been participating in a mothers' group, and so she decided to study it. The project eventually became her master's thesis, titled "Setting Stay-at-Home Standards: An Ethnographic Study of the Southland Mothers Association" (Freedman 1997).

Elliot Liebow wrote in the preface to his book *Tell Them Who I Am* that he had been diagnosed with cancer and had a limited life expectancy, so he decided to volunteer at a soup kitchen. As he put it, "I did not want to spend my last months on the 12th floor of a government office building, so at 58 I retired on disability from my job of 20-some years as an anthropologist with the National Institute of Mental Health" (1993, p. viii). Because he felt pretty good for a lot longer than he expected, he started volunteering at a homeless shelter as well. He became interested in the lives of the women at the shelter, so he began taking field notes and thinking about the shelters as a site in which to do research. Ultimately, he did an in-depth study of the lives of homeless women.

Other researchers, too, have written about how they developed their research interests. Lynn Davidman (1999) wrote about the experience of losing her mother to cancer when she was 13 and how that shaped her decision to study what she calls "motherloss." The point is, if you look around at your own environment, you may find the beginnings of a research topic.*

But should you stop there? What would happen if researchers began only with their own experiences and never considered others' perspectives? In framing research questions, it's important to remember that how people select research problems is not a neutral process. Rather, research questions always reflect *someone's* interests and priorities—either the researcher's or, if the researcher is getting funding from someone else, the people who are doing the funding. While this is not necessarily a bad thing, you do need to think about the variety of perspectives that different people bring to research projects.

Consider the following example: City officials in a midwestern city became concerned with drug use in a poor section of town. That section contained a low-income public housing complex, populated mainly by poor women and their children, that was in bad condition, with leaky roofs, dilapidated interiors, and crumbling steps. City officials convened a series of meetings at the housing complex to try to deal with the problem. A number of people attended the meetings, including the managers of the housing complex, members of an antidrug task force, various government officials, the police, a legal aid attorney, residents of the housing complex, and a few university researchers.

Over the course of the meetings, it became clear that the women who lived in the complex didn't see drugs as a major problem in their community. The main problem, from their perspective, was the dilapidated condition of the buildings they lived in. They also felt harassed by the complex security guards, most of whom were off-duty police officers. But the managers of the complex didn't see things in the same way at all. They felt that if the women could just "pull themselves up by their own bootstraps" and get jobs (or husbands with jobs), they would pay more rent and the buildings would soon be fixed. They felt the security guards were needed to protect the buildings and that if the women hadn't broken any laws then they had nothing to fear from the police. The legal aid attorney had yet another interpretation of the problem—as a civil rights violation. Finally, one graduate student researcher who was studying the meetings interpreted the dynamics between management, police, government officials, and the tenants in terms of state attempts to control poor women (Masuda 1998).

---

*If you're interested in learning more about how researchers come up with their topics, you might want to read some of the stories in *Qualitative Sociology as Everyday Life*, edited by Barry Glassner and Rosanna Hertz.

So whose interpretation of the situation was correct? What was the "real" problem? Was it drugs? Dilapidated housing? Police harassment? Social control? It depends on whose perspective you take. This is what I mean when I say that problems are never neutral. A problem is always a problem *for* someone. Sociologists sometimes refer to this as the "definition of the situation." In any social setting, people make assumptions about what they think is happening and how to interpret the actors and events. Researchers are also involved in a process of social interaction. They, too, make assumptions about what they think is happening and define the situation in diverse ways. How researchers choose to frame their research questions reflects their sense of what "the" problem is. What if you were going to research this situation? Whose perspective would you take into account? Why?

DECIDING WHAT TO RESEARCH

When you are first deciding what to research, you need to ask yourself a number of questions. First, what do you already know about the topic? And if you don't know very much, how can you get more information? Going to the library or searching the Internet are good ways to learn more about a topic (and we'll discuss these further later in the chapter), but they're not the only ways. You can also talk to other people, such as a professor or another student, who have an interest in the topic. You can visit places to get more information. For example, if you are interested in homeless people, you might volunteer at a shelter or visit the site.

A second question you need to consider is, How do you feel about your potential topic? Do you have very strong feelings about it? If so, your feelings might lead you to focus on one particular area and avoid others or blind you to other perspectives. You may be too biased to do a good job or to understand others' points of view. It's important to remain open to a variety of perspectives.

Being a member of the group you are studying can be both positive and negative. People often have strong feelings about the people and groups they are involved with. If you are studying a familiar group, you'll need to be especially careful to remain open-minded. For example, imagine that you are a member of a campus sorority or fraternity. You know that students who aren't involved in these groups often have negative opinions about them, and you want to do research to try to counter these stereotypes. Your involvement helps you gain access to members, and that is certainly positive. But you are so invested in showing the positive side that you aren't able to see any other points of view. In this case, being a member might hinder your ability to do good research.

As you develop your research project, you need to keep an open mind about the people and events in your research setting and to remain open to multiple definitions of the situation. If you close yourself off to alternative explanations too soon, you may miss important insights into your research setting.

How Do You Turn a Topic into a Question?

Once you've settled on a general topic, it's time to turn it into a research question. In qualitative research, your research question may shift once you begin your investigation. In fact, many scholars argue that a good qualitative researcher must have the ability to remain open to what the field setting or research site has to offer. They believe that the most important thing is simply to go out into the field to see what is out there. I argue that an initial focus is important. Even though your research question may change—and sometimes dramatically—once you begin work, you still need to start somewhere. Otherwise, you may have difficulty figuring out how to begin your research. As your research progresses, however, you need to keep an open mind to other questions that may arise in the course of your research—questions that may be even more important than the ones you initially devised.

As a first step, try brainstorming a list of questions about your topic. Then you can evaluate whether the questions can be answered using the resources you have at hand. Let's say you're interested in the general topic of abortion, but you're not sure how to narrow your topic down. Try asking some questions:

- What is the experience of abortion like for women?
- How do activists on both sides of the debate think about abortion? What do they think women's roles should be?
- How do abortion clinic staff deal with the threats of violence? Does it change the way they think about their work?
- How have media portrayals of abortion changed over time?

Notice how these questions are all answerable, at some level, with reference to the empirical world (the world of the senses). You could ask women who have had abortions what their experience is like; you could observe the staff in a clinic; you could examine news accounts of abortion to see how they have changed.

Compare those questions with, say, the following:

◆ Is abortion a good or a bad thing?
◆ Should women be able to choose to have an abortion?

These kinds of questions really can't be answered with reference to the empirical world. While they may be important *ethical* questions, they aren't amenable to social research. Thus, you need to consider whether the research questions you propose can be answered with reference to the "real" world.

You also need to ask yourself what your own assumptions about abortion and the women who have them are. If you have had an abortion yourself or know someone who has had one, that will certainly shape your thinking about the topic. If you have strong feelings pro or con, those will influence your initial question as well. You need to consider whether your own investments in the issue will allow you to investigate it with an open mind.

Is the Topic Interesting?

Next, you need to consider whether your research question is interesting. A good qualitative researcher can make just about any topic interesting. But if you are bored by or indifferent to your project, you probably ought to choose another one. Doing qualitative research can take a long time, and completing a research project—even one that you are interested in—can be difficult. It's tough to keep going when you're bored by your topic. Sometimes, beginning researchers pick questions because they think they will be easy or because their professor or adviser suggested the topic. These are poor reasons to choose a topic, unless, of course, you already have an interest in the topic. No research project is truly easy, and even the easiest research becomes difficult when you don't want to do it.

Whose Perspective Should You Take?

Once you've settled on a tentative research question, you need to think about how you will begin to approach it. At this stage, consider how taking different perspectives will lead you to embark on very different research projects. If your topic is homelessness, for example, you will find yourself moving down a very different path if you decide to study workers in homeless shelters than if you decide to study homeless people themselves. Similarly, you will find yourself doing a very different research project if you choose to conduct your research in a small shelter that houses homeless women and their families rather than a large shelter that provides temporary housing for single men. Try to list as many perspectives as you can before you settle on a tentative focus. But even then, it's important to keep a questioning attitude. And as you continue with your work, you should remain open to as many perspectives as possible.

You also need to consider how different paradigms might shape different approaches to your research. Although you do not need to settle on a paradigm at this early stage, it's helpful to think about how these choices will affect your research. With a social constructionist approach, for example, you would want to pay close attention to how individuals define and create social reality. With a critical approach, you would want to frame your research so that it would be useful in creating social change.

Let's consider the example of education in preschools and kindergartens. A feminist researcher might focus on gender relations in the classroom—perhaps on how boys and girls interact and how gender is produced through that interaction (see, for example, Thorne 1993). A social constructionist might focus on interaction as well. But this researcher might be more interested in exploring how children come to define the classroom as a "school" and how they learn the expectations for behaving in that setting (see, for example, Corsaro and Molinari 2000). A postmodernist might focus on the multiple and fragmented realities within and around the school setting: the realities of children, teachers, administrators, and others. This researcher might explore children's cartoons, commercial culture, and other texts that shape children's realities. A positivist might begin with a theory about education—for example, that children who attend preschool adjust better to kindergarten than those who do not—and focus the research on that question.

Is the Research Feasible?

Once you've settled on a tentative question, you need to ask whether you can actually do the research. For example, if you are interested in studying people in homeless shelters, you need to get permission from the shelter staff (probably the director) and from the residents themselves. Some groups are relatively easy to gain access to (such as other students); others are relatively difficult (such as people who are involved in illegal activities, like drug smugglers). You may also need to gain permission from an institutional review board at your school, which scrutinizes projects for ethical problems.

Once you've determined that you can gain access to the group you are interested in studying, you need to think about what other resources you will need. First, consider *time*. Doing qualitative research can take a great deal of time. If you are trying to study a group to which it may be difficult to gain access or that may be hostile to researchers, be sure you have enough time to develop the kinds of relationships you will need to do the research. For example, suppose you are interested in illegal drug use, as anthropologist Steven Koester is (Koester 1994). Specifically, you are interested in how HIV might be transmitted among street people who inject drugs. It will take a long time before they trust you enough to confide in you, so you need to consider whether you have enough time to gain trust.

Another important resource is *money*. Doing qualitative research can cost money. If you are going to do the research full-time, you still need to support yourself. If you are going to interview people, you need to purchase or have access to a reliable tape recorder and audiotapes. You also might have to hire someone to transcribe interview tapes, unless you plan to do it yourself. You may have to travel somewhere else to get to your research population or to find documents in an archive. You may need to purchase films or other texts to analyze. And there may be other costs as well.

The question of feasibility can be particularly difficult if you are trying to conduct a research project over the course of a semester. You may have great ideas for research projects, but the projects are too ambitious to be carried out over 14 or so weeks. Once you finally gain access to your research population or data, it is the end of the semester and time to wrap things up. Thus, you may find it easier to begin with a setting that you already know or can gain access to. But this means you'll have to be especially careful about the preconceptions and biases you bring to your work.

Is the Research Worth Doing?

A final issue is whether you *should* do a particular project. Just because you are interested and have the resources you need, it doesn't mean you should actually do the research. The key issue is whether the research has any potential uses or benefits. Will your research make a contribution, either to individuals or to a larger group or to our general knowledge base? Does it have the capacity to harm anyone—either yourself or the research participants? Before you begin any research project, you need to consider the potential benefits and risks. (These ethical issues will be considered in detail in Chapter 3.)

Again, let's say you are interested in researching people in homeless shelters. You think the study might have potential benefits because people might be more sympathetic to the problems of the homeless if they under-stood what their lives were like. They might be more interested in building affordable housing or having the government spend more money on subsi-dized homes. While the research might not have an immediate positive impact on the participants' themselves, you think that in the long run your work might help debunk stereotypes about homeless people.

DEVELOPING A RESEARCH STRATEGY

Once you've chosen a topic and framed a research question, you need to develop a research strategy. Specifically, you need to address these questions:

- How will you gather the data?
- What kind of population or setting will you study?
- Will you use in-depth interviews, or do an observational study, or work with "texts" (which can include things like books and maga-zines but also media such as TV shows, movies, and songs)?
- How will you begin to analyze and make sense of the data you have collected?

Different research traditions suggest somewhat different strategies. We'll consider these next.

Different Traditions, Different Starting Points

Depending on which research tradition you choose, you will begin your research from very different starting points. Before you get too far in your work, then, you need to consider which tradition(s) makes the most sense to you. According to the positivist paradigm, which we discussed in Chap-ter 1, the goal of social research is theory testing. Thus, in this tradition, you need to settle on a theory *before* you begin your research. Researchers who work within this tradition usually spend much time researching what oth-ers have found about their topic. They then develop *hypotheses,* or state-ments that can be tested, based on these theories, which often framed in causal language: "x causes (or affects) y" or "The more of x, the less of y." Then they develop a research design that they can use to test their hy-potheses. They use the results of their empirical tests to determine whether their theory is useful.

Let's say you're interested in rational choice theory (Friedman and Hechter 1988), which states that people act according to their best interests. Specifically, you're interested in applying rational choice theory to divorce. You think that, if people feel they will get more out of divorcing than staying in a marriage, they will choose to divorce. You're aware that raising children after a divorce can be hard, so you think that people with children have less to gain from a divorce than those without. Your hypothesis might be this: Couples who have children are less likely to divorce than couples who have no children. You could test this by comparing the divorce rate of couples who have children with that of couples who do not.

Qualitative researchers rarely work within this positivist tradition. That is, they are much less likely to test hypotheses than are quantitative researchers and are much more likely to work within one of the other traditions discussed in Chapter 1. Instead of *beginning* with a theory, qualitative researchers are more likely to begin with an examination of the empirical world. In the naturalistic and constructionist traditions, researchers immerse themselves in the social worlds of their research subjects. Only when they have been in a setting for a long time do they begin to develop theories. Some call this a *grounded theory* perspective (Charmaz 2000; Strauss and Corbin 1998), in which the aim is to develop theory grounded in the empirical world. If you choose this approach, your first step is to decide on a field setting or site for your research. At this stage, although you should do a library search to determine if others have studied the same kinds of sites, you should not try to develop testable hypotheses. Rather, you should focus on how you might gain access to the site and begin building relationships with the people there.

Researchers working within a critical research tradition might decide to do *action research*, in which the objective is to produce some kind of social change. For example, you might work with a coalition that seeks to end homelessness in your community. In this case, you first need to identify the stakeholders—the people who have a stake in eliminating homelessness. Obviously, people without homes do, but who else? Shelter workers? Community agencies? Neighborhood residents? You also need to identify who has the power to effect change and what the people you are working with think needs researching. For example, they might believe that the research should focus on the cost of housing in the community and on people's wages. In action research, rather than begin with a theory, you need to begin with a clear statement of the needs and priorities of the group.

While the discussion of research paradigms in Chapter 1 may have seemed abstract, the choice of a paradigm has real-life implications. The choices you eventually make will determine whether you turn first to the published research, or to the empirical world. In research that draws on the positivist tradition, you need to have well-developed hypotheses before you begin your research. In research that draws on the naturalistic or constructionist traditions, you need to frame a general research question and choose a site for your research. In research that draws on postmodernist traditions, you might focus on texts. In this approach, although it's a good idea to read at least some of the published literature before you begin (and many researchers, myself included, would insist that you do so), you don't begin with already formed hypotheses. Instead, you develop your theory and an increasingly refined research question as you conduct the research.

Types of Research Strategies

Once you have settled on a research question and research tradition, you need to decide how you will collect your data. Specifically, you need to address these issues:

- What research strategy will you use?
- What population or site will you study?
- What texts will you choose?
- What will your evidence consist of? Transcripts of interviews? Observational notes? Archival materials, like letters or diaries or an organization's records? Songs or videotapes of TV programs?
- How will you spend your time? Listening and talking to people? Observing? Going through published materials? Watching audio-tapes?

You can choose from several general research strategies. Which one you settle on depends on your research question, the research tradition you see yourself as working in, and your own individual preferences.

Observational Studies   In the naturalistic or constructionist traditions, you might conduct an *observational study*, in which you gather data by observing interaction in a particular site (such as a street corner or homeless shelter). Observational studies are useful when you want to understand how people behave in a particular setting or when you want an in-depth understanding of a particular culture or group. In an observational study, you might choose to participate. For example, you might volunteer at a homeless shelter, as Elliot Liebow, whom we discussed in Chapter 1, did. Or you might choose simply to observe in a public place (such as a shopping mall or a public park), without participating.

Interviews   Many qualitative researchers choose to conduct formal in-depth *interviews* with people. These can be relatively structured or unstructured. Interviews are good research techniques when you want to know what people think or feel about something. Researchers often combine observational techniques with either formal or informal interviews. In formal interviews, the researcher sets a particular time and place for an interview. Informal interviews tend to arise spontaneously in the course of observation. For example, you might decide to formally interview people who volunteer in a homeless shelter in order to understand their experiences, as well as to observe and informally interview shelter residents.

Unobtrusive Measures   Not all research involves talking with or observing people. *Unobtrusive research* involves examining human traces, or evidence of human activity. For example, if you want to know which magazines in the library are most popular, you might study which ones seem to have thumbed pages or seem to have been heavily perused. A number of researchers have studied public graffiti. Caroline Cole (1991), for example, analyzed the writing on walls in women's bathrooms, arguing that the graffiti there served as an alternative means of communication. Jeff Ferrell (1995) analyzed hip-hop graffiti in Denver, Colorado, combining participant observation of graffiti writers with visits to graffiti sites in other cities. He argues that hip-hop graffiti reflects young people's efforts to resist social control.

Sometimes, researchers study "texts" such as newspapers, books, organizational records, TV shows, and court transcripts. For example, Sharon Hays wanted to investigate what she called the "cultural contradictions of motherhood" (1996). To do so, she analyzed child-rearing manuals to identify the kinds of social norms for mothering contained in them and conducted in-depth interviews with mothers of small children to determine how they actually viewed their mothering.

Triangulation   Each research strategy has particular strengths and weaknesses. For example, in-depth interviews can provide insight into people's thoughts and feelings, but people's behaviors don't always match their words. Analysis of texts can tell you about social ideals for behavior, but the texts can't tell you how people actually respond to them. For this reason, researchers often use two or more research strategies. This is called *triangulation*. Because different data collection strategies have different strengths and weaknesses, research designs that include multiple research strategies tend to be the strongest ones.

READING THE LITERATURE

Whichever research tradition and strategy you choose, you should visit the library early in the process of designing your research. Although some naturalistic researchers caution against becoming too wedded to a particular theory or viewpoint before immersing yourself in your field setting, I think this concern is a little overstated. By knowing what other researchers have already said about your topic, you are in a better position to come up with a well-thought-out research plan. And at some point during the research process, you will still need to conduct a literature review to help you place your own research in context.

I recommend that you begin any research project by simply browsing. Look through the journals and books that seem most interesting to you, or browse through the databases available at your library. I usually skim through the abstract or the introduction quickly to see if I might want to read the whole article or book. Then I go through those readings that seem most useful in more detail. I recommend looking at as wide a variety of sources as you can. As you do so, be sure to take good notes (including accurate citations) so that you can locate the sources again as needed. There's nothing more frustrating than knowing that you had the perfect source but being unable to use it because you can't find it again.

Every library is different. Some have subscriptions to many journals and excellent on-line searching capabilities; others don't. Each library has its own special way of providing access to the materials. Some libraries have on-line search services, like EBSCOhost or Infotrac, which will deliver whole articles to you on-line. Others have a large selection of books and journals in print that you can browse through. Your librarian or professor will be the best person to help you search in your own library.

Most libraries will have access to Sociological Abstracts, either in print or on-line. One of the most important databases for sociologists, Sociological Abstracts summarizes the articles in the most important journals that sociologists publish in. By searching this index, you should be able to get a good idea of what others have said about your topic. Depending on your field and topic, you may also want to search databases such as Psychological Abstracts, ERIC, or Criminal Justice Abstracts. Again, I strongly recommend that you check with your professor or librarian to see what resources on your campus might be helpful for you.

Although this book can't help you search your specific library, it can give you some general tips on conducting a useful library search:

1. Try a number of different terms for the same thing. Different databases will often use somewhat different key words, and the same database may yield very different articles if you use just slightly different search terms.

2. If the term you've searched yields too many citations to look through, try narrowing it down. For example, I recently used the on-line version of Sociological Abstracts to search the term "working women." When I did so, I received 3669 "hits"—clearly, too many to look through. When I narrowed the topic to "working women and sexual harassment," I received 49 citations—still a lot to look through, but a much more manageable number.

3. Try a number of different sources, including the book catalogue, the journals (also called serials), and the Internet. Different sources will tend to give you very different kinds of results.

4. Once you've found a useful article or book, see if you can track down some of the sources the author used. They are often helpful.

5. Ask a librarian for help, especially if you're finding very little information about what you think should be a popular topic. But be sure you've already thought about some potential angles for your project. The librarian can't create a research topic for you, but she or he can help you find the right resources, given a specific topic.

EVALUATING WEB SITES

The Internet can provide a wealth of material for research projects. You can get information from a variety of government and private sources, as well as research reports, book reviews, and other useful texts. Many government agencies have Web sites, including the Census Bureau, the Bureau of Labor Statistics, and the FBI. However, the Internet can also lead you astray. A friend of mine says that the World Wide Web is like a huge catalogue—everyone wants to sell you something. Thus, you need to evaluate Web sites carefully before relying on them in your research. Here are a few questions to ask in judging the usefulness of various sites:

◆ Who sponsored the site? Is it maintained by a commercial enterprise or individuals who stand to gain something? Does it contain advertising? Is it maintained by a government agency or university or research institution? Or is it maintained by an individual? If so, what qualifications does the person have? Is she or he an expert in the field, or someone who is mainly trying to express a personal point of view?

◆ Does the site seem obviously biased? Does it use obviously inflammatory language? Is it published by a political or social organization with a particular agenda? Does it have a mission statement or statement of purpose anywhere on the site? What kinds of sites is it linked to?

◆ How often is the site updated? If it was published several years ago and hasn't been updated since, it probably is not a particularly reliable source.

As you continue to develop and refine your research project, you will probably need to return to the library a number of times. As your research changes, so will the literature that you find useful. But these tips at least will get you started.

THE RESEARCH PROCESS IN REVIEW

Developing a good research project is an ongoing process. There are a number of steps you need to take when embarking on a research project. Although the steps are listed in one order here, you will probably find that you need to go back and forth between the steps as your research unfolds. You should also realize that your project may shift its focus as you learn more and gather more evidence about your topic. At each of these stages, try to remain open to alternative paths.

1. Choose a general topic and try to refine it into a research question.

2. Evaluate whether your topic is interesting, feasible, and worth doing—and ethical. Chapter 3 discusses ethical issues that may arise in research.

3. Develop a research strategy. Decide on the kinds of data you will collect, and think about how you will try to analyze or make sense of them. Make sure that the strategy is consistent with the research question you pose and the research tradition you are working within.

4. Begin your search of the literature. Although you will probably need to return to the literature at other stages in the research process, you should begin with a good sense of what others who have studied the same topic have found.

5. Begin collecting and organizing your data. Chapters 4–7 examine different methods of collecting data, including observation, interviews, textual analysis, and action research.

6. Begin analyzing (or interpreting) your data. Although qualitative researchers usually move back and forth between analyzing and collecting data, it is sometimes helpful to think of the two as separate steps, at least initially. Chapters 8 and 9 discuss strategies for interpreting data.

7. Write up your research. In qualitative research, it can sometimes seem as if you are writing all the time. Certainly, the process of organizing data entails writing, as does interpretation. Qualitative researchers present their work in many venues: as journal articles or books, as presentations at professional conferences, at training sessions or in-service meetings for professionals, and as presentations for community groups. Chapter 10 focuses on strategies for writing up your research and presenting it to a larger community.

QUESTION FOR THOUGHT

Now is the time to consider where *you* stand in relation to your research question. Think back to the research traditions, or paradigms, outlined in Chapter 1. Which one(s) seem most convincing to you? Do you think researchers should take a critical position? Or does a more traditional orientation appeal to you? What do you think are the strengths and weaknesses of the various approaches? What personal insights do you have into your proposed research topic? What kinds of special knowledge might you have by virtue of your own life experiences? How might these insights shape the kinds of research you might do?

EXERCISES

1. As you go about your daily routine, try to pay particular attention to your surroundings. See if you can develop at least two research questions sparked by what you encounter in your daily life.

2. Evaluate one of your research questions in terms of whether it is interesting, feasible, and worth doing. Consider what kinds of resources you would need to complete the research.

3. Think of a general research topic that you might find interesting. Can you come up with three or four different perspectives on it? Try refining the topic into several different research questions.

4. Go to the library to see what information you can find about the research questions you developed. Locate at least five books or journal articles that you think might be useful.

5. Search the Internet to find at least two different Web sites of interest to you. Evaluate each Web site you've chosen in terms of its potential usefulness or bias.

6. Use several different research strategies to locate information about your topic. Try several different search engines on the Internet, such as Yahoo or Excite, and several academic databases, such as the card catalogue and Sociological Abstracts. (Check with your professor or librarian about the best methods for searching on your campus.) What different kinds of materials do you find using each strategy?

SUGGESTIONS FOR FURTHER READING

Creswell, John W. *Research Design: Qualitative and Quantitative Approaches.* Thousand Oaks, CA: Sage, 1994. A good introduction to research design, especially for those interested in comparing qualitative and quantitative approaches.

Glassner, Barry, and Rosanna Hertz (eds.). *Qualitative Sociology as Everyday Life.* Thousand Oaks, CA: Sage, 1999. A collection of essays by qualitative scholars that examine the linkages between sociological research and everyday life.

Lareau, Annette, and Jeffrey Shultz (eds.). *Journeys Through Ethnography: Realistic Accounts of Fieldwork.* Boulder, CO: Westview Press, 1996. A collection of researchers' accounts of doing qualitative research.

LeCompte, Margaret D., and Jean J. Schensul. *Designing and Conducting Ethnographic Research.* Walnut Creek, CA: AltaMira Press, 1999. Part of the Ethnographer's Toolkit, a seven-book guide to conducting ethnographic research.

3

Ethical Issues

Imagine that you have been researching radical environmentalists—those activists, like members of Earth First!, who believe that to achieve their goals they must sometimes break the law. You are interested in studying how these groups operate and how their members are like or unlike participants in other social movements. You have amassed hundreds of pages of confidential notes, transcripts of personal interviews, and other materials. Now imagine that a federal grand jury wants access to your confidential materials for a case it is developing against some of your informants. On the one hand, you guaranteed your research subjects confidentiality. They probably would not have agreed to talk with you otherwise, and they certainly didn't expect that you would be telling the police what they told you. On the other hand, you are being threatened with jail time yourself if you do not hand over the materials. What should you do?

The chances that you will be threatened with jail time or otherwise run afoul of the law while conducting research are fairly slim. But this is exactly the dilemma that sociologist Rik Scarce encountered in 1993 while studying the radical environmental movement (Scarce 1995). Scarce believed that his commitment to an ethical code meant maintaining his informants' confidentiality at all costs. Then a graduate student at Washington State University, Scarce was jailed for 159 days for refusing to share his confidential information with the authorities.

SLEEPING WELL AT NIGHT:
A PRACTICAL ETHICS

Researchers who study controversial groups are not the only ones who face ethical dilemmas. Because social research is conducted by, for, and about people, there is always the potential to harm others. For this reason, all social researchers need to think about ethical issues. We need to consider a number of questions, such as these:

- How should we conduct research so as not to hurt others?
- What kinds of relationships should we attempt to create with our research subjects?
- What kinds of power relations are there between those who are doing the research and those who are being researched?
- Who benefits from social research? Who *should* benefit?

In my own current research on at-home mothers, it's very unlikely that a grand jury will try to force me to reveal my informants' names. Yet I still worry about ethical issues. I worry about whether I have treated those I am researching well and whether they will benefit from my research. I worry about what happens when I develop friendships in the process of conducting research and about whether I am interpreting the women's lives in ways they might disapprove of. At a very practical level, I like to sleep well at night. To do so, I need to know that I have treated my research subjects ethically. But what is ethical treatment of research subjects? How do I know if I have conducted myself in an ethical way? Researchers answer these questions in a number of ways. There is no one "guaranteed" way to act ethically in a given research situation, and reasonable people—all of whom may think carefully about ethics—may disagree. My aim in this chapter is to encourage you to think about the kinds of ethical dilemmas that research can pose. I hope you'll consider how your own belief systems shape your responses to important ethical questions.

Ethical Codes

To help researchers make ethical decisions, most professional organizations to which researchers belong (such as the American Sociological Association [ASA] and the American Psychological Association) have ethical codes. Codes of ethics provide standards for behavior. The ASA, for example, has a detailed code of ethics that "sets forth the principles and ethical standards that underlie sociologists' professional responsibilities and conduct" (ASA Code of Ethics, p. 1). (You can read the complete version of the ASA code of ethics on its Web page: http://www.asanet.org. Parts of it are also reprinted in Appendix A.) Although much of the code is not necessarily relevant for beginning social researchers, it also contains many useful guidelines.

Confidentiality and Informed Consent

Two issues are of particular relevance for beginning researchers: (1) maintaining *confidentiality* and (2) obtaining *informed consent*. That is, researchers must ensure that participants freely agree to participate in the research, and they must protect the privacy of their research participants. They also must inform participants of all potential risks from participating in the research and gain formal consent before beginning. Although, as we'll see, the notion of informed consent may be especially tricky in qualitative research, there are important reasons for considering the issue carefully before beginning.

Concern for treating research participants ethically arose out of people's horror at the practices of Nazi medical researchers during World War II. For example, they injected Jewish prisoners with spotted fever virus to keep the virus alive, and they deliberately infected other prisoners with strep, tetanus, and gangrene. Some prisoners were placed in tanks of freezing water for up to 3 hours or forced to stand outside, naked, in below-freezing temperatures (Neutens and Rubinson 1997, p. 16).

In order to stop these kinds of abuses, judges at the Nazi war crimes tribunal developed the Nuremberg Code in 1947 (Shuster 1998). The code provided basic standards for conducting research on human subjects. First, and perhaps foremost, research subjects must voluntarily consent to the research. Second, the research must show clear benefits to society. Third, the research must be designed so as to minimize the potential of harm. Although the code contains other standards (for example, researchers must be qualified to conduct their work), the notion of informed consent has perhaps most influenced contemporary social scientists.

Nazi scientists have not been the only ones to engage in unethical practices—and, indeed, debates about the ethics of medical research continue today. Much closer to home is the Tuskegee Study funded by the U.S. Public Health Service. In this study, poor Black men who had been exposed to syphilis were left untreated for many years—even after penicillin had been developed and made widely available (Caplan 1992). About 600 Black men from Tuskegee, Alabama, were originally enrolled in the study. Promised free medical treatment (for diseases *other than* syphilis), lunches, and transportation, the men (at least, as one writer notes, those who were still living) were followed from 1932 to 1973 in order to determine what would happen if the disease were left untreated. (Syphilis is highly contagious and can lead to serious heart problems, blindness, paralysis, insanity, and, ultimately, death.) It wasn't until a Public Health Service officer named Peter Buxtun aired his ethical concerns to the press that the study was stopped. Outrage over the Tuskegee Study led Congress in 1974 to create the National Commission for the Protection of Human Subjects of Biomedical and Behavioral Research (Caplan 1992). This commission played a major role in the development of institutional review boards, or committees set up to consider ethical issues in research.

Clearly, medical research has the capacity to harm—or help—its research subjects in direct ways. But what about social research? Can it be considered in the same light? Some people argue that it can and that social researchers must follow strictly the same kinds of guidelines as medical researchers. Other researchers argue that there are crucial differences (Morse 1998). Two influential research projects have highlighted some of the ethical issues in social research. In each case, the ethical issues are complex, and social scientists have disagreed—sometimes heatedly—about what the researchers should have done.

CONTROVERSIES IN SOCIAL RESEARCH

Milgram's "Obedience" Study

One controversial study was conducted by psychologist Stanley Milgram in the 1950s (Milgram 1974). Milgram wanted to investigate how people are influenced by authority. He brought his research subjects into the laboratory and asked them to read pairs of words to another "subject" (really a confederate of the experimenter), who was sitting in another room, strapped to what looked like an electric shock machine. The research subjects sat in front of an elaborate control panel, with dials indicating voltages ranging from 15 to 315 and labels such as "extreme-intensity shock." The subjects believed that the object of the experiment was to see if the other person (the confederate) could remember the word pairs correctly. If the confederate answered incorrectly, the subjects were instructed by a researcher in a white lab coat to administer a shock. But the subjects couldn't actually see the confederate; they only saw the lights of the control panel indicating the answers and heard the responses to the shocks through an open door. As the experiment continued, the subjects were instructed to give what they thought were more and more intense shocks. When the subjects hesitated or refused, the researcher ordered them to continue. As the shocks became more intense, the confederate screamed in (feigned) pain, kicked on the door, and, finally, fell silent. When subjects finally refused to give additional shocks, despite the urgings of the researcher, the trial was over.

What Milgram was interested in was when people would stop administering the shocks. That is, once they felt they were hurting someone, would they refuse—even though a scientist, someone in a position of authority, pressed them to continue? Many of the subjects did continue, experiencing great stress in the process. Some begged the scientist to let them stop; others experienced physical symptoms of stress. Even though the subjects were not, themselves, subjected to electric shocks, many felt as if they had been.

This study highlights several ethical dilemmas. Should researchers be allowed to deceive their subjects? Under what conditions? Once Milgram knew that the subjects were experiencing stress, should he have stopped the experiment? Could he have obtained the information he wanted in any other way? These are just a few of the ethical questions raised in relation to Milgram's study—and there are no easy answers.

Qualitative researchers don't typically conduct experiments like Milgram's. Nonetheless, issues of deception can still come up—especially in types of research, like participant observation or in-depth interviews, in which researchers need to develop relatively close and trusting relationships with their research subjects. For example, should you tell your research subjects exactly what you plan to study? What if your findings are not necessarily flattering to your subjects? Or what if you are studying a group whose ideals you are critical of? Should you only study groups you approve of? For example, Kathleen Blee (1996) studied White women activists in racist groups such as the Ku Klux Klan and White supremacist groups. Blee describes herself as "decidedly unsympathetic" to the goals of the groups and, indeed, considers how her work could be used to help fight racism. Should she have informed her research participants of this before she began? If some of her research findings would help further the group's racist goals, should she share them? What should a researcher be obligated to tell his or her informants about the nature of the research?

Humphreys' "Tearoom" Study

A highly controversial study involving deception was conducted by Laud Humphreys in the 1960s and published as a book, *Tearoom Trade* (Humphreys 1970). Humphreys wanted to study homosexuality at a time when homosexuality was highly stigmatized (and illegal in most states) and when there was very little research about it. Specifically, he was interested in those men who had sexual encounters with other men in public bathrooms, or "tearooms." If he had tried to pass out questionnaires or even simply observe, the men likely would have assumed he was a police officer and left the scene. Given the stigma (and legal consequences) attached to homosexual behavior, he probably would not have been able to conduct his study if he had approached participants directly. So, Humphreys decided to participate in the scene by acting as a "watch queen," someone who kept watch for the police so that other men could engage in sex. Humphreys did not reveal his role as researcher; nor did he engage in sexual activities himself during the course of the study. But he secretly wrote down the license plate numbers of the men he observed. Later, under the guise of conducting another study, he was able to get the addresses of those men through a contact at the Department of Motor Vehicles. He then followed up with an in-person interview with the men, some of whom had wives and children, at their homes. He never revealed to the men how he had obtained their names and addresses or where they had encountered each other earlier.

Again, this study raises ethical issues. Should Humphreys have acted as a participant in an illegal activity? Should he have told the men about his research? Could he have obtained the information any other way? Should he have followed up with the interviews in the way he did? Did the benefits of his research outweigh the risks? These are just a few of the ethical questions about his study—and, again, there are no easy answers.

FEMINIST APPROACHES TO RESEARCH ETHICS

Many feminist scholars have criticized researchers for not paying enough attention to ethical issues in conducting research. Although there is no single feminist approach to research ethics, many feminist scholars believe that researchers need to address the power relationships that are embedded in research. Researchers, they note, often tend to be of a higher social class than the research participants. Researchers benefit from the research they conduct by publishing their findings and gaining public recognition, which helps them advance in their jobs. Researchers also determine how the research is conducted. In interviewing and other forms of data collection, they usually set the agenda and determine what is important, and they have the power to end the research relationship when they're finished. And it's their interpretations and analyses that get written up. The research subjects, while they may have the power to stop participating, do not have the power to leave the field that researchers do. Research participants can lie (and have lied) or exaggerate their stories, but they do not typically have the power to determine, ultimately, how the data are used.

Feminist scholars argue that researchers need to consider these power issues when doing research. Most feminist scholars agree that feminist research should contribute in some way, even if indirectly, to social change (Reinharz 1992). Many have urged the development of close, personal ties between researchers and subjects (Oakley 1981), although others have argued that such ties lead to a greater potential for manipulation and ethical dilemmas than other, more distant forms of research (Stacey 1996). Many believe that *reciprocity* can help reduce some of the power differences between researcher and researched. That is, researchers may be able to offer things that are of use to those being researched, such as giving rides or tutoring or doing other favors that place researcher and researched in a more reciprocal role. Still other feminist scholars believe that research should be more collaborative in order to level, as much as possible, the differences in power and status (Cancian 1996; Naples and Clark 1996). Many feminist scholars argue that researchers should share their findings with their subjects, and some believe that researchers should seek participants' responses and get approval from them before publishing their work. We will consider these issues further in Chapter 7, on action research.

INSTITUTIONAL REVIEW BOARDS

Most colleges and universities—and other institutions that do research on humans—have review boards to make certain that researchers follow ethical guidelines. These boards, called institutional review boards (IRBs) (or sometimes human subjects committees), review research proposals before the research begins to ensure that certain standards are followed. Each institution has its own special procedures, but all must follow federal guidelines. For example, all IRBs must include at least one member who is not a social scientist (for example, a lawyer or member of the clergy), and all IRBs must ensure that researchers have adequate procedures for obtaining informed consent. Sometimes, research that is conducted under the supervision of an instructor as part of a class is considered exempt; that is, it does not need special IRB approval. Other schools have special procedures for student researchers to gain approval. If you are planning to conduct research as part of your program or class, you should check with your professor to see if you need IRB approval before you begin.

IRBs are unpopular with many researchers. You might wonder about this. Why would anyone object to making researchers think about ethical issues? Who could *not* want research participants to be treated fairly? The problem is that many IRBs are more familiar with biomedical and behavioral research that is experimental in design (like Milgram's—which probably wouldn't be able to get IRB approval today). Many IRBs are not as familiar with qualitative research designs and the specific kinds of questions that arise. For example, much qualitative research is open-ended in nature. Unlike survey research, in-depth interviews are not wholly scripted. Thus, it may be impossible for a researcher to tell an IRB exactly the questions he or she plans to ask research subjects. Because of perceived (and sometimes actual) difficulties in receiving IRB approval, some researchers have shied away from controversial topics or innovative research designs.

ETHICAL CONCERNS IN QUALITATIVE RESEARCH

Some Problems of Confidentiality and Intimacy

Several features of qualitative research raise difficult ethical issues. The goal of qualitative research is typically an in-depth, detailed study. Instead of making statistical generalizations about a large number of cases, the goal is often to tell detailed stories (what some call "thick description") about a particular case or a small number of cases. And rather than use impersonal techniques of data collection, like surveys, which lend themselves to anonymity, the data are often collected after long periods (sometimes even years) in the field. Field researchers often develop close, intimate relationships with their research participants. Most qualitative researchers stress that the quality of the relationship between researcher and subject affects the quality of the research. Even when qualitative researchers conduct a one-time interview, it is still typically more intimate and personal. In a face-to-face interview, true anonymity is impossible. The researcher sees the interviewee in person, up close.

Under these conditions, it is often difficult to maintain confidentiality. Imagine that you are studying people in a small community. Chances are, providing only a few details about a participant—like job title, race, and age—might be enough information for others to guess the person's identity. In my first book, for example, I studied a small lesbian and bisexual community. One of the women I studied had a very unusual story. We both knew, when I was conducting the interview, that if anyone guessed the town in which the study was set, they would be able to tell who she was, even if I used a pseudonym (which I did) and changed identifying details (such as her occupation) in the book. We talked about the risks in the interview. In this case, she felt that her story was important, and she wanted other women to hear it. But what if she had felt otherwise? Would I have been obligated to leave it out of the book?

Judith Stacey (1996) has written about some of the ethical dilemmas qualitative researchers face when they develop close, personal relationships with their research participants over a long period of time. While the participants (and the researcher as well) may see the relationship as one of friendship, the researcher still gains from that relationship. At some level, this relationship can be exploitative. At the same time, some argue that those being researched may also benefit from the relationship. They may enjoy the opportunity to talk about themselves or like the fact that someone is interested in their lives. Indeed, Stacey acknowledged that her own research participants benefited in certain ways.

Although there may be other, more tangible benefits to participation, however, researchers typically have much more to gain. It is, thus, a lopsided relationship, one that researchers can end simply by leaving the field. In addition, when participants experience hardship or personal troubles, researchers are in an ambiguous role. Should they act as a friend? Should they observe and take notes? What does it mean when a "friend" takes notes about another's hardship and then benefits from it? When bad things happen to research participants, it may simply be, to researchers, "grist for the ethnographic mill," as Stacey (1996, p. 92) puts it. Ethnographic researchers may find themselves concealing information or telling half-truths and otherwise behaving in ways that leave them feeling very uncomfortable—and in ways that might disturb research participants if they knew. Thus, researchers must be aware of the contradictions and tensions involved in doing feminist and ethnographic research.

Some Problems of Informed Consent

Because of the open-ended nature of much qualitative research, it is also difficult to provide truly informed consent. In a one-time interview, it is not too difficult to anticipate the risks of participation and to gain informed consent before beginning. But what if you are observing an organization for a long period of time? You might gain consent at the beginning of the study, before you begin. But if new members join several months *after* you begin, should you continue to announce your research objectives? Also, people might forget that you are a researcher. If your informants come to see you as a friend, they might feel subtly coerced into participating. As one researcher has commented, "A major part of the problem is that informed consent changes almost as frequently as the weather" (Coy 1999, p. 2). In this type of situation, how do you negotiate and renegotiate informed consent?

You must also consider the types of settings in which you need to request informed consent. For example, you certainly need to gain consent in an interview or private setting in which all the members can be identified. But suppose you are observing a large public rally or demonstration—one with hundreds or maybe even thousands of participants. Should you attempt to gain consent from all the people there? Or suppose you are observing a private meeting with a large number of people. What steps can you take to inform people of your research? Should you make any distinctions between private and public settings? That is, do people have a greater right not to be researched in private settings than in public ones?

In addition to protecting confidentiality, researchers also need to be aware of some other privacy issues. At what point does social research invade the research participants' privacy? Because there are not always preestablished boundaries when conducting qualitative research, it's sometimes hard to tell when to stop collecting data. The line between collecting information for "legitimate" research purposes and invading respondents' privacy is a thin one. For example, suppose people share deeply personal information with you that, at least as far as you can tell, seems unrelated to your study. Should you encourage them to continue? Should you try to subtly change the subject? Or suppose people tell you intimate details about *other* people's lives—maybe people you know or other people involved in your study? What are your ethical obligations to *them*?

Overt Versus Covert Observation

Is it ever ethical to carry out research covertly—that is, without the participants' knowledge? Some researchers believe that deception is sometimes necessary for the research to take place at all. Humphreys' "tearoom" study would never have been done without it, for example. Others argue that deception is rarely or never ethical (see, for example, James Richardson's 1991 discussion of covert research in new religions). Richardson argues that covert research isn't really necessary most of the time—and probably isn't as effective, ultimately, as overt research methods.

I tend to agree that covert research is *almost* never ethical, although there may be times when deception is necessary. But sometimes deception is crucial. Let's say you want to study whether bankers practice racial discrimination in their mortgage lending practices. One of the best ways to do so is to send out matched testers—people with identical credentials but from different racial/ethnic groups—and see if they are treated differently when they apply for mortgages. The mortgage lender can't give informed consent; otherwise, the test won't work. Is this ethical? It probably is ethical to use deception when the intent is to uncover some kind of abuse or bad practice. What about in other situations?

Before choosing a covert research strategy, I would encourage you to think carefully about the dilemmas involved. You might want to consider how *you* would feel if you found out that a researcher was studying you without your consent. When do you think you should reasonably expect privacy—which presumably includes the right *not* to be researched? In your home? Your car? Your place of employment? In public places like shopping malls or restaurants? What about in a classroom? In general, when people can reasonably expect privacy, you must attempt to gain informed consent. In public places (like shopping malls), where people reasonably expect that others might see them and in which informed consent might be impossible to obtain, covert research may be fine.

Sometimes, beginning researchers think that they must conduct research covertly because if people know they are being observed they will act differently. While this may be true, there are things you can do to minimize the effect. (Chapter 4 will deal with this issue in detail.) You should also be aware that you miss important details when you conduct research covertly, because you are typically less free to ask clarifying questions or to take notes. In addition, the stress of researching covertly may subtly shift your interactions and make you inhibited around the people you want to study. Still, the issue of covert versus overt strategies is not always clear-cut, and researchers continue to debate the issue, often passionately (see Mitchell 1993; Punch, 1998).

PRACTICAL CONCERNS IN PROTECTING PRIVACY

Researchers need to be careful about protecting participants' confidentiality while collecting and analyzing the data and when publishing it or otherwise disseminating their results. While collecting your data, there are several things you can do to try to protect your respondents' privacy. First, you can make sure that you don't leave their names or phone numbers or e-mail addresses lying about where others can see them. (This might seem obvious, but for those of us who tend to be messy, it's sound advice.) It's a good idea to keep this kind of information in a locked file cabinet. Some researchers, especially those who are working with members of controversial groups, are careful *not* to keep lists of participants, or they discard them as soon as possible. If you share a computer with others or use the Internet to correspond with research participants, you should take special steps to preserve your participants' privacy.

A relatively easy way to help protect your subjects' privacy when you are writing notes and transcribing interview tapes is to assign a code number or pseudonym and use that instead of the person's real name. (And, if you do attempt to do "high-risk" work—for example, research on groups that break the law—it's absolutely crucial.) My own students have found this important in their class research projects. One group was conducting a campus study on student cheating. They knew that student participants wouldn't be honest if they thought that professors might learn their identities. If the research was going to yield anything of value, the student researchers had to be scrupulous about protecting their informants' privacy. But I also had to read the student researchers' field notes and interview transcripts in order to evaluate their course work. By omitting names from those documents and by asking me not to observe a focus group session, the students were able to protect their informants.

You also need to think about how to discuss your work with others while you are doing it. If you are excited about how your data collection is going, it's often difficult *not* to talk about it. But you need to consider whether you are giving away important identifying details. For example, a former student of mine and I presented a paper based on some ongoing field research in an urban housing project in Kansas City (Masuda 1998). The conference was in Iowa. We didn't reveal the name of the housing project (there were a number in the city), the management company, or any of the people involved. Yet at the end of the session, someone came up to us and asked if one of the participants in the study was "Jan" (I won't give you her real name, but he had guessed it correctly). It sometimes takes very little information for someone even slightly familiar with the setting to guess another individual's identity. This may be even more crucial in a college or university setting if you are conducting a research project on campus.

When you are presenting your research—either as a presentation or a published piece of writing—you need to be especially careful to protect your participants. Most social researchers use pseudonyms for participants and vague descriptions for the actual place in which they do research. Thus, William Foote Whyte (1943) wrote about "Cornerville," which he revealed years later to be the North End of Boston. Judith Stacey (1991) located her respondents in Silicon Valley—a large enough geographic region to protect the confidentiality of her informants.

TALKING ABOUT ETHICAL ISSUES

Ethical issues may occur at all stages of a research project. In the early stages, you should plan to minimize any harmful consequences to your research participants. You also need to consider what you can give back to the people you are studying. As your research unfolds, new ethical challenges may arise as your work goes in new and unexpected directions. At all stages, it is important to talk with others about these ethical challenges. Others may see ethical problems you hadn't considered, or they may offer novel solutions. By talking with others, you may gain greater insight into how to handle ethical dilemmas.

QUESTIONS FOR THOUGHT

1. Some researchers have gone to great lengths and some have even broken the law to conduct their research. For example, Jeff Ferrell (1995) was arrested for "graffiti vandalism" in the course of his participant observation with hip-hop graffiti writers. In doing research on sex workers, Wendy Chapkis (1997) spent an afternoon selling sex to women clients (legally) in Amsterdam. Much closer to home, some students have gone to parties where illegal substances have been present. How far would you go in your research? Would you break the law? Do something that some consider unethical? Why or why not?

2. What would you do if you observed someone doing something illegal or unethical in the course of your research? Why? What would you do if a research participant told you about doing something illegal (but you didn't observe it)? Would your reaction be different? Why?

3. Imagine that you have been interviewing students about a whole range of controversial issues, including their religious beliefs, their use of alcohol and drugs, and their sexual behaviors. How can you protect their privacy and confidentiality? What if you want to interview students whom you already know? Is this ethical? What kinds of special precautions should you take?

4. Imagine that you are conducting research on sexual violence. You have been interviewing students and observing at a rape crisis shelter. One of your research participants becomes upset during the interview, visibly shaking and crying. What should you do? Suppose that she names someone you know or have heard of as her attacker. What should you do?

5. Imagine that you have been doing an in-depth study of personal relationships in a small community. You have been observing and conducting taped interviews. Suppose that in one of your interviews your subject freely talks about a number of people whom you know through your research. What should you do? Suppose that in the course of conducting one of your interviews, you become very attracted to the person you are interviewing. Is it ethical to ask him or her for a date?

EXERCISES

1. Find out the procedures for getting IRB approval on your campus. Do students have to get special approval for their research projects? What procedures must they follow?
2. Choose one of the research questions you evaluated in Chapter 2. Develop a plan for protecting research subjects' confidentiality and gaining informed consent, if appropriate.
3. Following the model in Appendix B, develop a form for obtaining informed consent from a potential research subject.

SUGGESTIONS FOR FURTHER READING

Fine, Michelle; Lois Weis; Susan Weseen; and Loonmun Wong. "For Whom? Qualitative Research, Representations, and Social Responsibilities." Pp. 107–131 in *Handbook of Qualitative Research*, 2nd ed., edited by Norman K. Denzin and Yvonna S. Lincoln. Thousand Oaks, CA: Sage, 2000.

Punch, Maurice. "Politics and Ethics in Qualitative Research." Pp. 156–184 in *The Landscape of Qualitative Research*, edited by Norman K. Denzin and Yvonna S. Lincoln. Thousand Oaks, CA: Sage, 1998.

Richardson, James T. "Experiencing Research on New Religions and Cults: Practical and Ethical Considerations." Pp. 62–71 in *Experiencing Fieldwork: An Inside View of Qualitative Research*, edited by William B. Shaffir and Robert A. Stebbins. Newbury Park, CA: Sage, 1991.

Stacey, Judith. "Can There Be a Feminist Ethnography?" Pp. 88–101 in *Feminism and Social Change: Bridging Theory and Practice*, edited by Heidi Gottfried. Urbana: University of Illinois Press, 1996.

Wolf, Diane L. (ed.). *Feminist Dilemmas in Fieldwork*. Boulder, CO: Westview Press, 1996.

4

Observation: Participant and Otherwise

You observe all the time—on your way from home to school and work, during class and meals, and so on. But how much do you really see? If you're like most people, much of what you observe in your day-to-day life you ignore. Your eyes don't really focus, or you don't think much about what you're seeing. You forget almost as soon as you move on.

Here's a quick test I sometimes do with my students. I ask them to close their eyes and tell me the color of the walls and the floor of the classroom. Usually, most of them don't know. Can you remember the color of the classroom where your methods class meets? Probably not. This shouldn't be a surprise. After all, you don't really *need* to remember its color, and so you don't. But you probably *do* remember the topic from your last assignment— or at least could bring it to mind if you thought about it. In class, you're expected to focus on the substance of the course, and not on your physical surroundings. You're likely to remember more about the topic because you have been focusing on it.

How much more do you see when you really pay attention? How much more can you recall when you make a mental note to remember something or when you take the time to write things down? When you focus on observing, you see so much more. In qualitative social research, you need to train yourself to look, to *observe*. This isn't that much different from what you do the rest of the time. It's more a question of degree.

Observation—looking in a focused way—is at the heart of qualitative research. This chapter focuses on the ways in which scholars use observation to understand social life. *Observational studies* are very different from surveys or experiments or even interviews. Instead of asking people questions about their thoughts and behavior or conducting experiments in a laboratory, these researchers go to the "natural" settings in which social life takes place and observe what people "really" do in those settings. In observational studies, researchers play a much more prominent role than in other kinds of research. They usually immerse themselves for relatively long periods of time in a specific setting, getting to know the people there intimately.

Researchers have used observation to study many different groups of people in many different kinds of settings. William Shaffir, for example, used participant observation to study ultra Orthodox Jews in Israel and Montreal (Shaffir 1991). Alma Gottlieb lived for 15 months among the Beng people of West Africa with her husband, fiction writer Philip Graham. They wrote about their experiences in an award-winning book, *Parallel Worlds: An Anthropologist and a Writer Encounter Africa* (Gottlieb and Graham 1993). Closer to home, researchers have studied lesbian communities in the Midwest (Krieger 1983) and Northeast (Esterberg 1997), low-income women in the Boston area (Dodson 1998), families in California's Silicon Valley (Stacey 1991), and children in elementary schools in California and Michigan (Thorne 1993). Researchers have used observational methods to study taxi drivers, jazz musicians, biker gangs, and police officers, among many others.

ETHNOGRAPHY

Scholars from different traditions use somewhat different words to describe this kind of work. Some, especially those from anthropology, use the word *ethnography*. Often, those who do ethnography—called *ethnographers*—supplement their observations with in-depth interviews (which we'll deal with in Chapter 5) and archival research (which we'll consider in Chapter 6). Historically, sociologists have used the term *participant observation*, although an increasing number call it ethnography as well. Still others call it *field research* or *field studies*. Whatever you call it, this kind of research entails immersing yourself in the social life of a group, observing, and writing about what you see.

Many of those who have traditionally done ethnography have argued that the study of culture is—or should be—the central concern of this kind of research (Geertz 1973). There are many debates about what ethnography (and culture) is; one anthropologist defines ethnography as "the study of the customary social behaviors of identifiable groups of people" (Wolcott 1999, pp. 252–253). In this sense, the challenge for ethnographers is to gain insight into the lives of particular people within particular social settings, to understand social behavior in context. By observing and participating, they try to understand how the participants themselves view social life.

By participating, ethnographers hope to develop an understanding based on first-hand experience (what some researchers call "lived experience"). They learn more by participating than they would by other means, such as simply asking others questions. They can use all of their senses: sight, hearing, smell, taste, and touch. Let's say, for example, you want to understand what life is like for men in a homeless shelter. You will have a much better idea if you actually go to the shelter and talk to the men there than if you simply ask questions over the phone. You will be able to see, hear, and smell what the men themselves do and thereby get a much richer understanding of shelter life. Your understanding will be deepened if you actually spend the night and experience some of the same things as the homeless men. And if you hang out and observe at the shelter for an extended period of time—not just once—your understanding will be further enriched. By sharing experiences with the men over time, you can gain insight into their lives. Will you actually begin to experience life exactly as the homeless men do? Not as long as you have a home that you could go to. But you will come much closer to their experiences than you would otherwise.

Ethnography developed out of an impulse for westerners to understand what they thought of as "primitive" people. Traditionally, ethnographic researchers were encouraged to study groups of people in distant communities or, at least, groups of people who were very different from the researchers themselves. Thus, anthropologists typically studied groups in far-off places, and sociologists studied hoboes, slum dwellers, prostitutes, and the like. Ethnographic researchers were not encouraged to study themselves or people like themselves. While ethnographers still study marginalized groups, they often do so with the explicit aim of giving voice or bearing witness to their experiences. Many ethnographers hope that their writing will dispel stereotypes or help increase understanding of the group they are studying.

More recently, some scholars have created what they call *autoethnography*, or ethnography of the self. The purpose of this kind of ethnography is to try to understand the researcher's own experiences by using introspection and recalling personal experiences (Ellis 1999). Autoethnographers focus on their own thoughts, feelings, and experiences. By exploring their own lives, autoethnographers like Carolyn Ellis (1999) hope to shed light on the lives and experiences of others.

Although ethnographers work in a variety of settings and see themselves as having somewhat different purposes, at heart researchers who do this kind of research all do the following:

1. Immerse themselves in a field setting, usually for an extended period of time
2. Participate in a variety of ways
3. Observe while they are participating
4. Take notes about what they are observing
5. Conduct informal (and sometimes formal) interviews
6. Take more notes (and more notes and more notes and more notes)
7. Analyze their notes
8. Write up their analysis, often in the form of a story or extended narrative

PARTICIPATING AND OBSERVING

When I discuss participant observation with my students, they often focus more on the observation side and less on the participation side. That is, they think they have to spend all their time watching and taking notes, and not much time joining in. They often don't understand what I mean by participating in the life of the group. One research group in my class, for example, studied the parking problem at our university. They spent many hours watching people drive in and out of the parking lots. They took lots of notes while they were observing, but they didn't really talk to anyone while they were doing their observations. No one knew that they were observing the parking lots, and—because parking lots are a public place—no one seemed to care.

In this case, the students took primarily an observational role. That is, they didn't interact much with others in the setting, and no one changed their behavior as a result of their observation. But were they really pure observers? That is, were they *not* participating in the setting at all? Actually, they were participating, for they were all students at the university, and they all had experiences of their own trying to park their cars on campus. Even though they had little contact with others while they were observing the lots, they still brought their own experiences as students and as drivers to their observations. These experiences clearly shaped how they thought about parking on campus, what they noticed while they were observing, and how they interpreted what they saw.

Some researchers study groups that they are already involved in. For example, Patricia and Peter Adler decided to study after-school groups because of their experiences as parents (Adler and Adler 1994). As parents, they were already involved with school-aged children in a variety of roles; they added the role of researcher to study the after-school programs more systematically. Other researchers enter into field settings specifically to study them. Once in the setting, they figure out what role to play and how best to participate. For example, William Foote Whyte spent several years observing and participating in Boston's North End during the late 1930s (Whyte 1943). Prior to his study, he had had no contacts with the community. He picked the neighborhood he called "Cornerville" for study because he was interested in what he then called "slum districts." (In an appendix to the third edition of his book, Whyte wrote about how he came to study "Cornerville," what roles he played, and how he was able to gain access.)

How much observing should you do, and how much participating? While it is possible for you to participate minimally in a setting and for participants to be unaware that you're observing, most researchers participate at least in some ways. And while it may be ethical to engage in covert observations in very open and public places, in more private places covert research may be unethical.

You might think of participation as having multiple dimensions (Atkinson and Hammersley 1998). The researcher might be completely known to those being researched, a little known, or completely unknown. Those being researched might know a little bit or nothing about the research, or they may be actively involved in setting the agenda for the research, as they would be in field studies conducted from a critical perspective. While in the field setting, the researcher might engage in a variety of tasks, from strictly observing (as the students in my parking group did) to being completely engaged in the scene. How much observing and how much participating you do depends on your own inclinations and on the research setting. The balance between observation and participation can also change over the course of a research project, as you become more and more familiar with the setting and the people in it.

THE SELF AS INSTRUMENT

In observational research, you are the research instrument. What's important is what *you* observe, what *you* see and hear. Clearly, you cannot observe everything at one time; you have to decide what to focus your attention on. However, unlike in survey research, you do not have an interview guide or schedule to fall back on. There's no list of things that you *have* to focus on. And humans are moving targets! They don't simply stand still and wait for you to record their behavior or jot down what they just said. By the time you've noted a behavior, the people in the setting have moved on.

Sometimes, students think that if they could just record everything—either by hand or with a tape recorder—they would somehow have a complete and objective record of "what happened." As beginning researchers soon discover, however, they miss much of what people say or do. There's simply no way that they can record everything that is going on in the setting. But even if they could somehow magically record everything, they would still have to figure out which of the things they saw or heard were important. In qualitative research, you have to use your judgment to figure out what to focus on. You have to decide what is important in the setting and what you should focus on.

At the same time, your own personal qualities—how well you get along with other people, whether you're outgoing or more reserved, whether you have a sense of humor, and so forth—will dramatically shape how people react to you in the field and, thus, what kind of evidence you collect. Your own qualities shape what you can see in the field setting. As we'll discuss shortly, developing personal relationships is one of the crucial tasks of fieldwork. In this sense, ethnographic research is very personal research. Who you are and what qualities you bring to your work matter.

THINKING ABOUT SETTINGS AND SELECTING A SITE

One of the first tasks in an observational study is to pick a research setting. Where are you going to observe? What do you hope to see? You also need to consider the physical place in which you plan to conduct your research. As you are considering potential settings, you need to ask these questions:

- Is this an appropriate place to study what you want to study?
- How can you define the boundaries of your field setting?
- Who are you in relation to this site? What kinds of connections do you already have to it?
- How can you gain access to this site?
- What kinds of ethical dilemmas will you need to consider in using this site?
- What kinds of risk are inherent in this setting?

Is This an Appropriate Place to Study What You Want to Study?

One of the first things to think about is the kind of setting that will be appropriate for your topic. Some kinds of topics are more amenable to observational study than others. For example, if you want to know how the media depicts urban teenagers, you probably shouldn't do an observational study. You'd be much better off doing a systematic study of the media, such as newspapers and TV programs. But if you want to know how teens themselves think about their lives, then you might do participant observation with a group of urban teenagers—at school, in their after-school hangouts, on their jobs, and at home.

Suppose you want to know what women who receive public assistance think about their experiences. It wouldn't make sense to observe the social workers who administer benefits. While that may end up being a part of your study, you would be much better off beginning with the women themselves. But if you are interested in how social workers think about their clients, you will want to find a location where social workers interact.

In general, good sites for participant observation tend to be relatively small-scale. You couldn't do a good job observing an entire country, for example, or even a state. But you could observe a small town, a relatively self-contained neighborhood within a city, or a workplace. At the same time, good settings should also include some kind of face-to-face interaction. Although it is increasingly possible to observe virtual communities on the Internet, these studies can be problematic (Rutter and Smith 1999). Settings without any people in them do not make good sites for observing social behavior!*

What Are the Boundaries of This Site?

Once you've established a general setting, you need to consider the boundaries of that setting. Where, exactly, do you intend to observe and participate? Will all your observations be made in one single location, or will you participate in a number of places? Some topics seem to suggest settings with relatively clear boundaries. For example, one group of students I worked with was interested in the question of how (and what) people ate in public. They wanted to see if people ate differently when they were with

---

*Of course, a great deal of information about social behavior can be gleaned from physical traces or archival materials even when living people aren't present. But these kinds of materials are studied using somewhat different strategies.

people than when they were alone, and they wanted to see how different groups of people negotiated dining halls. Their field setting was relatively straightforward: They observed in the school cafeterias, a relatively well-bounded place.

Other settings seem more amorphous. For example, if you are interested in how social workers think about their clients, you might want to spend some time observing in social workers' offices. Yet much of the work that social workers do is carried out in the field. Therefore, you might also ride along with the workers as they go about their daily business. In addition, you might attend any gatherings outside of work, such as informal social get-togethers or special events, that the social workers engage in. In this case, your field setting may include many different physical sites.

As you begin your fieldwork, you should try to define as clearly as you can where you will be observing and what you will be doing. Although the boundaries of your setting may very well change, as will your level of participation, it is best to begin with at least a general idea of what you hope to be doing.

Who Are You in Relation to This Site?

You also need to consider what personal connections you have to the setting. What do you already know about this place? What kinds of stereotypes might you have about the place and the people in it? Do you already know people in the setting? Do they know you? What do you think they think about you? Does the setting have any personal meanings for you? Does it evoke any particular emotions or feelings?

Some people suggest that you shouldn't study a place you are too familiar with. They argue that your familiarity with the setting will make it hard for you to see anything new. This can certainly be a danger. For example, one of the students in my parking lot group had difficulty seeing that there was anything to study in her setting. She didn't really believe that there was anything new to see, and so her first field notes were very thin. A bunch of cars were parked, she noted; some came in, and some went out. She wrote that she didn't expect to see anything, and indeed she didn't.

Being familiar with a setting can give you some hints about where to begin. For example, if you already volunteer at a homeless shelter, you may have an idea of what's important to the people who stay in it. The shelter residents may also feel more comfortable about your presence in the shelter and your research role. You may have access that you wouldn't be able to get otherwise. However, the shelter residents may have some preconceived notions about your role. They may have a hard time thinking of you as a researcher, and not as a volunteer. If you decide to do your research in a setting where others already know you, you need to think about how they may see you, for that will certainly affect your research.

Janet Theophano and Karen Curtis wrote about their experiences doing fieldwork in an Italian American community (1996). In studying the relationship between food and ethnicity, they shared family meals in their field site over an extended period of time. One of them, Theophano, was married and had a child; the other, Curtis, was single. They found that they were treated differently in the field because of their different statuses. Because she was a mother, Theophano was "expected to eat the leftover foods that mothers eat; in contrast, [Curtis] was seen as a daughter and provided with newly prepared foods at each meal" (Theophano and Curtis 1996, p. 159).

You should also consider whether the setting has any personal meanings that may influence your study. For example, if you have been homeless yourself, you may find that studying a homeless shelter evokes powerful emotions. The existence of these feelings isn't necessarily a signal that you shouldn't do your research in the setting. Sometimes, these emotional cues can help you uncover profound truths about your setting—and yourself. But you should at least consider whether you want to put yourself in a position to have those experiences. If you do decide to proceed, you should be careful to distinguish your own feelings about the setting from those that the participants themselves may have. Although they may be similar to yours, they may also not be.

How Can You Gain Access to This Site?

Especially for students, who may only have a semester or two to complete a project, the question of access is paramount. You need to think about whether you can gain access to the setting. Whom might you need to ask for formal permission? Do you have connections that can help you gain access? Who are the *gatekeepers*, the people who can make your entry easier or stop your research completely?

In public places where you don't intend to announce that you are observing, such as shopping malls or parking lots, you may be able to observe without asking formal permission. Access in these cases is easy: You simply enter like any other member of the public. Thus, the students in my parking lot group merely sat in their cars or at the edges of the lot and observed. Similarly, in her research on public spaces such as airport waiting areas, Lyn Lofland simply sat down in the waiting rooms like any other passenger (Lofland 1985).

Although it is possible to do covert research in more private spaces, you need to consider whether it is ethical to do so. (Chapter 3 discusses some of the ethical concerns.) You should also be aware of the stress that doing covert research can place on the researcher—and the likelihood that a covert researcher can actually "pass" in the setting.

Richard Mitchell discussed his experience as a covert researcher among right-wing survivalists (1991). He recounts: "We had come as covert researchers, hoping to blend in. We arrived driving a late-model diesel-powered Peugeot station wagon, 'disguised' for the occasion in freshly pressed discount-store duck-hunting outfits over preppy L.L. Bean pants, Patagonia jackets, and Nike trainers." Rather than blend in, he found that "our disguises were taken as signs of naïve enthusiasm. (Who else would wear such ludicrous costumes?) We were accepted, treated with gentle respect, even praised. But we were never overlooked" (Mitchell 1991, pp. 105–106).

Yet clothes were not the least of it. One evening, Mitchell found himself in a small group doing guard duty at a Christian Patriots Survival Conference. As the group began swapping violent racist and homophobic stories, Mitchell found himself in the difficult position of having to tell one himself in order to be accepted. He closed his account of the event in this way: "If there are researchers who can participate in such business without feeling, I am not one of them nor do I ever hope to be. What I do hope is someday to forget, forget those unmistakable sounds, my own voice, my own words, telling that Nine O'clock story" (Mitchell 1991, p. 107).

In most cases, you need to ask formal permission before you can do research in more private places. And even in some public places, if you are going to observe over an extended period of time, you would do well to ask permission. (Your professor or the institutional review board at your school can help you determine what is appropriate for your own research.) Before entering the field, you need to determine who can grant you permission to study a particular site. You may find that you need to go up several levels in the hierarchy. Suppose you want to observe a classroom in a school. Perhaps you know the teacher and feel you have a reasonable chance of getting her permission. She may refer you to the principal, who might, in turn, refer you to the superintendent of schools. The superintendent may decide that you need to ask permission from the parents before you can begin. At each level, it may take weeks or even months to gain approval to do the research—and you may ultimately be turned down.

Sometimes, the person who can formally grant you permission may not be the same person who can actually gain you access to people within the setting. Often, people act as gatekeepers. Because of either their formal position or their personal characteristics, they can influence others in the setting to either accept you or not. In many offices, for example, secretaries and other clerical workers are the ones who can ensure that you actually get in to see executives. In an informal setting, such as a group of friends, one person may be central, an informal leader. In an unfamiliar setting, it may take you a while to figure out who the informal gatekeepers are.

You may also find that choices you make early in your fieldwork affect the kinds of relationships you can develop later on. For example, imagine that you are studying worker relations in a factory. If you are introduced to workers by a boss or manager, they may not trust you and think you are there to spy on them. If you are introduced by a union steward, they may think you are a part of the union, and those who are distrustful of the union may not trust you. Although it is possible to overcome these early impressions over a long period of observation, you should carefully consider how early choices may shape later access.

You also need to think about your own personal characteristics and their potential effect on your access to the site. An African American or Asian American researcher, for example, will have enormous difficulty gaining access to racist groups like the Christian Identity movement or the Ku Klux Klan. Women might find that they have very different kinds of access than men to college football players or fraternities. Similarly, men may not have the same kind of access to feminist action groups, sororities, or women's athletic teams as women do. Does this mean that you can never study groups of people who are different from you? Certainly not. But it does mean that you need to think about how your personal characteristics might shape how those in a field setting view you and what kinds of access you might (or might not) be able to get.

What Kinds of Ethical Dilemmas Might Arise in This Site?

When evaluating your field setting, you need to consider whether there are any special ethical issues. We've already talked about the ethical considerations involved in choosing to do covert research, but there may be other issues as well. If there is any possibility that participants could be harmed by your work, you need to make sure that you minimize it. For example, if the researcher who studied radical environmentalists (discussed in Chapter 3) had released the names of his research participants to the federal grand jury, they might have faced criminal charges (Scarce 1995). Sometimes, simply bringing attention to a group might change how it functions, perhaps in negative ways. If the harm to participants is great, you may need to abandon the research project.

Some field researchers have chosen to do their research among people who are breaking the law, like Daniel Wolf, who rode with "outlaw" bikers (Wolf 1991), and Patricia and Peter Adler, who studied drug traffickers (Adler 1985; Adler and Adler 1991). In such cases, you need to think about your own limits in terms of the types of activities you feel comfortable observing. If you observe an illegal activity as part of your research, what should you do? Are you obligated to tell someone? Under what circumstances? While you might think that this kind of ethical dilemma is far-fetched or confined only to professional researchers, student researchers encounter it, too. For example, my students are often interested in studying student drinking on campus. What should they do if they encounter, in the course of their research, underage students drinking? Should they write down what they saw in their field notes? What if they see someone drinking and driving or someone who seems to have a serious problem with alcohol? Although you cannot predict in advance all of the ethical problems you may encounter, you do need to think through the kinds of issues that may arise in a given setting.

What Kinds of Risks Are Inherent in This Setting?

Finally, you need to evaluate the risks inherent in the setting you have chosen. In most settings, the potential risks are relatively minimal. But in some field settings, the risks are substantial. Again, Adler and Adler's study of drug traffickers and Wolf's study of motorcycle gangs come to mind. Before you enter into a setting, think carefully about whether there are any personal risks and whether you are willing to take them.

GETTING IN AND GAINING ACCESS

Once you've settled on a field site and obtained formal permission to begin your research, what do you do next? Every field site is unique, and so a textbook like this one can only give you general advice. You might find it useful to read stories that other researchers have written about their early days in the field. (See, for example, the accounts published in *Journeys Through Ethnography* or *Experiencing Fieldwork;* the full citations are given at the end of this chapter.) "Hanging out" is typical behavior of ethnographers. But in any given setting, what does hanging out entail?

The early days in an observational research project are often puzzling and can be overwhelming—even if you are studying a site with which you are familiar. It's not necessarily clear what you should be focusing on or what you should be doing. Even if you have already selected a general topic, it can be difficult to figure out exactly what you should be observing. For example, let's say you're interested in how kindergarten-age children develop social relationships. You've received permission to observe in a classroom setting. When you first go to the classroom to observe, where do you situate yourself? What vantage point should you take? Do you sit still or move around? If there is a lot of activity going on in the classroom (as is typical in such settings), where should you direct your attention first? What kind of role should you play? How do you explain what you're doing to the children?

Developing Relationships

Gaining trust and developing relationships with the people in your setting is your main task. Especially in the early days, people may not trust you or pay much attention to you. And if they do notice you, they may wonder what you are doing there and not let you "in" to observe at all. Hanging out, after all, is rather unusual—and even suspicious—behavior in many settings.

Again, a textbook can give you only a very general idea about how to develop relationships. Certainly, in general, it's better to be courteous and polite than rude. It's better to act interested than bored. It's better to listen to others than to talk about yourself. It's better to be unobtrusive than splashy. But in specific field settings, you still need to figure out what role you should play.

Some ethnographers play the "naïve incompetent" role. That is, they adopt the persona of someone who is nice but doesn't really know very much about the people in the setting and is willing to ask what might seem like dumb questions. The goal here is for people to take pity on the researcher as someone who needs instruction.

In any human relationship (research-related or not), there is usually give-and-take. As a researcher, you are taking up people's time. You are asking them to give you information and to help you out in your research. Why should anyone take the time to talk with you or let you follow along? Sometimes, people appreciate the opportunity to talk about their lives; they feel that they have an important story to tell and that the researcher can help them do that. Other times, ethnographers can do small favors: giving rides, buying meals, and so forth. Patricia and Peter Adler talk specifically about reciprocity and exchange (1991, pp. 175–176). They note that researchers "can turn the norms of reciprocity to their advantage, offering assistance to subjects (or potential subjects), thereby hoping to build feelings of trust and indebtedness" (Adler and Adler 1991, p. 176). In their study of drug traffickers, they offered small loans, babysitting, and dinners.

Whatever role you play, it's helpful to remember that the people in the setting are the true experts on their own lives. As an ethnographer, you are trying to learn from them. You can learn more by showing an interest and by being open to what they have to say and to show you.

Cultivating Informants

As you spend time in your field setting, you may find yourself developing special relationships with certain individuals. Some individuals may seem more knowledgeable about the scene and be more willing to share their insights with you. Others may take you "under their wing," so to speak, and help you gain access. These individuals are sometimes called *informants* (or *key informants*, for those who play a particularly special role). In his study of Boston's North End, William F. Whyte (1993) described the relationship he had with a key informant named Doc. Until he met Doc, he was unable to get any insight into "Cornerville." Once Doc introduced him around as his "friend" and was able to vouch that he wasn't a government official, he was able to enter places that had formerly been closed to him.

It is important to remember that each informant will have her or his own perspective on the scene and access to somewhat different groups of people. They may, of course, even lie to a researcher. Thus, it's usually a good idea to try to develop relationships with more than one key informant.

Developing a Cover Story

It's important to create a relatively brief description of your research so that you can tell people what it is you're doing and why you're hanging out. Most people will simply be curious about why you're there and what you're doing, but they don't usually want an extended response. (Think about it: When you ask someone, "How are you?" do you really want a long, detailed response? Probably not.) It's important that your description be appropriate for your audience. For example, a teacher may want a more extended version than kindergarten students will.

Should you tell people exactly what it is you're studying? It depends. Usually, people in the field won't want to know all the details of your research, although sometimes they may. There are also instances in which telling people exactly what you're studying might negatively affect the research. For example, let's say you're interested in gender relations in the classroom—specifically, in whether the teacher treats male and female students differently. If you tell the teacher exactly what you're interested in, she may change her behaviors. In that case, you may want to provide a more general description of your work ("I'm interested in student-teacher relationships").

Should you ever tell an outright lie about the purpose of your research? Probably not. In doing fieldwork, your aim is to develop relationships. If you have lied to the people in your setting, how can you expect them to tell you the truth? Nevertheless, researchers sometimes find themselves telling "polite" lies or lying by omission—for example, not telling details about the purposes of the research or not disclosing details about their personal lives. This can be a source of tension. As a researcher, how much should you disclose about yourself? After all, your research participants might disapprove of some aspect of your identity or social life that you think is not relevant to the research. Sometimes, researchers know that they will be critical of the group in their write-up. This, too, can be a source of tension. In fact, it is just this kind of tension that led William Shaffir and Robert Stebbins to describe fieldwork as one of the "more disagreeable activities that humanity has fashioned for itself" (1991, p. 1).

Becoming Invisible

Won't people change their behavior if they know that a researcher is watching them? Most of us don't like outsiders to see us doing something socially unacceptable. If we knew that someone were watching us, we would probably behave much better than we would otherwise. In a classroom, for example, a teacher might pay special attention to her lesson plans if she knows she is being observed. The children might act differently as well—perhaps more or less well behaved.

Because people will change their behavior, my students often argue that covert research is better. If people don't know you're observing them, they won't change. But this isn't necessarily the case. In ethnographic research, the researcher typically stays in the field for an extended period of time. Over time, those in the setting become habituated to her or his presence. People often forget that the researcher is actually gathering data while hanging out. The researcher may be of so little importance to those in the field that they simply don't attend to his or her presence. Or the researcher poses no threat to their everyday activities, so they pay her or him no mind.

While those in the setting may never accept the researcher as one of them, they can come to accept the *role* that she or he plays in that setting. Besides, it's difficult for people to be on their best behavior for very long periods of time. If you spend enough time in the field, it's likely that people will eventually come to behave as they ordinarily would, or at least approximately so.

Dealing with Emotions

Emotions are part of all life experiences, including field research. As you go about your fieldwork, you'll likely experience various emotions, including boredom, disgust, anger, and pleasure. You may feel anxious about being accepted by your informants or about figuring out your role in the field. You may become bored, as my students who observed the school cafeterias eventually did. You may become angry at or feel manipulated by your informants, as Patricia and Peter Adler sometimes did in their study of drug traffickers (1991, p. 170).

Researchers in the positivist tradition typically have argued that emotions are too subjective and have little place in social research because they affect researchers' objectivity. But other researchers argue the opposite: that it is crucial to pay attention to your emotions when you are conducting qualitative research. Sherryl Kleinman (1991, pp. 184–185) suggests that if you don't pay attention to your emotions they will still shape the research— you just won't know exactly how. Emotions provide important clues to what is actually happening in the field. For example, in doing field research with a support group of at-home mothers, I consistently felt anxious or guilty about my own parenting in the presence of one of my informants. A careful analysis of my field notes led me to an important insight into insider-outsider dynamics within the group.

WRITING FIELD NOTES

Developing Observational Skills

How do you learn to observe? How do you learn to remember what you have seen? And how do you learn to make sense of what you are observing? Like all skills, observation can be learned. You get better at it by practicing. As a first step, I recommend that you work through some of the exercises at the end of this chapter. You might also be interested in a 1998 book by Valerie Janesick, *"Stretching" Exercises for Qualitative Researchers*, that provides a number of activities to help beginning researchers become better observers (see the "Suggestions for Further Reading"). Finally, the practice of writing field notes can help you develop your observational skills.

In fact, one of the most important tasks you will engage in during field research is writing field notes. Why write field notes? For one thing, writing things down helps you to remember them. Because field research usually takes place over many months, if not years, you simply cannot remember everything you see without writing it down. Many field researchers argue that if you don't write something down it's almost as if you didn't observe it. The field notes become your written record of what you observed.

In addition, writing is a way of making meaning. You begin to organize your thoughts and make sense of what you are observing by writing about it. Thus, as Robert Emerson, Rachel Fretz, and Linda Shaw argue, writing field notes "is not so much a matter of passively copying down 'facts' about 'what happened.' Rather, such writing involves active processes of interpretation and sense-making: noting and writing down some things as 'significant,' noting but ignoring others as 'not significant,' and even missing other possibly significant things altogether" (1995, p. 8). As you write, you make judgments about what is important in your setting.

When to Write?

Should you write in the field or should you wait until you are out of people's presence? Some researchers find it awkward to take notes in front of those whom they are researching; they feel that taking notes in the field interrupts the flow of action. Sometimes, note taking is clearly inappropriate. For example, if you are observing a very emotionally charged event (such as a funeral or a wedding), it might seem rude or disrespectful to take notes. At other times, and in other settings, it seems perfectly natural. For example, if you are observing in a school cafeteria or a shopping mall, it may feel perfectly appropriate to take notes. Some researchers who take notes openly in the field argue that it gives them more freedom to ask questions. It may also reinforce, in the minds of participants, their role as researcher.

Whether you take notes openly or not, I recommend that you carry a small notebook with you and try to jot down key words or phrases while in the field. If you're in a setting in which you feel it is inappropriate to take notes, you can sometimes leave the scene briefly or take a quick break to jot key words. What should you jot down? You can use mnemonics (words that will help you to remember), memorable quotes, and a few details about the interaction. Some researchers carry a tape recorder with them. Then, on their drive back from the field setting, they record as much as they can remember.

Immediately upon leaving the field, whether you have recorded notes afterward or jotted down notes in the field, I recommend that you write up full field notes. These are your fullest, most complete descriptions of what occurred during your period of observation, including the events, the setting, and the participants. They may also include your initial sense of what is happening in the setting or what the events mean to the participants. Even if you use a tape recorder or are able to write fairly complete notes in the field, I still recommend that you write up full field notes as soon as possible after leaving the field.

What to Write?

Your notes should reflect your growing understanding of the social scene you are studying. You should take notes about the physical setting and the people within it, as well as the behaviors you observe. When you first enter a field setting, you should take notes about your initial impressions. You might want to draw a map of the site as well. Then jot down notes about what the place looks like, what kinds of things immediately stand out, what the people look like, how they are dressed, and how they interact with each other. Although your impressions are likely to change as you gain experience in the field, these initial impressions are crucial. After you have been in the setting for a while, you will become habituated. That is, you won't see certain things that you take for granted, just as you don't really see the color of the walls and floor of your classroom.

The following is an early field note on the "Parker Gardens" Section 8 Housing Complex, on which Kazuyo Masuda based her master's thesis (1998). (This study was described in Chapter 2.) Notice how this excerpt helps set the scene. It describes the housing complex in which much of the action takes place but does not provide details about any action.*

> Parker Gardens is a complex of two-storied apartments, covering two by two square blocks, or four blocks in total. There are no through streets cutting through the complex, but parking lots in the middle and on the west side. The complex starts at V St. on the east, and climbs the street, up 23rd and 24th, to the next north-south street, the one with Jefferson High School on it. The main floor of the buildings is brick, and the second floor is wood siding, with the kind of early 1960s window trim that is a three-sided curb around the win-

---

*A number of researchers were involved with this research in the early stages of the project. Anthropologist Ken Erickson, Kazuyo Masuda, and I all contributed field notes. This excerpt was contributed by Ken Erickson.

dows. The buildings are in need of paint; some have screen doors and some do not. The management office and the "community room" next to them are in one of the buildings, apparently with an occupied apartment above them. (We could hear footsteps this morning, Ms. R. and I, and she mentioned the four-bedroom apartment above us.)

Sometimes, you'll want to describe people as well, as Masuda did here:

> Mr. M. wears expensive socks and expensive loafers and expensive silk shirts and he drives a Mercedes. He wears a gold bracelet and a rather big gold ring, too, and he has round, wire-rim glasses.

In your ongoing field notes, you should note what people say and do and what the things they say and do seem to mean to them. When possible, you should provide direct quotations or paraphrases of what people say. Sometimes, you'll write scenes or stories. (For an excellent discussion of the kinds of things you might include in your field notes, see *Writing Ethnographic Fieldnotes.*) The hardest thing for most beginning researchers is providing enough detail. You probably cannot have enough description in your field notes.

The following excerpt, also from the "Parker Gardens" project, tells the story of a tutoring session for children from the housing complex that never really got off the ground. Masuda wrote the following notes after her first day as a volunteer tutor. It is a Monday, shortly after school has begun in the fall. Most of the action occurs between herself and "T.," the service coordinator for the building.

> As I was walking up to the office, I saw children running around. When I walked in the office, Mr. M, T., and another man were there. They were discussing the adult education program. T. told me since this was the first day of the after school program, no kids would show. . . . When we walked into the meeting room together, a man and a woman with a child were working with another man. They appeared to be in an adult education program.
>
> There were two loaves of bread, peanut butter, jelly, juice, muffins, cups and napkins laid out on the table. However, T. began to put them back in the refrigerator as soon as we were there. He said, "It's the first day, you know." He and I chatted about school. . . . After the conversation, he said to me, "You can help them [the kids at the complex]." I offered to stay until 5 p.m. He said, "Well you don't need to. We will see what happens between now and 4 p.m."

T. left for somewhere. I sat down and began to read my book.
A middle-school-age boy came in and opened the refrigerator and
looked in. He left, then another boy came in and did the same. After
this one left, a school-age girl came in and did the same. T. came back
and the two boys came with him. Two girls (one elementary school
age) wandered in. "Get the cups out," said T. The kids got the juice
out and drank. One boy said, "This is good!"

T. began asking the kids questions about their homework. First girl
said, "We get homework twice a week in creative writing class. Other
classes, it depends." Another girl mumbled something I could not
hear. T. told the children to bring their homework next time. "And if
you don't have homework, bring something else." Then he realized
the kids were drinking up all the juice and told them, "It will be there
tomorrow." He put the cups back in the cabinet.

The boys were talking all the meanwhile. T. asked them, "Then
Tuesdays and Wednesdays are not good days [for the after-school pro-
gram]? Did you go to school today?" First boy answered, "Yeah." The
kids began discussing which school they go to. Second boy said he
was kicked out from one school and did not get to go to the school
he wanted to. . . .

T. said he would have a program for them on Tuesdays and
Wednesdays. Second girl argued: "Tuesdays and Thursdays, that's what
on the flyer." T. said, "NO! I wrote it. I know. . . ." She ran to the office
bulletin board and said, "Look at this." T. and the kids went over. I
heard paper being ripped from the bulletin board and tossed in the
trash can.

After the kids left, T. came back and said to me, "I will have something lined up for you next week. You can go if you want to." He left.
I thought about staying longer. I decided not to stay and walked out
shortly after. I saw T. driving off as I was leaving the office. There were
several children playing around the apartment building.

Arguably, not much is happening here. But after observing in the field for an
extended period of time, Masuda noticed that many of the programs and
initiatives begun by the service coordinator ended in this way: in little actually happening and few children becoming involved. The observation that
children were playing outside as Masuda both entered and left the scene,
while a small detail, is important. It's not for a lack of children that the after-
school program falters.

What should you *not* write down in field notes? Even though it's often
difficult to avoid, you should try to avoid generalizations (Emerson, Fretz,
and Shaw 1995). For example, let's say you are observing people eating in

a cafeteria. You shouldn't say that a research participant "always" gets a tray. You can only report what you observed today: that in this instance, someone (let's call him "X") took a tray. You should also try to avoid judgmental statements, such as "X eats a lot" or "X is a glutton." Rather than interpreting his or her behavior, write about what X is *doing:* "X took four sandwiches, a bowl of soup, and a large bag of chips; he then returned for two cups of milk, an ice cream, and a package of cookies." Finally, try to keep your opinions out of your jotted notes. "X ate very quickly, using both hands. Crumbs dropped on the floor and down his shirt" is better than "X ate like a pig."

Avoiding generalization is difficult—even for experienced researchers. For example, go back to the field note describing Mr. M. on page 75. What does "expensive" mean? To one person, an expensive pair of shoes might be bought at Walmart. To another, expensive shoes might mean a designer label pair bought in a department store like Bloomingdale's or Macy's.

How to Write?

You should date each field note and note the time and location in which the observation took place. It's often helpful, too, to list the participants. (Of course, sometimes there are too many to list or the participants change; you will need to decide what is helpful to you.) You may want to use pseudonyms, initials, or code names for your study participants. I always recommend writing full field notes using a word processor and placing them in a three-ring binder. This may help you in your subsequent analysis.

Use quotation marks for direct quotes—things you heard people say and were able to write down exactly (or almost exactly) as they said them. Use paraphrases when you can't remember exactly how someone said something but do recall the gist of it.

In addition to recording what happened, I also encourage my students to write about their own feelings and initial hunches about the data. But I recommend that you separate your own feelings and impressions from more direct observations. When I write field notes, I usually use brackets to separate my own feelings and thoughts from my actual observations. Some people like to write in two columns—one column for their thoughts and feelings, the other for their observations. Others prefer to use different typefaces or colored type to distinguish the two.

People use a variety of styles for their field notes. I generally try to use complete sentences, and I usually start chronologically (what happened first) but then shift around as my writing sparks new memories. Sometimes,

writers will begin with a big event and then move on to smaller, less important ones. You'll develop your own style as you write. What's most important is that you keep on writing.

LEAVING THE FIELD

At some point, you need to stop observing and leave the field. When should
you leave? Ideally, you should leave when you feel you have little more to
gain by observing longer. Perhaps your field notes seem to be saying the
same things over and over, or additional informants seem to be telling you
the same kind of things. Perhaps you feel stale or bored in the setting. Or
perhaps you feel that you have learned all you can, at least for the time
being. If this is the case, it's probably a good time to leave. In most cases,
however, external factors will play a major role in determining when you
leave the field. The summer ends, and you need to go back to the classroom.
Or the semester is over, and the final paper is due. Or the funding has run
out. Ideally, you should stay in the setting until you feel it's time to go. More
practically, you will find that you often leave prematurely.

As you prepare to leave the field, you need to consider your future relationships with those whom you have been researching. Will you want to
return to the setting later for additional study or clarification? If so, you
should be sure to leave on good terms. A general rule is that ethnographers
shouldn't "spoil" the field—make it impossible for future researchers to
return.

Some people believe that researchers should share their findings with
their informants or solicit their comments on the final analysis and write-up.
Judith Stacey (1991) allowed her informants to have—literally—the last
word. As the last chapter in her ethnography of postmodern family life, she
printed an interview with one of her informants on her reactions to the text.

You also need to consider the obligations you may have incurred during
the course of your study. Have your informants come to rely on you in any
key ways? If so, can you continue to provide the kind of support they have
been getting from you? Or can you find alternative ways for them to get it?
The relationships that ethnographers develop with their informants often
are in many respects like friendships. Some researchers see themselves as
friends with those they are studying (and vice versa). But there's a peculiar
imbalance of power in these relationships, for the researcher can leave
whenever she or he wants to. The informant, in contrast, typically cannot
leave her or his own life. Judith Stacey (1996) argues that, because of the
greater intimacy possible in ethnographic research, much greater exploita-

tion is possible than in more distant kinds of research, such as brief surveys. In exiting the field, you need to think carefully about the kinds of expectations your informants may have of you—and you of them.

FOCUSING YOUR OBSERVATIONS

How do you begin to figure out what is important in your setting? How do you begin to narrow your observations and make sense of the relationships you are documenting in your field notes? As in any other kind of research, your data will not "speak for themselves." You have to interpret—figure out—what the evidence means. Researchers often leave this as a last step. They focus for an extended period on gathering data and observing in the field. Then, on returning "home" from their fieldwork, they begin to analyze their materials and develop a final, written report of their research. Because ethnographers typically generate hundreds, or even thousands, of pages of written data (field notes, interview transcripts, documents, and so forth), analysis can seem a daunting task.

It's best not to wait until you have finished your observations before beginning to make sense of them. If you begin your analyses while you are still in the field, you can focus your observations on the questions that arise during your analysis. Chapters 8 and 9 deal specifically with data analysis. For now, however, I'll discuss some ways that you can begin to make sense of the materials you have collected.

Making Meaning

I like to think of data analysis as answering the question "So what?" Why is your research interesting or important? Why should people care about it? What is the larger sociological significance of your study? Even something as mundane as parking cars can have sociological significance. My parking lot research group, for example, came to argue that at least part of the parking conflict on campus was about social status. Students complained about not being able to find convenient parking spaces. As customers—people who were paying for their education—they felt that they deserved access to good parking spots as part of their tuition and fees. They argued that their tuition, in effect, pays faculty wages; thus, they felt entitled to better parking spaces than the faculty. Faculty members, in contrast, felt that they deserved better parking spots because they had higher status than students.

This kind of analysis is called *interpretation*. Not only do you have to write good descriptions in field research, you also have to interpret what the evidence means. How do you begin? I recommend that, after you have been observing for a while, you read and reread your field notes and write memos or notes to yourself. (We'll discuss memos in greater detail in Chapter 8.) Try to read with a questioning mind. Then, jot down your thoughts, hunches, and feelings about the ongoing research. Sometimes, these memos will help you to make sense of what you're observing. Other times, they will help you explore how you're feeling about your research. Sometimes, they may point you in a new direction. Don't worry if at early stages you seem to be bouncing around among many different ways to think about your material. What these early explorations do is help you tease out different possibilities.

Coming to See Multiple Realities

At heart, observational research is about looking—and seeing—from multiple perspectives. No two individuals have exactly the same understanding of social reality. Anthropologist Harry Wolcott gives a good example (1999, p. 66). He invites us to consider how a real estate developer, a hunter, and a biologist might appraise a prime piece of rural property. The developer might focus on the possibilities for construction and development, the hunter would mainly be interested in the possibilities for hunting and recreation, and the biologist would be more interested in the flora and fauna. In all three cases, the piece of land remains the same. But how people think about it—what they see in it—differs. As social observers, your task is to try to understand the multiple ways in which individuals perceive reality.

QUESTIONS FOR THOUGHT

1. Imagine that someone (maybe a teacher?) has been covertly studying you. This person has been taking notes about how you dress, what you say, how you interact with others. The notes are fairly detailed and sometimes embarrassing, because you didn't know you were being observed. How would you feel about this? Would you feel any differently if you found out that the research was going to be published? Would you want to be able to have a say in what was said about you?

2. Some people argue that ethnography should be more objective, like the natural sciences. Others think it should be more subjective, like the humanities. What do you think? Why?

EXERCISES

1. Consider the following field settings. What strategies might you use to gain access to the site? What difficulties might you encounter?
   a. Recruits in the police academy
   b. A community of recent immigrants
   c. A disability rights group
   d. A student organization
   e. A women's soccer team

2. Now imagine that you are a member of another racial/ethnic group. (If you are White, imagine that you are Asian American or African American, for example. If you are Asian, imagine that you are African American or Latino/a, for example.) How might your strategies for accessing the groups in Exercise 1 change? Would access be harder or easier? In what ways?

3. Now imagine that you are a member of the other gender. Again, how might your strategies for accessing the groups in Exercise 1 change? Would access be harder or easier? In what ways?

4. Practice describing yourself to (a) a teacher, (b) a parent, and (c) a friend. How do your self-descriptions change for each audience? What do these self-descriptions say about how you "really" are?

5. Have a teacher or friend place a few inanimate objects in the middle of a table or desk. Sitting in one place, spend 5 minutes observing and writing down what you see. After the 5 minutes is up, move to another location, and again spend 5 minutes observing and writing down what you see.* What did you see from each perspective?

6. Go to a public place where you can observe without disturbing the scene (for example, a waiting room, cafeteria, or mall). Spend about 15 minutes observing and taking notes. Then go home and write up full field notes. Try observing again in the same place at least one or two additional times, each time writing up full field notes. How do your observations change over time?

7. Find a setting where there is a lot of social interaction (for example, a party, a ball game, or a public park). Try to observe intensively without taking notes. Remain in the setting for at least 30 minutes. When you return home, write up full field notes. What are you able to remember?

---

*This exercise is adapted from one in Janesick 1998.

SUGGESTIONS FOR FURTHER READING

Burawoy, Michael, et al. *Ethnography Unbound*. Berkeley: University of California Press, 1991.

Emerson, Robert; Rachel Fretz; and Linda Shaw. *Writing Ethnographic Fieldnotes*. Chicago: University of Chicago Press, 1995.

Janesick, Valerie. *"Stretching" Exercises for Qualitative Researchers*. Thousand Oaks, CA: Sage, 1998.

Lareau, Annette, and Jeffrey Shultz (eds.). *Journeys Through Ethnography: Realistic Accounts of Fieldwork*. Boulder, CO: Westview Press, 1996.

Lofland, John, and Lyn Lofland. *Analyzing Social Settings*, 3rd ed. Belmont, CA: Wadsworth, 1995.

Shaffir, William, and Robert Stebbins. *Experiencing Fieldwork: An Inside View of Qualitative Research*. Newbury Park, CA: Sage, 1991.

5

Interviews

Interviewing is rather like marriage: everybody knows what it is, an awful lot of people do it, and yet behind each closed front door there is a world of secrets.

—ANN OAKLEY (1981, p. 30)

Have you ever been interviewed? If you have a phone in your name or have spent much time in a shopping mall, chances are, somebody has tried to interview you to get your opinion about some product or service. Maybe you were interviewed as part of the process of getting into college or obtaining a job, or maybe you have been interviewed by a local newspaper or television program about an accomplishment.

Valerie Janesick defines an *interview* as "a meeting of two persons to exchange information and ideas through questions and responses, resulting in communication and joint construction of meaning about a particular topic" (1998, p. 30). There are many different kinds of interviews, each with somewhat different techniques and purposes. Journalists conduct interviews to get information for a news story. Market researchers conduct interviews to figure out what products are likely to sell. Businesses conduct job interviews to try to find employees. Social scientists conduct interviews for their own somewhat different purposes. But what all these approaches have in common is the attempt to gain information from individuals on some topic.

Interviewing is at the heart of social research. If you look through almost any sociological journal, you will find that much social research is based on interviews, either standardized or more in-depth. In fact, some argue that it is the most popular form of data collection in sociology (Denzin 1989). Examples of interview research abound. William Finlay and

James Coverdill (1999), for example, used interviews with corporate head-hunters to determine who benefits most from the use of such recruiters: the managers who use them or others in the firm, including human resource departments. They found that the managers who used headhunters tended to benefit the most, not only because headhunters are able to find prospective employees who are happy in their current jobs (and thus not likely to be looking for work) but also because the managers are able to exercise greater control over the process. In a very different setting, Dana Britton (1999) interviewed correctional officers who worked in men's and women's state prisons to determine why prison guards prefer to work in men's prisons and what that might say about sex segregation in the labor market.

Many researchers combine participant observation with in-depth interviews. (In fact, many textbooks treat the two together.) During the process of observing, researchers naturally ask questions about the ongoing action. Sometimes, these interviews may be informal, as when a researcher spontaneously asks questions of an informant. Other times, they may be more formal, as when a researcher prepares a list of questions. Some researchers use both. Finlay and Coverdill, for example, conducted formal interviews with the headhunters, which they tape-recorded and transcribed. They also did over 300 hours of fieldwork, during which they asked questions more informally (Finlay and Coverdill 1999, p. 14).

INTERVIEWING AS A RELATIONSHIP

Most methods textbooks treat interviewing as a conversation between two people—the interviewer and the interviewee. The interviewer asks questions, and the interviewee responds to them. But if you think about it, this is a peculiar kind of conversation. In an interview, one person—the interviewee—reveals information about him- or herself; the other does not. One person—the interviewer—directs the conversation, often with expectations for what should happen during that conversation and for what constitutes a "correct" answer; the other does not. One person—the interviewer—decides when the questions have been satisfactorily answered and closes the conversation; the other does not. In this sense, an interview is an odd type of conversation indeed. In what other kind of conversation is there such a lopsided exchange?

I prefer to view interviewing as a form of relationship between two individuals (or, in the case of focus groups and group interviews, more than two individuals). The individuals may be close or, perhaps more typically, distant. The interview may be prolonged, repeated over time, or very brief. In each case, however, two individuals come together to try to create meaning about a particular topic. While participating in this relationship, they also draw on established social conventions. For example, questions and answers usually follow one another, with individuals taking turns speaking and observing rules for finishing conversations (Schegloff and Sacks 1974). In most interviews, one person does most of the questioning, with the focus on the person being interviewed. (As we'll see, however, some interviews are far less structured and more like a "real" conversation.) The other characteristic of the interview is that it is focused around the production of *talk* (DeVault 1999). Thus, while interviews may be a peculiar form of conversation, they still focus on language and its social organization.

TYPES OF INTERVIEWS

There are several types of interviews, including structured, semistructured, and unstructured. Interviews vary according to the amount of control exerted by the researcher during the interview and to the degree of structure.

Structured Interviews

At one end of the spectrum are *structured interviews*, the most formal and the most rigidly controlled type. Structured interviews are more likely to be used in survey research, in telephone interviews, and in market research and political polling. In structured interviews, the sequence of questions and the pace of the interview tend to be preestablished. Although at least some of the questions may be open-ended, allowing interviewees to respond in their own words, they may also be closed-ended, forcing interviewees to choose between fixed responses. In structured interviews, the interviewer usually is not allowed to deviate from a rigid protocol (or interview schedule). The questions must be asked exactly as written, and follow-up questions (also called probes), if they are allowed, are standardized. And if a respondent doesn't understand the question, the interviewer typically does not rephrase it in the respondent's own words. Instead, he or she simply repeats the question, perhaps with minor changes in phrasing.

The following extract gives an example of a segment of a structured interview. Notice that the instructions for what the interviewer should say to the respondent are written out.

First, I'd like to ask you some questions about your household. Then I'm going to ask you some questions about your daily activities.

1. Besides yourself, how many people usually live in this household?
2. Are there any children under the age of 18? [If yes] How many?
3. Of all the people living in your home, how many are full-time students?
4. How many people work outside the home, for pay?

I'd like to get a sense of what a normal weekday in your household looks like.

5. What time do you typically get up in the morning?

In structured interviewing, interviewers typically do not reveal any personal information about themselves, even if asked directly. Rather, they seek to remain as neutral as possible in how they present themselves. Personal revelations on the part of the interviewer are said to produce *bias*, because interviewees will tend to give the responses that they think the interviewer wants to hear. This is sometimes called *social desirability bias.* That is, respondents will want to give the response that they think is socially acceptable. So, for example, respondents may underestimate how often they engage in behaviors seen as socially undesirable, such as drinking alcohol or using illegal drugs, or they may overestimate how often they engage in socially desirable behaviors, such as exercising or eating healthy foods or attending church (Presser and Stinson 1998). Researchers who study stigmatized groups or topics that are typically considered private—such as sexual behavior—face additional constraints. If respondents believe the interviewer disapproves of a behavior, they are much less likely to respond honestly.

Researchers use structured interviews far more often in quantitative than in qualitative research. While some qualitative researchers may incorporate elements of the structured interview in their research, many reject this type of interviewing for philosophical reasons. Structured interviewing allows the researcher to retain a great deal of control over the interview process. Yet many qualitative scholars believe that structured interviews grant *too much* control to the interviewer. Because the interviewer controls what questions are asked and how they are worded, he or she can overlook issues that may be more important to the interviewee. In addition, respondents may misunderstand what is being asked, and they may lack opportunities for clarification. The researcher assumes that all interviewees will understand the questions in the same way and that the questions address the interviewees' reality. But the questions may have different meanings for different interviewees, and if the questions are not meaningful to the research participants, the interview data will not be useful. Structured interviews can thus risk missing what's most important to the interviewees.

Imagine, for example, that you are asked in a structured interview what your favorite flavor of ice cream is. The interviewer gives you a series of choices: chocolate, vanilla, peppermint, coffee, or chocolate chip. If your favorite flavor happens to be mango, how will you respond? What if you don't like ice cream at all? What if you really want to talk about sorbet or sherbet or gelatti? If these choices aren't offered, then the interview won't reflect how you really feel. Of course, survey researchers have a number of strategies for avoiding these problems. (If you're interested in finding out more about survey research, see Babbie 1990.) Still, most qualitative researchers choose semistructured or unstructured interviews for the greater depth of insight they give into the lives of their research participants.

Semistructured Interviews

Semistructured interviews (sometimes called in-depth interviews) are much less rigid than structured interviews. In semistructured interviews, the goal is to explore a topic more openly and to allow interviewees to express their opinions and ideas in their own words. As Michael Quinn Patton (1990) reminds us, we can't observe everything we might want to know. Thus, we interview people to understand what life is like from perspectives other than our own. We try to move beyond our own experiences and ideas and to *really* understand the other person's point of view. Although the researcher typically begins with some basic ideas about what the interview will cover, the interviewee's responses shape the order and structure of the interview. Each interview is tailored to the research participant. Semistructured interviews thus allow for a much freer exchange between interviewer and interviewee.

In semistructured or in-depth interviewing, the researcher needs to listen carefully to the participant's responses and to follow his or her lead. The process resembles a dance, in which one partner (the interviewer) must be carefully attuned to the other's movements. Because the interviews are not prescripted, they can sometimes take surprising turns. Thus, in-depth interviews are particularly useful for exploring a topic in detail or in constructing theory. A number of feminist scholars have argued that these interviews are a particularly good way to study women and other marginalized groups (DeVault 1999; Reinharz 1992). Because women historically have been silenced, they have not always had the opportunity to tell their own stories. In-depth interviews allow them to do so.

As I'll discuss in greater detail shortly, researchers have different opinions about how much of themselves they should reveal in an interview. Some believe that the exchange should be more like a "real" conversation, with interviewer and interviewee both participating in the dialogue (see Reinharz 1992, pp. 32–35). From this perspective, the goal of the interview is to jointly construct meaning on some topic. These researchers, who are more likely to share a postmodernist or critical approach to social research, may not hesitate to present their own opinions and beliefs. They tend to call those whom they are studying their research *participants*, to emphasize their greater role in shaping the research process.

Other researchers, however, feel that the emphasis should remain firmly on the research subjects, with the interviewer playing a much more neutral role. These researchers suggest that the interviewer should tailor his or her presentation of self to the research situation. The interviewer should dress neutrally, so as to "blend in" as much as possible. If an interviewee asks a personal question about the interviewer, the interviewer might politely deflect the question or try to answer it after the respondent has presented his or her own point of view. The question of how much of the self to present in an interview hinges in part on the nature of the research. If the researcher is logging many hours in the field, with interviews a secondary component to observation, the participants are likely to have much greater knowledge of and a more personal relationship with the interviewer. If the interview is a one-time encounter, then the relationship between interviewer and interviewee is likely to be much more impersonal. The researcher's personality also influences the level of self-disclosure. Some researchers are much more reserved, and others are outgoing. These personal qualities have an impact on the kinds of relationships the researcher develops.

The following excerpt is from an in-depth interview conducted with an at-home mother. In this interview, notice that the interviewer begins with a general question and follows the respondent's lead.

> INTERVIEWER: Can you talk a little about what it was like for you when you were both working and a new mom? What was that like?
>
> RESPONDENT: First of all, finding day care was very, very difficult for me. I interviewed a dozen people. Um. Most of them were young, young ladies with new babies themselves. And it was very stressful to think about leaving my son, leaving him to be raised with somebody else. I ended up finding a day care person who was in her mid-50s. She was really a nice woman, and I felt very comfortable with her. And the whole surrounding . . . And my husband would drop him off in the morning so I didn't have to deal with that separation thing, which was kind of nice. And then I would pick him up at

night, so I got that opportunity. The day care woman was really nice; she very rarely called me for any trivial things. I kind of wish she would have—you know, you hear now about the day care people keeping logs, you know, about what they ate or how many times their diaper was changed or whatever. So I don't really have a history from, you know, I went back to work when he was 3 months and I quit when he was 9 months. So there's a whole 6-month gap there. It was hard there, it really was.

INTERVIEWER: What was the hardest thing for you?

RESPONDENT: Just the fact that, you know, he would be smiling for the first time without me seeing it. And just the fact that, you know, she would be giving him his first cereal. I don't know. I don't know. It was hard.

INTERVIEWER: Hard. And how did you make the decision to quit your work? Your paid work.

RESPONDENT: Well, both my husband and I are in finance, so we kind of did it financially. You know, that was our way to make it seem okay. We sat down and put everything to paper. Where we were, what we could afford to do. And then the decision after that was easy. You know. That's us, though. We do everything with paper and pencil. Okay, how are we going to do this, let's figure this out. But it was more an emotional thing because every day it was so hard to get up. I mean, I was getting up at 5 o'clock in the morning, I would work out, then I would take my shower, get him up, and I was nursing. And I was also expressing milk at work. It was really hard. So it was an emotional thing. And that's kind of what set us to putting it down on paper. Like, how could we do this? What could we do to make this happen? So, you know, we just cut down on a few things, we paid off both our cars, we cut back on all kinds of things.

Unstructured Interviews

As the label implies, *unstructured interviews* are the least structured of all. Unlike structured interviews, which tend to be preplanned and may be tape-recorded, unstructured interviews are often conducted in a field setting, in conjunction with an observational study. They tend to be more spontaneous and free-flowing, with topics arising from the situation or behavior at hand. The interviewer typically does not have a set of questions prepared in advance. Instead, questions arise more naturally. For example, if you are conducting a participant observation study in a fast-food restaurant, you might ask questions about the work itself or about the workers' feelings about the job during the course of your observation. Of all interview types, unstructured interviews tend to be the most like "real" conversations.

CLOSENESS AND DISTANCE
IN INTERVIEW SITUATIONS

Survey researchers and authors of structured interview texts suggest that there should be distance between interviewer and interviewee. From this perspective, the interviewer is akin to a mechanical recorder, trained to extract information in an efficient, detached, yet pleasant manner. To avoid bias, the interviewer needs to reveal as little about him- or herself as possible. Interviewers are (within some constraints) seen as more or less interchangeable. The implication is that any interviewer, if adequately trained, can extract the same information from the interviewee. It's as if there are nuggets of "truth" embedded in the interviewee, and all the interviewer has to do is pick them up using a set of mechanical tools.

Yet interviewers—and interviewees—are *not* interchangeable. They each bring different qualities to the interview, based on who they are and the experiences they've had. Because interviewing is essentially a personal relationship, *who* the participants are matters. Thus, many feminist researchers have stressed that being similar in crucial ways to their interviewees was important in gaining access to them. For example, Patricia Zavella writes about how she informally made her interviewees—Mexican American women workers—aware of similarities between them and herself (1996, p. 146). By disclosing her own ethnic identity and her status as a working mother with a young child, she hoped that her informants would open up to her as well. Similarly, in her study of Appalachian women and domestic violence, Patricia Gagne emphasized her similarities to the women she was studying by sharing information about her own experiences in an abusive relationship (Tewksbury and Gagne 1997).

Presenting the appearance of similarity can also aid in developing rapport. For example, Lauraine Leblanc (2000) studied punk girls in North America. She had been involved with the punk scene prior to becoming a graduate student, and she still retained elements of her past involvement, such as tattoos, hairstyle and hair color, and wardrobe. Her appearance as a punk and her familiarity with the scene (she notes that she was sometimes seen as an "old punk") was crucial to her acceptance by the girls.

Must researchers always be similar to their research participants? If this were the case, then we could never know about people different from ourselves, and most research would be about White, professional-class academics. Clearly, then, not all researchers study those who are like themselves—nor should they. But the skills involved in developing relationships across social boundaries are complex. Thus, Carol Stack, a middle-class

White academic, writes about how she came to do research among both urban and rural African American women, often poor, who were very different from herself (Stack 1974, 1996). At one point, she describes a group discussion about her research on men and women who were migrating back to the South. Finally giving her support to Stack's project, one woman declared, "You see here a white woman capable of learning" (Stack 1996, p. 103). A standardized survey, in which all the questions were prearranged and selected, would clearly not have served Stack well in her attempt to transcend boundaries of race and class.

From a feminist standpoint, Ann Oakley (1981) argues that interviewers must be willing to risk disclosing personal information and developing real relationships with their research participants. In her research on the transition to motherhood, she found that she simply could not follow the advice of traditionalists in response to her interviewees' questions. In this research project, Oakley interviewed women many times, both before and after giving birth. She was also present at a number of the births—certainly one of the more personal and intimate times in a woman's life. Because of the intimacy that developed over time, she found it artificial, and even impossible, to maintain emotional distance. Traditionalists argue that researchers should try to laugh off requests for personal information in interviews or state that they have never really thought about the question. But, Oakley wondered, how could she laugh off or not respond to questions like "Why is it dangerous to leave a small baby alone in the house?" (Oakley 1981, p. 48) Her interviewees wanted to know if she, herself, was a mother, and she saw no reason to withhold that information. Furthermore, Oakley argues, her own experiences of mothering gave her special insights into her participants' lives and helped shrink the distance between herself and her subjects. As a mother herself, she had experienced many of the same things as her interviewees. And these shared experiences were critical for her research.

Because interviews are relationships between people—however artificial they may sometimes feel—interpersonal skills are crucial to being a good interviewer. If the person you are interviewing doesn't trust you or feel comfortable in your presence, then the interview is unlikely to go well. After all, why should someone take the time or effort to interview with you? What's in it for them? Even if participants do agree to an interview, they may not be willing to talk honestly or discuss intimate details about their personal lives if they do not feel some level of trust. This is especially true in attempts to research those who are different from you or those from stigmatized groups.

The development of trust between interviewer and interviewee is often called developing "rapport." Traditional interview texts suggest that you should develop enough rapport to get people to talk to you, but not so much that you actually develop friendships with your participants or disclose too much about yourself. The image is almost one of "tricking" research participants into talking to you.

More recently, many scholars, especially feminists, have argued that this image of the interview tends to ignore issues of power in the interview situation (Acker, Barry, and Esseveld 1996; Reinharz 1992; Stacey 1996). Ann Oakley suggests that the traditional focus on extracting information from passive research subjects is "morally indefensible" because it treats those being researched as objects. In the traditional view of interviewing, researchers define the boundaries of the relationship; thus, they do not necessarily keep interviewees' best interests in mind. In fact, the researchers' desire to get research participants to reveal intimate details may directly conflict with the participants' desire to keep information private. Oakley argues that the traditional way of thinking about interviews rationalizes inequality: "What is good for interviewers is not necessarily good for interviewees" (1981, p. 40). In addition, she suggests that the preservation of distance and hierarchy between interviewer and interviewee makes for poor interviews. How can researchers expect intimacy when they are not willing to reciprocate?

PREPARING FOR THE INTERVIEW

Before beginning an interview, you need to make choices about the interview process. Specifically, you need to address questions like these:

- What kind of relationships do you hope to develop with those you are studying?
- How intimate a relationship is desirable?
- How will you gain access to potential interviewees?
- What kinds of information are appropriate to disclose about yourself?
- Will you conduct relatively structured or unstructured interviews?
- Is the interview process a method for gaining information from research subjects or a process of jointly sharing information and creating meanings?

Your decisions about these questions will shape how you prepare for and conduct your interviews.

Deciding Whom to Interview

Methodologists tend to worry a lot about *whom* to interview, and their concern makes sense. If you don't choose appropriate people to interview, you won't get the information you are looking for. Survey researchers and quantitative social scientists tend to use techniques that will ensure what they call a random sample of the population. These techniques allow them to generalize the results of the study to a larger population. But these kinds of sampling methods are not as useful for qualitative research. In qualitative research, we are more often interested in understanding a particular case in great detail. We want to know a lot about a relatively small number of people. Thus, we tend to sacrifice breadth for depth. We typically don't interview thousands or even hundreds of respondents, as quantitative scholars do. Instead, we might interview only twenty-five or fifty people for our research. Some studies are conducted with even fewer participants. Judith Stacey, for example, studied two kinship networks very intensively over an extended period of time (Stacey 1991).

Qualitative researchers usually choose research participants for the specific qualities they can bring to the study. In general, you should choose those interviewees who can give you the greatest possible insight into your topic. Sometimes, after an extended period of field observation, you will recognize that there are several different groups within your field setting. In a fast-food restaurant, for example, the distinction between part-time and full-time workers may be important. If so, you will want to interview people from both groups. Sometimes, you know in advance that you want several different perspectives on a topic. For example, you may want to explore the perspectives of old women and young women on domestic violence, or those of Asian Americans and Latinas. This is sometimes called a *purposive strategy*, in which you intentionally sample research participants for the specific perspectives they may have.

At other times, especially in the beginning stages of a research project, it's helpful to use what is sometimes called *snowball sampling* or *chain referral sampling* (Biernacki and Waldorf 1981). In this technique, you begin with an initial interviewee—often, a key informant. Then you ask that person to refer you to friends or acquaintances or others who might be appropriate to interview. In this way, your sample "snowballs." In fact, for "hidden" populations or groups of people who engage in stigmatized behavior, this may be the only way to recruit interviewees. For example, suppose you want to investigate people who use illegal drugs. Chances are, if you advertise in a newspaper or bulletin board, you will get few (if any) responses. Potential interviewees need to know that you are trustworthy. Thus, having a friend or acquaintance vouch for you may be crucial in gaining access. For certain kinds of research, snowball sampling may be the only way to gain access.

If you do use snowball sampling, it is often helpful to begin your recruitment efforts in somewhat different social locations. For example, if you are studying men who have tested positive for HIV, you might want to gain initial contacts with men from different clinics and social service agencies, in addition to seeking out men who are not affiliated with these agencies at all. One of the risks of snowball sampling is that the participants may be too similar to one another to give you the diverse perspectives you want.

Lisa Groger, Pamela Mayberry and Jane Straker (1999) caution that as researchers you need to consider those who refuse to participate in an interview or those to whom you can't gain access. What might you *not* learn, they ask, because of who would not talk to you? In their research on African American elders and their caregivers, they experienced numerous problems gaining interviewees. There were numerous gatekeepers, some of whom may have had a vested interest in not providing access. Some of the elders may have had particular reasons not to be interviewed. They suggest that qualitative researchers need to think carefully about how the choices they make in soliciting research participants may shape the conclusions they come to.

Preparing an Interview Guide

In in-depth interviewing, the researcher typically prepares an interview guide to help focus the interview. Unlike a questionnaire or a precoded survey instrument, which provides a rigid order and specific wording for the questions that the interviewer must follow, an interview guide helps the interviewer focus the interview. The interview guide lists the main topics and, typically, the wording of questions that the researcher wants to ask. It also usually includes some ideas about follow-up questions (or probes). But the researcher does not follow the guide rigidly in conducting the interview. Rather, she or he adapts the questions during the course of the interview, changing both the phrasing and the order of the questions. The interviewer might ask additional questions based on the participant's responses. Some researchers like to create two interview guides: a relatively long one that includes many detailed questions and a short schematic that summarizes the main topics. The detailed guide serves primarily to help the researcher prepare for the interview; the summary helps him or her remember the key topics during the actual interview.

Deciding What Kinds of Questions to Ask

Not all topics are amenable to interviews. It doesn't make sense to ask interviewees about things they can't answer, and some kinds of questions will make for more productive interviews than others. For example, it doesn't really make sense to ask native English speakers when they first learned to speak English, because they probably don't remember. If you want to know about what people actually do, rather than what they say they do, you should probably use observation. But you can legitimately ask people questions about the following (Patton 1990, pp. 290–293):

- Their experiences or behaviors
- Their opinions or values
- Their feelings
- Their factual knowledge
- Their sensory experiences
- Their personal background

important!

Let's say that you are researching workers in a fast-food restaurant, and you want to ask them about their daily routines. You might ask, "What do you normally do when you begin a shift?" Or you might inquire about a particular experience: "Have you ever been stiffed by a customer? Can you tell me about it?" These questions point to *events* or *experiences* that research participants have had.

You might also be curious about research participants' *opinions* or *values.* In the case of fast-food workers, you might ask them how they think customers (or the workers themselves) should be treated. For example, you might ask, "Some people use the saying 'The customer is always right.' What do you think about that?" or "What do you think about how workers are treated in this restaurant?"

Sometimes, you will want to explore the interviewees' *feelings* or *emotions* about a particular topic or event. In this case, you might ask, "How did you feel when you were yelled at by a customer?" or "What do you like about your work?"

Other times, you may be interested in *factual information*—what the interviewees know. Thus, you might ask, "Have you heard about proposed legislation to raise the minimum wage?" Be aware that factual questions may not lead to an in-depth discussion. But they can sometimes be used to figure out whether to continue a line of questioning. For example, if you only want to find out *what* employees have heard about the proposed legislation, you won't want to continue that line of questioning if they haven't heard of it.

You can also ask questions about the *senses*—what the interviewees see, hear, touch, smell, and taste. An appropriate question here might be, "What does the kitchen smell like at the end of the shift?" These kinds of questions can be especially useful in setting the scene and trying to figure out what the interviewees' daily reality is.

Finally, you can ask *background* questions—questions about, say, family background or social class or income. You might ask, "How many children do you have? How old are they?" Some background questions are especially tricky—for example, questions about income. Sometimes, interviewers will include a short questionnaire for these kinds of information to avoid having to ask about them face-to-face.

Structuring and Ordering Questions

In developing the interview guide, it's often useful to brainstorm a list of questions and topics that you think might be useful to include. Then you can put them in some kind of logical order. For example, for your research in the fast-food restaurant, you might put questions about how the work is actually done in one section and questions about relations with coworkers in another. Keep in mind, though, that the precise order will depend in large part on the interview itself—it's best to follow the interviewee's lead. But it's also a good idea to at least think in advance about the kinds of questions that seem to go well with other questions and to consider some potential follow-up questions. As a general rule, you should place easier, less threatening questions at the beginning and save more controversial or sensitive questions for the middle or end, once you have developed some rapport and established some trust.

When I'm preparing an interview guide, I usually brainstorm a fairly long list of topics and questions. Then I circle all the topics and questions that seem related, make sure the questions and topics don't overlap, and delete redundant questions. Finally, I work on the phrasing of the questions, trying to craft open-ended questions that will help spark discussion, rather than close it down. I often find it helpful to work with a key informant or another researcher at this stage, someone who can help me sort through potential redundancies. I usually try to gather feedback early on and pretest the questions before using them on a larger scale.

Box 5.1 shows an excerpt from a brainstorming list for my research on stay-at-home mothers. Notice how the items in Box 5.1 are expanded into an interview guide in Box 5.2. In the actual interviews, I didn't necessarily

---

BOX 5.1 **Brainstorming Topics for an Interview Guide for At-Home Mothers**

Questions about what the day looks like
--structure of day
--who does what work

Ideals about mothering
--where did ideal come from?
--compare self to ideal

Support
--go for help

Feelings about self: what was it like to quit job
--how others reacted, too

BOX 5.2 **Excerpt from an Interview Guide for At-Home Mothers**

A. Typical Day
1. What does a typical day look like for you?
2. What are the greatest stresses in your day?
3. What are the greatest pleasures in your day?

B. Household Work
4. Tell me about the household work in your family. Who does it?
   [Probes: Different areas of household work: dishes, cooking, laundry, cleaning, car repair, yard work. Does your partner/spouse help out?]

C. Transition to Being at Home
5. What kind of work did you do before becoming an at-home mom?
6. What did you like about it?
7. What did you not like about it?
8. What was it like for you to stop working for pay? How did you feel about it?
9. When you first decided to stay at home, how did others react?
   [Probes: Get reactions of partner/spouse, parents, coworkers, friends.]
10. Did anyone support you in your decision? Who?

ask the questions in order; nor did I use the exact words listed. As an inter-viewer, I wanted to follow the interviewee's lead. Still, the list provided guidance for the topics to be covered.

Making Questions Open-Ended

Remember that your purpose in in-depth interviewing is to explore the research participant's reality. You need to make sure that the questions make sense to your research participants and are phrased in language that is appropriate for them. The questions should open up discussion, not close it down. Patricia Zavella (1987), for example, conducted her interviews in whatever mix of Spanish and English was most comfortable for her inter-viewees. If you know that the group you are studying uses specific terms for various things, you should use them. But it also doesn't make sense to take on another group's jargon unreflectively. Think how silly I would sound, for example, if I tried to use teenagers' expressions.

Beginning researchers often try to use relatively formal language, which looks good on paper but sounds awkward in speech. In the first draft of an interview guide, for example, one group of students included a question about whether their interviewees had ever "engaged in the use of alcoholic beverages at parties." While technically correct, this question sounded stilted when they asked it. It sounded much more natural when they rephrased it to ask if their respondents "ever drank at parties," clarifying as needed that they were referring to alcoholic beverages ("like wine or beer or hard liquor").

You also need to consider that how you phrase questions will shape interviewees' responses to you. Especially in in-depth interviewing, you need to make sure your questions are open-ended. Try to create questions that encourage your participants to talk, not shut down. There are a number of tricks you can use to try to keep your interviewees talking.

Avoid Dichotomies   Try to avoid questions that can easily be answered by a simple "yes" or "no." These questions, called *dichotomous questions* because there are two possible answers to them, can bring a conversation to a halt be-cause they do not encourage interviewees to continue. Here is an example:

INTERVIEWER: Do you feel college drinking is getting out of hand?

RESPONDENT: No.

Avoid Leading Questions   Dichotomous questions can often be *leading questions*—that is, questions that lead interviewees to give a particular response. You should avoid these questions because they don't encourage the interviewee to say what she or he actually thinks. Be especially wary of questions that begin with "Don't you think . . . ?" or "Wouldn't you agree . . . ?" Look at this example:

Leading question: "Don't you think that college drinking is getting out of hand?"

You can revise dichotomous and leading questions to make them more open-ended. For example, you can reword the question this way:

Revised question: "What do you think about college drinking?"

Ask Both General and Specific Questions   Asking general questions gives your interviewees the opportunity to reflect on what's most meaningful to them. With a general question, you can focus on those aspects of the topic that are most salient. General questions also allow your interviewees to move at their own pace and indicate that you are interested in what they have to say. So, for example, you might want to ask your interviewee questions like these:

General question: "Can you describe a typical day at work for me?"

General question: "What do you usually like to do after school?"

At the same time, it's often helpful to ask more specific questions, ones that require your interviewees to draw on their own experiences. More specific questions can also serve as good follow-up questions. For example, compare these two questions below. The first invites respondents to think more abstractly about college drinking, and the second asks respondents to reflect on their own campus.

General question: "What do you think about college drinking?"

Specific question: "What do you think about drinking on this campus?"

Whenever possible, try to ask questions that encourage respondents to draw on specific experiences. For example, if a respondent has trouble imagining a "typical day," you might ask her or him to describe a specific day: "What about the last day you worked? Can you describe what happened that day?"

Take Care with the Question "Why?"   Be cautious about using the question "Why?" People don't always know why they do things, and they may feel defensive when asked to provide an account of their actions. This doesn't mean that you should never ask "Why?" in an interview. As a researcher, you are certainly interested in figuring out why people do things or hearing the accounts they give. But it does mean that you should think about whether the wording of the question is useful.

Consider the difference between these two questions:

Potentially threatening: "Why did you get drunk at that party?"

Potentially less threatening: "Can you talk a little about your drinking at that party?"

The second question might also be followed up with several more specific questions—for example, "How did you begin?" and "Do you remember how you made the decision to keep drinking after you felt tipsy?" Sometimes, simply asking "How come?" instead of "Why?" will make a question less threatening. In general, if you can normalize the experience you are asking about and show that you are not being judgmental, you will be less likely to threaten the interviewee.

Pretesting Your Interview Guide

You should always try to pretest your interview guide, because what may seem like a good question in the abstract may turn out not to be in practice. Sometimes, the language is too formal or informal, or the question simply doesn't make sense. As a first round of pretesting, you might try the questions on your classmates. Then you might try the questions on a key informant, one who can help you make adjustments. In large-scale interview studies, researchers may do a round of pretesting on a smaller group of subjects before using the interview questions on a large scale. Whether you do a formal or informal pretest, be sure that you are familiar with the questions you want to ask. By the time you interview "real" research participants, you should have the questions basically memorized. That way, you can focus on what the interviewee is saying, not on whether you remember the questions.

BEFORE THE INTERVIEW

Once you have completed your interview guide and pretested it, you are ready to set up the actual interview. It's best to set up the interview in advance. You should have some idea of how long the interview should take, based on your pretest. Make sure you allow more time than you think you will need for the interview. When you set up the interview, be sure to tell potential interviewees about what you are researching and why. Give them an estimate of how much of their time you will need, as well as a phone number or way to contact you if they need to cancel or change plans. If you've made a date for the interview far in advance (say, several weeks), it's a good idea to call the day before to remind them that you'll be coming. And if you are conducting the interview at an unfamiliar place, be sure to get directions!

Establishing a Location

The location of the interview can vary, depending on you and your interviewees' preferences. Interviews can take place in an office, in an interviewee's home or workplace, or in a coffee shop or other public place. Ideally, you should do the interview in a fairly quiet place where you won't be disturbed. If you can, try to turn off cell phones and pagers and other potential sources of interruption. Realistically, however, it's often difficult for some people to find a quiet place. For example, when I was interviewing at-home mothers, I typically came to their homes. Because the women were caring for their children at home, they tended not to have baby sitters or other child care. The interviews thus were often interrupted so the women could attend to children's needs. While the interviews often felt disjointed and were difficult to transcribe, they also gave much more insight into the texture and quality of the women's lives than an interview in a sterile, artificial environment would have.

Constructing a Face Sheet

Often, interviewers construct a *face sheet* that includes demographic information about the interviewee and information on the set-up of the interview: the name or code number of the interviewee, contact information, the place and time of interview, and so forth.

Deciding What to Bring

My "interview packet" includes a face sheet, an interview guide, consent forms (and pens), and any other material I think I might need, such as informational handouts for the interviewees. If you are taping the interview, be sure to bring extra batteries and more tapes than you think you might need—and make sure your tape recorder is working. Most interviewers have suffered the unhappy experience of having a tape recorder stop in the middle of the interview and thereby losing irreplaceable interviews. Some interviewers like to record the date, location of interview, and name (or code number) of the interviewee at the beginning of the tape. That helps them test the recorder, as well as keep track of their interview tapes later on.

Dressing Appropriately

At the risk of sounding like an old fuddy-duddy, I strongly advise you to think about issues of dress and appearance for the interview. What you wear, how you style your hair, and how you adorn your body send clear messages about who and what you are. And interviewees are no less susceptible to these messages than other people. Thus, you need to consider the kinds of messages you want to send. You'll clearly make different choices depending on your interviewees. If you're interviewing other students, for example, you can probably keep your body piercings in and dress a little more informally. But if you're interviewing residents in a nursing home, you probably should cover up your tattoo and dress more formally. The key is to know your audience. What kinds of assumptions will they make about you? How will they respond to certain kinds of dress or appearance? If you are interviewing students in a sorority or fraternity, wearing a Greek letter pin will give them one impression. (If you don't legitimately have one, though, I wouldn't recommend it.) Wearing a heavy metal tee shirt will give them another. When in doubt, dress a little more conservatively or more neutrally than you think you might need to.

DURING THE INTERVIEW

Before you actually begin the interview, take time to describe your study and your interviewee's role in it. You should make sure your interviewee knows that she or he can stop the interview at any time or refuse to answer any question. I always inform my interviewees that I'm interested in their viewpoints and that there aren't any right or wrong answers. Some interviewees are not used to structured interviews or are convinced that there's a "right" answer. During the interview, they may ask things like "Is this what you're looking for?" I try to reassure participants that I want to hear about their experiences in their own words. Also make sure that you answer any questions the interviewee might have. Sometimes, for example, interviewees want to know why you have selected *them* for the interview. If you have a consent form, make sure the interviewee signs it before beginning.

If I am tape-recording interviews, I often find it helpful to move the tape recorder close to the interviewees while going over the consent forms and providing preliminary information. I usually reiterate that they can stop the interview at any time, and I show them the "stop" button on the tape recorder. I also let them know that they can erase any part of the tape they like. Essentially, I give them control of the tape recorder.

Warming Up

Interviewees often are nervous about the interview or about being tape-recorded. Many researchers find it helpful to chat for a few minutes before beginning the interview. For example, I asked mothers about their children in my interviews with at-home mothers. Some interviewers like to establish rapport with their interviewees by finding things they have in common.

Keeping the Conversation Rolling

In-depth interviewing is an art as well as a skill. More than any other research technique, in-depth interviews require active listening skills. Conducting an in-depth interview entails sending out the message that what your interviewee has to say is important. It's not simply a matter of mechanically asking questions and giving responses. Instead, it involves actively listening to what your interviewee has to say, following up, and keeping the conversation rolling. Think of it as more like a meandering river and less like a game of Ping-Pong.

You can encourage conversation through body language and verbal cues that indicate active listening and genuine interest in what your respondent has to say and through follow-up questions and prompts. Some people are naturally better at interviewing (and, more generally, at conversing) than others. Still, interviewing is a skill that you can learn through practice.

One way to encourage the flow of conversation is through the careful use of transitions. How can you move the interview smoothly from one topic to the next? Suppose you are interviewing a fast-food worker about her relationships with coworkers, and you want to turn to her relationship with the manager. You might try a transition like this: "You said you tend to get along with your coworkers pretty well. Is that the case for your manager, too?" Sometimes, there won't be a graceful transition. In those cases, it's still a good idea to let your interviewee know where you're heading in the interview—for example, "We've been talking about how you get along with your coworkers. Now I'd like you to think about how you get along with customers. Can you talk a little about that?"

Thinking on Your Feet: Follow-Ups and Probes

In an in-depth interview, you have to "think on your feet." The interview guide gives you a place to begin your questioning, but it's important to remember that your goal is to follow your interviewee's lead. This means that you don't have to go through your questions in lockstep order. Instead, if a question leads the interviewee to talk about something that is farther down on your interview guide (or isn't on the guide but seems relevant), don't hesitate to jump to that topic.

Sometimes, interviewees are reticent or simply don't know how much information you are looking for. You can use follow-up questions and probes to clarify responses or to obtain additional information. Some follow-up questions are planned; others are unplanned. You might want to follow up when an interviewee uses an unfamiliar term, or when you need more information to understand a story, or when you simply want more details. The wording of probes and follow-up questions usually flows from the specific topic you are investigating. Still, there are a number of general probes that you might find helpful, including these:

- What happened?
- When did something happen?
- Who else was there?
- Where were you?
- How were you involved?
- How did that happen?
- Where did it happen?
- What was that like for you?

Probes

One follow-up question I use frequently when I want to know more is simply "Can you tell me a little more about it?"

As a final question, I usually like to ask respondents if there is anything they want to add or any aspect of their experience that the questions didn't cover. I usually also ask if they would like to ask me anything before I go.

Speaking and Keeping Quiet

One of the hardest things for many beginning interviewers to do is to deal with periods of silence in the interview. But some people think faster than others. Sometimes, people need time to gather their thoughts and sort through what they want to say or simply to remember something. If you rush in to "fill the gap," you may stop their thought process or cut them off.

They may feel that you're not really interested in what they have to say or that they're going into too much detail. If long silences in conversation make you uncomfortable, you need to find some way to stop yourself from rushing in. Sit on your hands. Count silently to yourself. If someone really doesn't understand the question, he or she usually will say something or look confused or otherwise indicate a need for clarification. However, don't jump in with a clarification until you're absolutely certain that it's necessary.

Look for subtle cues that the person is really finished speaking before moving on to the next question. Sometimes, for example, interviewees might repeat the answer or give a verbal cue that they're done, such as saying "That's all" or "Is that what you mean?" They might look away while they're thinking and then make eye contact when they're ready to speak (or done speaking). If you're not sure if someone has finished speaking, you can always ask if she or he wants to add anything else. Whatever you do, make sure you allow the interviewee lots of time to think. A slower-paced interview will usually give you much richer information than a fast one.

In a similar vein, don't rush in to tell your own stories. Sometimes, an interviewee's story will remind you of some of your own experiences, and you may be tempted to jump in. But I strongly recommend that you do not. Instead, keep the focus on the interviewee.

Communicating Nonverbally

Not all meaning is communicated verbally. A skilled interviewer also watches for body language, which can provide important clues to the respondent's meaning. For example, a fast-food worker might say, "I l-o-o-o-v-e my boss," and then roll his eyes, indicating the opposite. You need to pay attention to *how* people say things, as well as to *what* they say.

You also need to monitor your own nonverbal communication. Your body language can send the message that you're interested in what your interviewee has to say—or bored by it. Be an active listener. That is, lean in toward your interviewee, nod your head, and say, "Uh huh." These "minimal prompters" communicate that you are listening intently to what your interviewee has to say. Sometimes, restating what the interviewee has just said is a good check to make sure that you understand—for example, "You said you don't like working the front counter, right?"

Keeping on Track

What if your interviewee goes "off track"? How much control should you try to exert during the interview with a very talkative interviewee? Most first-time interviewees are too concerned with asking all their preplanned questions in order and keeping interviewees "on track." But some of the most important insights come from the spontaneous parts of interviews. For this reason, I recommend that you allow your interviewees a fair amount of leeway. The most important thing is to let participants speak, not to keep them rigidly on track. That said, there are times when an interviewee wanders very far afield from the topics at hand. When that occurs, it's best to gently guide the conversation back on track.

Taping and Taking Notes

Should you tape-record the interviews? Take notes? Do both? Some interviewers feel very strongly that you should tape-record all interviews; others feel equally strongly that you should not. In informal, unstructured interviews, such as may occur during participant observation, it may actually be impossible to record the responses. In these cases, taking notes (written or mental) may suffice. In more structured interviews, I recommend tape-recording unless the interviewee seems so unnerved by the process that the interview does not get off the ground. Some interviewees are afraid that they will seem ignorant or say something they'll regret having on tape. Others become painfully self-conscious. Still others—such as those involved in illegal activities—may be concerned that the tape will fall into someone else's hands and be used against them.

My experience is that most interviewees eventually forget about the tape recorder. Taping enables you to listen more fully to what the individual is saying. If you are frantically trying to take notes, you cannot make eye contact or give the interviewee full attention. Taping also enables you to go back and listen again and again to the interview—a big help in conducting the analysis. Taping also lets you pay attention to small details or to particular ways of phrasing things that you might otherwise miss. Marjorie DeVault (1999) reminds us that *how* someone says things may be as important as what they say. The tape recording provides a record of this.

Should you take notes during the interview as well? Many interviewers do. Notes can help you remember details about nonverbal gestures or questions of emphasis. They can help you remember where the interview has gone and avoid repeating topics. You can also jot notes about follow-up questions that you want to ask. If you take good notes, then you can reconstruct the interview if the taping fails. I generally do not take many notes during the interview itself, though I keep pen and paper handy. Despite my best intentions to take notes during the interview, I find it hard to concentrate on what people are saying if I'm writing. But others have the opposite experience: The act of writing keeps them focused on what is being said. You should use your own judgment about what works for you.

AFTER THE INTERVIEW

Writing Field Notes

As mentioned previously, I recommend writing detailed field notes immediately after an interview. I often end up taking notes in the car a few blocks away. In those notes, I try to recall as much as I can about the small details of the interview. I try to recall the setting and the appearance of the interviewee, as well as any details about the interaction that strike me. I also try to record my impressions about how the interview went. The following is an excerpt from field notes that I wrote after an interview with an at-home mother:

> I just came from interviewing 009, who lives in a rented town house in Mill City. She strikes me as depressed. At least more than a little unhappy and isolated. It seems to me that given how much she has moved around and how she hasn't been able to finish her schooling, no wonder she is unhappy. . . . I was struck by how she talked about her unhappiness in mothering right in front of her daughter.
>
> When I got to her house, her daughter was watching television. The house is small, worn, definitely not new. They're saving up for a down payment for a home of their own, which she hopes they'll be able to buy next spring. We sat at her dining room table near sliding doors. She apologized for the view (the next door neighbor's back yard, which had a lot of junk in it). She's definitely not happy with the house—no yard for her daughter to play in, not enough room. . . .
>
> At the end of the interview (and I could see she was nervous about the tape recorder), we talked a little. She said something like "now let's turn the tables. I'll interview you. Tell me about your childhood!" She's uneasy about her mothering, and I felt like I needed to reassure her. I think she thinks that all other mothers are perfectly happy, that other mothers have perfect children, etc. I gave her some info about some of the hard times other mothers have described.

Transcribing and Making Sense

If you do tape-record the interviews, you should transcribe the tapes as soon as possible after the interview. Don't wait until you have many tapes piled up, or the job of transcribing (and subsequent analysis) will become overwhelming. If you're lucky and have a research grant to hire a transcriptionist, you can delegate that work. But chances are, you'll have to do the transcribing yourself. Transcribing interview tapes is hard work. Even if you are an excellent typist, it still can take many hours to transcribe one interview tape. A tape player with foot pedals and variable speeds is an enormous help. Still, according to one estimate, it takes a fast typist about 4 hours to transcribe each hour of interview tape (Morse 1998). A 1-hour interview can yield twenty-five pages of typed transcript or more.

What should you transcribe? How much detail should you go into? How should you record the stuttering, repetitions, silences, laughs, and awkwardness of spoken language? In general, you should transcribe in as much detail as you can muster. Be sure to include both the questions and the responses—what you say, as interviewer, is a crucial part of the conversation. But you need to make a decision about how much detail to go into. Some researchers, called *conversation analysts,* pay attention to *how* things are said (Schegloff and Sacks 1974). They are interested in the rules that structure conversation, and they have developed very complicated methods for transcribing tapes, including symbols to indicate pauses between turns, intonation, and overlapping speech. For your purposes, you probably won't need to go into that much detail. Still, it's useful to reproduce the speech as faithfully as you can. I don't recommend "cleaning up" the speech too much (for example, don't correct grammar or transform spoken language into standard written English). Spoken language, after all, is much less formal than written language, and it's important to preserve the flavor of what was said.

Some interviewers give a copy of the tape or transcript to the interviewees afterwards to let the interviewees make any corrections or additions. For example, Sharon Thompson interviewed over 400 teenage girls over a 9-year period on the subject of romance and sex (Thompson 1995). After each interview, the participant could decide whether to allow Thompson to include the tape in her research. The girls were encouraged to call her later if they changed their mind.

GROUP INTERVIEWS

The Role of the Focus Group

Not all interviews are conducted with only one person at a time. Some researchers conduct interviews with small groups, typically with fewer than ten people. Sometimes called *focus groups,* small-group interviews are used extensively by market researchers and political pollsters. Although the techniques for focus groups were originally developed in the 1940s and 1950s, they subsequently fell out of favor among most social researchers (Morgan 1988). In the past two decades, however, the use of focus groups by social researchers has become much more commonplace.

Social scientists often use focus groups to evaluate programs (such as job training programs or drug and alcohol treatment programs). Public health researchers, and individuals interested in "social marketing," or trying to introduce desired behaviors such as sexual practices that decrease the risk of HIV, also use focus groups (Morgan 1996). Sometimes, focus groups are used alone; but more often, they are used in conjunction with other methods, such as individual interviews or surveys. Social scientists have used focus groups to explore a variety of topics, including fear of crime among Latinas (Madriz 1998), people's experiences with natural disasters such as Hurricane Andrew (Belgrave and Smith 1995), the coping strategies of HIV-positive mothers (Marcenko and Samost 1999), and women's feelings about sexuality (Montell 1999).

Group interviews, like individual interviews, can be relatively structured or unstructured. They are useful when you want to know about people's opinions or attitudes, rather than people's actual behavior. They are also useful when you want to understand group processes—how people arrive at decisions. When they work well, focus groups can be an extraordinarily rich source of data, as focus group members build on one another's ideas and opinions.

One of the advantages of small-group interviews is that they allow for the collection of a fairly large amount of data in a relatively short period of time. With group interviews, you can typically sample a larger variety of opinions in a shorter period than in individual interviews. Overall, they can be less time-consuming (and thus cheaper) than individual interviews. In addition, some researchers find that focus groups are especially helpful for studying transient populations. For example, if you want to conduct interviews with migrant farmworkers, who move from place to place picking crops, it will take you a long time to conduct individual interviews. By the time you are partway through, the workers likely will have moved on. Focus groups provide you with a way to gather interview data more quickly.

Some feminist researchers argue that focus groups are especially helpful in reducing the imbalances of power between the researcher and those being researched (Montell 1999). By enabling women to speak with others who have had similar experiences, focus groups help empower women. Esther Madriz sees focus groups as a form of "collective testimony," a way for women to break their silence and confirm their experiences with other women (Madriz 1998, 2000).

A focus group typically consists of a small number of participants—usually less than 10. Often, the focus group is relatively homogeneous with regard to age, ethnicity, gender, or some other characteristic important to the study. What's most important in forming a focus group is finding a group of people who will feel comfortable interacting with one another and who will express their opinions freely. Sometimes, groups are composed of people who are already familiar with one another, such as parents in a particular school or workers from the same workplace. Other times, the participants are unfamiliar with one another.

Recruitment can be a difficult problem for focus group researchers (Morgan 1995). Unless the topic is of great intrinsic interest to potential participants, they may not be motivated to participate. And once they have agreed to participate, there is still the possibility that they will not show up. Yet, unless at least a minimal number show up, the focus group won't be as productive and may even have to be canceled. Thus, experienced users of focus groups often use extensive follow-up procedures (written and telephoned reminders, for example), offer incentives (food or money), and typically over-recruit. One rule of thumb is to invite at least two more participants than you think you will need (Morgan 1995).

The Role of Moderator

Focus groups can be more or less structured. Morgan (1996) argues that it's helpful for moderators to control the session in terms of two dimensions. First, moderators may play a more or less directive role in regard to the questions asked. In a more structured focus group, the questions are relatively specific, and the moderator controls what topics are brought up. In this group, the moderator may move group discussion away from topics that are not of interest to the researcher. In a less structured group, the questions can be very general, and the moderator allows topics to emerge according to the group's interests.

The second dimension of structure involves group dynamics. In a relatively structured group, the moderator plays a more directive role in terms of group dynamics. The moderator can intervene to encourage quiet or shy participants and at the same time tactfully discourage more forceful individuals from dominating the group. Some experts suggest that it's helpful to have two moderators: one to focus on group processes and keep the conversation moving and the other to observe and take notes.

Because each group member must be allowed time to participate, a group interview will typically deal with fewer topics than an individual interview. Most focus groups last between 1 and 2 hours. In that period, only a relatively small number of topics can be introduced. Sustaining discussion is easier if the participants are legitimately interested in the topic. Some experts argue that it can be helpful to begin with questions that are likely to be of most interest to participants, even when those topics aren't the most important to the researcher (Morgan 1995).

Stimulating free and open discussion is one of the greatest challenges of the moderator. One risk of focus groups—especially when they include individuals of differing power and status or when they focus on controversial topics—is that participants might censor themselves and defer to group opinion so as not to "rock the boat" or make others feel uneasy. This phenomenon, called *groupthink* by Irving Janis (1982), can be avoided. One way is through the use of "devil's advocates"—individuals whose specific role is to question the group's ideas and decisions and thus to spark free discussion (MacDougall and Baum 1997). Another possibility is to include only those who are of similar status in the group, thereby avoiding the problem of lower-status group members censoring themselves. Esther Madriz argues that it may be important for the moderator to be of the same racial/ethnic background as the participants (1998). Sharing important similarities, she suggests, leads to rapport, which enhances the likelihood of a successful focus group session.

Ethical Issues in Conducting Focus Groups

Focus groups have some specific ethical issues. Unlike in individual interviews, the researcher is not the only one who needs to respect confidentiality. In the case of group interviews, all the other group participants need to maintain confidentiality as well. Participants won't speak freely if they believe that what they say will not be held in confidence. This is especially important in focus groups that deal with sensitive issues, such as sexuality. Bruce Berg (2001) suggests that all participants in a focus group sign a confidentiality statement in which they promise not to reveal information outside of the group. Others suggest beginning the focus group with a statement of the ground rules for participation, including the confidentiality pledge.

Recording the Focus Group

How should you keep a record of the conversation? Group conversations are complex: People sometimes interrupt or talk over one another, and the conversation may move rapidly from one side of the room to the other. Audiotapes are useful, but they do not indicate who the speaker is—something that can cause problems in the analysis. Written notes are usually necessary to augment audiotaped focus groups. Some focus group facilitators video-tape the session. (Market researchers, who are typically far better funded than academic researchers, may have access to plush video conference rooms with one-way mirrors so that researchers can view the session. If you have access to resources like these, of course you should use them!) Whatever method of recording you use, it's useful to keep written notes as well, and tapes (just like individual interview tapes) should be transcribed as soon as possible.

MAKING MEANING

What do you do when you're finished transcribing the tapes? How do you begin to make sense of the data you are collecting? We will deal with strategies for analysis in detail later in the book, especially in Chapter 8. In the meantime, you should listen to the tapes and read over your transcripts several times. Try to listen closely to what your research participants have been saying. It is only through immersing yourself in their words that you will begin to make sense of the conversation you have been a part of.

QUESTIONS FOR THOUGHT

1. How much of your own opinions do you think you should share in an interview situation? What might be some of the consequences of sharing personal information with an interviewee? What might be some of the consequences of *not* sharing?

2. What kinds of topics might be better suited to an individual interview than to a group interview? What kinds of topics might be better suited to a group interview? Why?

3. How do you see yourself? Are you extroverted and relatively outgoing? Or are you shy and introspective? What personal challenges do you think you will face in trying to conduct interviews? What strengths do you think you have?

EXERCISES

1. The purpose of this exercise is to develop your listening skills. You'll need to do this one with a friend. Have your friend talk for 3 minutes

(use a timer) on any topic that interests her or him. Your job is to listen as carefully as you can without interrupting. When the time is up, try to recall as much detail as possible about what your friend said.

2. Observe someone who is actively listening to another person. Pay attention to the body language that they use: leaning in, shaking their head, and so forth. What kinds of nonverbal cues tell you that someone is listening? What kinds of nonverbal cues tell you that someone is not paying attention?

3. Develop an interview guide on a topic you are interested in. When you have completed an initial draft, go through the questions looking for dichotomous questions and leading questions. If you find any, rewrite them.

4. Try out your interview guide on a friend or fellow student. As you're interviewing, pay attention to which questions seem to stimulate discussion and which seem to shut it down. When you have finished, revise your interview guide based on your experiences. It's often helpful to have a third person act as an observer and give you specific feedback on what went well and what could be improved.

5. Develop a set of questions for a focus group that you could conduct with a group of fellow students. Campus life is full of potential topics. After you have developed the questions, try conducting a focus group with your classmates as participants.

6. Imagine that you are interested in studying youth violence. Develop a strategy for recruiting participants for either a focus group or an individual interview. (Alternatively, develop recruitment strategies for studies of police harassment, worker safety in small businesses, or parents who homeschool their children.)

SUGGESTIONS FOR FURTHER READING

Fontana, Andrea, and James H. Frey. "Interviewing: The Art of Science." Pp. 47–78 in Norman K. Denzin and Yvonna Lincoln (eds.), *Collecting and Interpreting Qualitative Materials*. Thousand Oaks, CA: Sage, 1998.

Holstein, James A., and Jaber F. Gubrium. *The Active Interview*. Thousand Oaks, CA: Sage, 1995.

Madriz, Esther. "Focus Groups in Feminist Research." Pp. 835–850 in *Handbook of Qualitative Research*, 2nd ed., edited by Norman K. Denzin and Yvonna S. Lincoln. Thousand Oaks, CA: Sage, 2000.

Morgan, David L. *Focus Groups as Qualitative Research*. Newbury Park, CA: Sage, 1988.

Oakley, Ann. "Interviewing Women: A Contradiction in Terms." Pp. 30–61 in *Doing Feminist Research*, edited by Helen Roberts. London: Routledge & Kegan Paul, 1981.

Seidman, Irving. *Interviewing as Qualitative Research: A Guide for Researchers in Education and the Social Sciences*, 2nd ed. New York: Teachers College Press, 1998.

6

Unobtrusive Measures

Analyzing Texts and Material Artifacts

The average person throws away 2.1 pounds of garbage a day, much of it paper and plastic (Rathje and Murphy 1992). What would people find if they systematically rooted through your garbage? No doubt lots of paper, some food wrappings, some leftover food, and maybe some worn-out clothes or empty printer cartridges. How much evidence of fast-food consumption would they find? What about fresh vegetables, or milk, or soda? What might they be able to tell about your study habits? Your work habits? Your choices in recreation?

That's exactly what William Rathje, an archaeologist and director of the Garbage Project at the University of Arizona, does. Project researchers systematically identify and analyze what households in Tucson, Arizona, throw away. They also examine landfills, sometimes digging down deep to analyze trash from earlier decades. By systematically analyzing household garbage, they have learned a great deal about people's habits and behaviors—especially those that people don't necessarily want to talk about, like drinking alcohol or eating processed foods (Rathje 1992, 1993). They have even devised ways to estimate the size and composition of the population based on garbage. For example, they can fairly reliably tell how many babies live in a given neighborhood by the number of diapers they find in the trash.

The work of the Garbage Project is a good example of using *unobtrusive measures* to study human behavior. Unobtrusive measures involve any form of studying human behavior that does not rely on asking people directly (such as interviewing) or on observing people (such as doing

, int observation). These may include studying human physical traces, as the Garbage Project does, or analyzing written records and documents, the media (like television or radio), or the Internet.

PHYSICAL TRACES

One way in which you can study people without interacting directly is through the study of physical traces (Webb, Campbell, Schwartz, Sechrest, and Grove 1981). Humans leave physical traces of their various activities behind as they go about their daily lives, and you can use this evidence to make inferences about them. In my neighborhood, for example, you can buy a Chinese-language newspaper from a box on the street alongside the local English-language paper; you can also buy national newspapers in English, like *USA Today* and *The New York Times*. This fact tells us that there is a large enough population of Chinese-speaking people in the community to support a Chinese newspaper. In the same neighborhood, you can see many Italian groceries and bakeries alongside Vietnamese noodle shops. Again, this gives us some information about the neighborhood and the ethnic groups living there. A cemetery in a neighboring town shows a similar pattern. Most of the tombstones in the oldest part of the cemetery, dating from the late 1700s, contain English names. In a somewhat newer part of the cemetery, you can read Irish and Italian names on the gravestones. In the newest part of the cemetery are a few Asian, Armenian, and Portuguese names, along with large numbers of Italian and Irish names. A careful social observer can learn something about the migration patterns of ethnic groups by looking at the environment.

Generally, physical traces are either measures of accretion or measures of erosion. Measures of *accretion* entail the accumulation of layers. The Garbage Project is a good example of this. Garbage builds up in layers as people throw things out. By studying the layers, you can get information about how a society or group of people within it change over time. In the top layers, for example, you might see computer monitors and other parts of discarded personal computers in landfills. You certainly wouldn't find evidence of these if you dug down a little deeper; instead, you might find construction debris, bottles, and cans (as you would still find today). If you looked carefully, you might find pull-top tabs from beer and soda cans from the 1960s or eight-track tape players from the 1970s.

Another good example of accretion is graffiti (Lee 2000), which can include "official" signs and notices such as stop signs or no-parking signs. These signs, some argue, serve as a continual reminder of the state's regulation of social life. Sometimes, graffiti can be more political in nature or express pressing social concerns. For example, stop signs have been spray-painted to read "Stop Rape" or "Stop War." Recently, concerns about globalization have also been expressed in the form of graffiti. Graffiti can also serve to demarcate social boundaries, as in gang graffiti. Public art, including murals, can also be considered a kind of graffiti. And all of these physical traces can be analyzed.

Measures of *erosion* entail studying how people gradually wear down facets of their environment through daily use. By studying patterns of wear, you can gain information about people's activities. For example, a landscape architect might place a walkway in an area where people don't habitually walk, but the paths worn in the lawn indicate where people *actually* walk. In a library, the most frequently used periodicals might be heavily thumbed and worn looking. In a museum, footprints might be worn into the floor of the most visited exhibits, whereas the floors near little-viewed sites might be clean and shiny.

Your imagination is the only limit in devising ways to study people's physical traces. In general, this evidence can help you figure out what people *actually* do, rather than what they say they do. Because this method does not entail interacting directly with people, it also enables greater anonymity for the researcher (Webb et al. 1981). In addition, the biases of this research method are likely to be very different from those of other methods, such as participant observation and interviewing. For this reason, studying physical traces can be a very useful addition to more traditional sociological methods.

But this method has drawbacks. Most important, we need to ask, What is the likelihood that any given object will actually survive? For example, vegetables decompose far more quickly than bones. Thus, unless you sift through garbage quickly, you will have more difficulty gaining evidence of vegetable eating than of meat eating. In addition, some physical accretion and erosion may be so small as to be unmeasurable. Walking on a soft surface, like a lawn, will yield more traces than walking on a hard surface, like concrete. You might not be able to measure the erosion of concrete in a short span of time. Finally, because these methods tend not be very systematic, they often are paired with other, more systematic methods.

MATERIAL ARTIFACTS

One form of studying physical traces is the study of *material artifacts*, the objects that people produce, like pots and pans and cars and computers. Archaeologists and historians may be more accustomed to studying material artifacts, but sociologists can use them as well to help make sense of the social world. Social scientists have studied tattoos (Sanders 1989), graffiti (Cole 1991), and Zippo cigarette lighters collected in Vietnam (Walters 1997), among many others.

Analyzing material artifacts can be far more complicated than analyzing written texts. First, material artifacts are less logical than formal language, in the sense that they don't have a formal grammar. You can't make a comprehensive dictionary of all the meanings that an artifact might possess. Furthermore, the meanings of material objects often remain implicit (Hodder 1998, p. 117). Thus, we need to understand the social contexts in which material artifacts are made, used, discarded, and reused (Hodder 1989, 1998). This means that the act of interpreting material culture has to be tentative. It expresses as much about the analyst—about who you are—as the material culture itself.

Second, the meanings of material artifacts may change over time, as may the contexts in which they are produced. When automobiles were first produced, for example, only the wealthy could afford them. Car ownership takes on very different meanings when most people can afford to own one.

Third, material artifacts are harder to "read" than a written text because they are not linear. In reading a set of field notes or a transcript of an interview or any other written document, you know to read from left to right and from top to bottom. (Of course, the conventions for reading vary from one language or culture to another. If you were reading a document in Japanese or Hebrew, you would move from right to left, from what feels to an English speaker like the back to the front.) With material artifacts, there is no necessary order to your analysis. Imagine that you are interested in contemporary fashion and want to understand the meanings of a pile of clothes. There is no necessary order in which you should "read" those clothes. From top to bottom? Left to right? Back to front? Analyzing material artifacts is not a linear process.

In addition, in analyzing material artifacts, you have to figure out what things mean without having access to the person (or people) who produced them or used them. This is especially true if you are working with historical artifacts. Thus, you may not have an "insider's" perspective on the meanings of things and have to interpret them using contextual clues. Even if you do have an insider's perspective, people are often not articulate about why they do things. Think about it: Why is an exam book usually blue, and why do we still call it a "blue book" even if it is not blue? Why do we usually use a mug for hot drinks like coffee or tea, and a cup or glass for cold drinks? Why not use the same container for both? Having the advice of an insider—one who uses blue books or coffee mugs or glasses—probably won't help you much.

Interpreting material artifacts thus involves a *hermeneutical* process, a process of making meaning. You need to try to situate the artifact both in the context in which it was made and produced and in the context in which you (as analyst) are situated. You need to try to understand not only how the item was produced but also how it came to your attention for analysis. Why was this particular artifact (or type of artifact) preserved, and not others? At one level, this is a physical process. Some kinds of things (like vegetable matter) decompose relatively quickly; others (like ceramic or bone or stone) do not. Yet the preservation of things is also a social process, one that involves human choices about what should be preserved and what should not. What things are seen as *worth* keeping? For example, you probably don't think twice about throwing out or recycling a Coke can or a bottle that water came in. In another culture, in which material goods are less plentiful, these items would be carefully preserved and reused for a different purpose.

How do you go about analyzing material artifacts? It is certainly not easy, nor are there any general guidelines. Analyzing these artifacts always involves the study of local, particular cultures. One analyst states, "There is nothing easy in our work, but its basic strategy is not hard to state. We hunt for patterns" (Glassie 1991, p. 255). Archaeologist Ian Hodder suggests that the analyst of material artifacts must work "between past and present or between different examples of material culture, making analogies between them" (1998, p. 121). To do this, you need to immerse yourself in the specific historical context (Tuchman 1998), and you need to know enough about the cultural context in which something has meaning. Specifically, you need to address these issues:

- Where and when was this item (or group of items) produced?
- What do you know about the society in which it was produced?
- What kinds of people made the object you are analyzing? How? Who used it?
- How was it sold or distributed?
- Did different people use the object in different kinds of ways? How?
- How was the meaning of the object transformed in different contexts?
- What kinds of personal meanings might the objects have had, as well as larger social meanings?
- What kinds of things were used in similar ways?
- What are the economic and political systems in which the items were produced?

These are just some of the questions you might ask to get you started.

You also need to consider what historical theories might help you understand the material artifacts you are trying to analyze (Hodder 1998). How have different theorists thought about the time period or the type of material culture you are interested in analyzing? It's important to immerse yourself in what others have said about the historical period (whether it is an earlier period or today) and the social context.

Finally, you should try to confirm the account you have made. That is, you should ensure that your account is internally coherent, logical, and plausible. You also need to consider any potential alternative arguments. And you need to ask whether your account leads you to understand similar objects and opens up new lines of questioning.

Ian Walters' research into Zippo cigarette lighters provides a good example of the analysis of material culture (1997). Zippo lighters were issued to American and Australian military personnel during the Vietnam War (or, as the Vietnamese call it, the American War in Vietnam). Many service personnel engraved the lighters with their date of tour, location of service, or the year. Others engraved them with short sayings or quips. Many thousands of these lighters survived. Today, there is a thriving market in Zippo lighters in Vietnam's tourist markets, and people buy them as war memorabilia. Interestingly, most of the lighters available in Vietnam are fakes—not the actual Zippo lighters from the war era. Yet the sayings engraved on them replicate the engravings of the service personnel.

Thus, these lighters have retained meanings far broader than their simple function: to light cigarettes. These lighters can be interpreted in multiple lights. As Walters argues, "As personalized icons, signifiers, they still speak to us long after their original owners have ceased to be fighters in the war zone" (1997, p. 64). In fact, the "life history" of the Zippo, Walters suggests, contains several stages. The lighter began life as a commodity—something to be bought or sold. It was sold to the army, issued or sold to individual soldiers, and used as a lighter (and as a war weapon). With the engraving, the lighter became a sign of unit identity or a personal statement. When it passed out of the owner's possession, it became either junk or someone else's souvenir (or perhaps someone's functioning cigarette lighter). In contemporary Vietnam, it reentered the commodity market as something else to be bought and sold. But it also became a memento (perhaps for soldiers who had served in the war and who returned decades later to buy the souvenir, or perhaps for other tourists), a museum piece (for those Zippos shown to be "actual" war-era items rather than fakes), an item for research, and even an object for discussion in a research methods textbook.

Walters argues, "Vietnam Zippos tell us stories. They become speech, for they mean something. Vietnam Zippos give us insights into the soldiers who annotated them and used them, loved them, laughed at them, and lost them" (Walters 1997, p. 73). But the lighters also tell stories about modern Vietnam and the world economy. To understand the meanings of the Zippo lighter, we need to immerse ourselves in the context of both the American War in Vietnam and contemporary Vietnamese life.

Analyzing material artifacts is clearly difficult—especially for those of us who are used to working with written texts. Because the analysis is so contextual, there are no simple rules that you can apply. You need to learn about the culture and history of the objects you want to analyze. But it is very worthwhile work, for it can lead you to understand human behavior in greater depth than can studying words alone.

DOCUMENTS AND RECORDS

Another way you can study human behavior unobtrusively is through written texts in the form of documents and records. *Documents* and *records* are any written materials that people leave behind. These might include things like private letters and diaries, corporate records, and government documents. These might also include media accounts, such as television programs, newspapers, and magazines. In more recent years, they might also include electronic texts, such as e-mail lists and Web sites. Although the different kinds of texts might involve somewhat different technologies, we can study them using similar methods. This chapter focuses especially on methods for obtaining written documents and records and on some of the associated problems in doing so. Chapter 8 examines methods for analyzing texts and making sense of documents and records. (The procedures for analyzing texts are typically called *content analysis*.)

Public Records

Many researchers distinguish between two kinds of written texts: documents and public records (Lincoln and Guba 1985; Macdonald and Tipton 1993). *Public records* include those materials produced for "official purposes" by social institutions like governments, schools, and hospitals. They document official transactions, like births or marriages or sales of houses. While many public records are numeric (a good example of this is U.S. Census Bureau materials) and are often used by economists and other quantitative social scientists, many others are text-based, including things like court transcripts and congressional debates.

For example, Linda Gordon (1988) used welfare records to try to understand family violence. As a historian, she was interested in how social conceptions of family violence had changed over time. She used case records from social work agencies to investigate this trend. Using these records from social welfare agencies, Gordon was able to document family violence among poor women, who typically did not leave private letters or diaries or other materials that would give insight into their experiences of violence. Without them, she probably would not have been able to document their experiences at all. But because she relied on social work records, she had only the perspective of the welfare workers who managed their cases. She lacked direct access to the women's own thoughts and feelings.

The federal government is one of the largest sources of official documents. But state, county, and city governments also generate records that can be used in qualitative analysis. Many of these documents are a matter of public record. And with the growth of the Internet, many records are now available on-line. You might want to explore, for example, Census Bureau materials (www.census.gov) or a general jumping-off point for federal government resources (www.info.gov). Remember, though, that Internet addresses tend to change rapidly. You may want to check with your librarian for other suggestions. Many libraries will bookmark helpful sites for searching government documents and other public records.

You might also want to examine public records in combination with participant observation. Schensul, Schensul, and LeCompte (1999) argue that archival data (which they define as records originally collected for bureaucratic purposes but used for research purposes) can be a very useful source of demographic information. Records such as voting lists, municipal listings of births and deaths or marriages, real estate transactions, and area maps can help field workers gain insight into the community they are studying. They argue that field workers should always attempt to gain access to these kinds of data to help describe the population and the way it has changed over time, as well as features of the physical environment.

Documents and Private Papers

Documents and private papers include things like letters, diaries, and personal papers. These may be personal in nature, such as the kinds of papers an individual gathers and generates over a lifetime—credit information, pay stubs, letters and other correspondence, news clippings, fliers, photographs, diaries, and so forth. Organizations, too, generate papers, including office memos, mission statements, and correspondence. While these kinds of private papers may be more difficult to obtain and interpret than publicly available government documents, they can provide invaluable insight into individuals' lives. Diaries and letters, for example, can provide important information about what individuals think and feel and about the texture of daily life. Financial records give clues about the economy and people's standard of living. Organizational records may give clues about how organizations function.

Personal papers and documents are sometimes seen as the province of historians. Still, sociologists have put them to good use as well. For example, Theresa Montini (1996) collected a variety of archival materials in her research on breast cancer informed-consent laws. In addition to transcripts of testimony at legislative hearings, copies of breast cancer informed-consent laws, and editorials and letters to the editor of medical journals, she collected documents from activists and former breast cancer patients, including letters, videotapes, and other personal papers. She combined her documentary research with participant observation and interviews.

Sociologist Nancy Whittier (1995) also drew on archival materials in her study of women's movement organizations in Columbus, Ohio. Along with in-depth interviews with activists, she analyzed the papers of a feminist organization, the personal files and correspondence of activists, and media reports of women's movement activity.

Primary and Secondary Sources

Most social researchers who do documentary analysis distinguish between primary sources and secondary sources. *Primary sources* are the original sources, like letters or eyewitness accounts of an event. *Secondary sources* are one step removed from primary sources (hence the name) and include things like historians' or sociologists' analyses, as well as the accounts of people who were not eyewitnesses and are not scholars. As Shulamit Reinharz puts it, primary sources are the "'raw' materials of history" while secondary sources are the "'cooked' analyses of those materials" (1992, p. 155).

The distinction between primary and secondary sources can be a little tricky. Historians will usually include things like magazines and newspapers as secondary sources, because they rely on the accounts of journalists and writers. But social scientists will sometimes use those sources as the primary source of data, as when a researcher studies the representation of domestic violence in women's magazines (Berns 1999).

Media Accounts

Media accounts include things like newspapers, magazines, books, films, and television programs. Qualitative social researchers have long used media accounts to investigate social life. These accounts are useful for understanding how groups of people are represented in public discourse or what norms and ideals for behavior exist in a particular time and place. They can tell us about changes (or stability) in social mores. Using media accounts, researchers have studied such varied topics as race and sex stereotyping in children's books (Clark, Lennon, and Morris 1993), gender in advertisements (Barthel 1988, Goffman 1976), fear of crime in the news (Altheide and Michalowski 1999), portrayals of animals in television advertisements (Lerner and Kalof 1999), and sexual nonconformity in television talk shows (Gamson 1998).

A strength of media accounts is that they are easily accessible and often cheap or free. Many media sources have existed for a long period of time—often decades, as in the case of major newspapers and mass market magazines. This makes them especially useful for looking at changes over time. Their easy accessibility can be a boon to beginning researchers (especially for projects like senior theses). One of my students, for example, compared how girls and women were portrayed in *Sports Illustrated* and *Sports Illustrated for Kids* (Elsinger 1998). She found that women and girls were much more frequently featured (and more likely to be shown as athletes rather than spectators) in the children's version of the magazine.

With media accounts—as with all written documents—you need to be careful about sources of bias. First, factual errors might creep into media accounts. For example, a newspaper might make a mistake about people's age, the spelling of names, or places (Macdonald and Tipton 1993). Although newspapers often print retractions, the original version of the story tends to stand. (Who reads retraction notices, after all?) More important, you always need to consider who published a particular account, for what purpose, and for what intended audience. A media source might be biased in a particular direction; for example, an editor might have a conservative or liberal slant and publish news that fits with his or her preconceived biases. You also need to consider the audience for whom the account is published. *The New York Times*, for example, is written for a wholly different audience than the *National Enquirer.*

Some suggest that analyses of texts—like TV shows, magazines, or newspapers—should be combined with studies of the producers and the audiences. Thus, Joshua Gamson combined interviews with TV talk show producers, interviews with show guests, participant observation at tapings, and analysis of transcripts of the shows (1998). The combination of methods made his research, published in a book called *Freaks Talk Back*, far richer and subtler than it would have been otherwise.

ELECTRONIC TEXTS

As the Internet and electronic texts have become more widely available, social researchers have begun to rely on them as sources of data as well. For example, researchers use the Internet to recruit research participants for both electronic interviews and more standard phone or face-to-face interviews. Documents posted on the Internet on listservs and electronic bulletin boards may be treated in ways similar to other documents and material artifacts. The Internet is also a site for participant observation. A researcher need not even be physically copresent to conduct participatory research in interactive sites (Kendall 2000).

For example, Joan Fleitas (1998) conducted research with children who had chronic illness or disabilities. She recruited participants via a Web site that she created specifically for her project, medical listservs, and listservs for parents of children with disabilities, as well as through more traditional techniques (including snowball sampling). Although she also conducted face-to-face focus groups, she collected most of her data through e-mail and on-line focus groups convened in chat groups established specifically for that purpose.

In a very different way, Lori Kendall conducted participant observation in an on-line format known as a *MUD* (multiuser dungeon) (Kendall 2000). A MUD is much like an on-line chat room. Instead of storing messages that were posted at an earlier time (as in an electronic message board or an e-mail listserv), a MUD involves real-time conversation, albeit in written form. Kendall was interested in how participants created raced and gendered identities on-line. She participated in the on-line chats, interviewed some of the participants, and read other on-line materials related to the MUD.

In another example of Internet-based research, Emily Noelle Ignacio (2000) examined messages posted on a newsgroup to understand how Filipina women created and negotiated identities in a newsgroup dedicated to Filipino culture and issues. Among other things, Ignacio was interested in seeing how the women might challenge stereotyped thinking about Filipinas.

As a research tool, the Internet has both strengths and weaknesses. One advantage is that the Internet can encourage open expression of thoughts and feelings because it does not involve face-to-face communication. In Fleitas's research, for example, children with physical disabilities were able to communicate without worrying about how their bodies would be perceived. In addition, because the Internet is global, researchers can recruit participants from a much larger geographical area than they might otherwise (Binik, Mah, and Kiesler 1999; Fleitas 1998).

However, not everybody has access to computers and the Internet. Internet users tend to be younger, wealthier, more technologically savvy, and better educated than nonusers. Males are more likely than females to be Internet users, as are individuals in wealthier nations with a better-developed infrastructure (Binik, Mah, and Kiesler 1999). Thus, research conducted with participants drawn from the Internet is likely to involve a more privileged sector of the population. Kendall (2000) found, for example, that most of her research participants were young, white, and male, with a few women and a few Asian Americans.

In addition, in conducting research on-line, researchers cannot pick up on nonverbal cues. Although people can insert graphics and pictures into text files to allow for both visual and text-based responses, researchers do not have access to the full range of nonverbal cues, such as shrugs and winks and yawns. Internet users sometimes attempt to re-create many of these nonverbal cues, with symbols like :) to indicate a smile or ;) to indicate a wink. Still, much is missed. Indeed, researchers typically can't even verify who the research participants are. For example, Fleitas (1998) couldn't verify that the e-mails actually were sent by disabled children. Because individuals may be more anonymous on the Internet, they may be more inclined to "play" with identities, presenting themselves as holding different genders, races/ethnicities, or other identities than they may in fact possess.

Researchers also use the Web for more traditional content analyses—for example, of electronic bulletin boards, Web sites, or e-mail listservs. Using the Internet in this way poses particular challenges. For example, Nalini Kotamraju (1999) suggests that, because the Internet has developed so recently and changes so rapidly, it is subject to "time compression." Change on the Internet comes about far more rapidly than in other spheres of life. This causes problems for researchers. Archival data may disappear as newer technologies and newer sites update "old" ones. Kotamraju argues, for example, that a researcher can't even find out what kind of jobs were available on-line a mere 3 months ago. Thus, sociologists who wish to use the Internet for research purposes must adapt the strategies historians have developed for dealing with the issue of time. For example, unlike sociologists, historians tend to expect that much of their data may be missing or

BOX 6.1 Some Useful Web Sites

General Sociology Research Sites
www.socsciresearch.com
www.sociolog.com
www.wcsu.ctstateu.edu/socialsci/socres.html

Government Sites
www.info.gov (a general jumping-off site for government agencies)
www.census.gov (U.S. Bureau of the Census)
www.cdc.gov (U.S. Centers for Disease Control and Prevention)
www.ed.gov (Department of Education)
www.fbi.gov (Federal Bureau of Investigation)

Qualitative Research Methods
www.ualberta.ca/~jrnorris/qual.html (QualPage: Resources for
    Qualitative Research)
www.nova.edu/ssss/QR/web.html

Associations
www.asanet.org (American Sociological Association)
www.latrobe.edu.au/www/aqr/index.html (Association for Qualitative
    Research)
www.coe.uga.edu/quig (Qualitative Interest Group)

impossible to find. They have thus developed strategies for gathering diverse forms of evidence.

At the same time, others argue that the Internet provides a wealth of materials for historians and other researchers (Donnelly and Ross 1997). In an article published in the *Historical Journal of Film, Radio & Television*, Donnelly and Ross provide a number of sources that researchers interested in the history of the media might access, including the Media History Project (www.mediahistory.com), Vanderbilt University's Television Archives (http://tvnews.vanderbilt.edu), and the University of Maryland's Broadcast Pioneers Library (www.itd.umd.edu). Box 6.1 lists some other sites that may provide useful starting points for research on the Internet.

The Internet can be a wonderful source for research projects, with literally hundreds of potentially useful Web sites. However, the Internet can also lead you astray. You need to assess whether the information on any given site is valid or whether the site simply wants to sell you something or express someone's personal feelings. Certainly, you might sometimes want to analyze how individuals express their feelings on a personal Web site. But you shouldn't mistake that subjective impression for anything else. You thus need to evaluate Web sites very carefully when relying on them in your research. You may find the guidelines set forth in Chapter 2 useful in evaluating potential sites for research.

Using the Internet for research also raises some novel ethical issues, with privacy and confidentiality issues paramount (Binik, Mah, and Kiesler 1999). For example, what parts of the Internet might reasonably be considered private? Is an on-line chat room public or private? What about a moderated e-mail list? An unmoderated one, which anyone can join? When do you need to gain informed consent? When simply viewing Web sites? When participating in an on-line chat or e-mail list? Whom should you ask permission from? In an e-mail listserv that changes membership frequently, how often do you need to remind participants that you are researching them? Ignacio (2000) notes, for example, that she posted a letter on the newsgroup she was studying every few weeks to inform participants. Not all newsgroups and e-mail lists allow researchers, however. Many moderated e-mail lists specifically request that participants not circulate or use the e-mail for any purpose other than personal use.

The nature of Internet participation also causes problems with consent issues. It's difficult to verify that the person giving consent is actually able to do so or that he or she is actually an adult. What kinds of assurances of confidentiality and anonymity can researchers reasonably give to their research participants? For example, while research participants might believe that their e-mail responses will be held in confidentiality, someone else (through either legitimate means or illegitimate ones) may gain access to information sent on-line. How can researchers minimize the chances that their participants' privacy will not be breached? This is especially an issue with sexuality research or research on other sensitive topics (Binik, Mah, and Kiesler 1999).

HISTORICAL RESEARCH

What is history? Sociologist Gaye Tuchman (1998) invites us to consider that question, arguing that history is more than merely a series of easily memorized dates and facts. In trying to incorporate historical perspectives in our research, we need to ask what it means to live in a particular time period. We need to identify what assumptions we can make about how people live, what are the meanings of things in particular times and places, and how the past impinges on the present.

In many respects, historical analysis is very much like the analysis of material artifacts and documents. Historical research involves the analysis of secondary and, especially, primary sources. Sociological researchers may do so as well, but they also tend to rely on the work of historians (and secondary sources created by them) because historians tend to have much better access to and training in the use of archival materials. In addition, sociologists tend to ask somewhat different kinds of questions, often less specific or more theoretical ones.

In general, we may want to use historical methods to understand "big picture" types of questions. How did major social changes take place? When? Why are social arrangements different in various places and times? We might want to know, for example, how the women's movement emerged in various times and places. How is it different in, say, the United States and Mexico? To answer this question, we would need to know a little bit about the histories of both countries. It isn't enough merely to understand the present moment; we need to know how the movement developed over time.

Doing Historical-Comparative Research

Some researchers do what they call *historical-comparative research*—research that focuses either on one or more cases over time (the historical part) or on more than one nation or society at one point in time (the comparative part). Comparative researchers tend to compare a relatively small number of cases (Ragin 1994). They want to understand the cases in depth, as well as compare their similarities and differences.

One example of historical-comparative research is Nader Sohrabi's study of revolutions (1995). Sohrabi compared the Young Turk Revolution of 1908, the Iranian Constitutional Revolution of 1906, and the Russian Revolution of 1905 to try to understand their similarities and differences. Another example of historical-comparative research is Marshall Ganz's study of farm workers' organizations (2000). Specifically, Ganz was interested in why one organization, the United Farm Workers (UFW), succeeded while another one, the Agricultural Workers Organizing Committee of the AFL-CIO (AWOC), failed during the period 1959–1966. He focused on how differences in leadership, organizational influences, and creative strategies affected movement success.

In both of these examples, the researchers systematically compared the cases across a variety of dimensions. They used a variety of primary and secondary materials in their research, including newspaper articles, copies of legislation, published memoirs, proceedings of meetings, and historians' accounts.

In beginning to do comparative research, you first need to distinguish the cases by asking what these are cases *of*. Cases should be, in some sense, members of the same class or category. It wouldn't make much sense, for example, to compare the city of Boston with the nation-states of Honduras or India. But it might make sense to compare social movements in different nations—for example, the labor movement in Sweden, the United States, and Poland. Then, you need to consider the important facets of the cases you might compare. For example, are you interested in characteristics of the leadership? Political strategies? You might want to compare state support for the labor movement. Is it high in one place and low in another? As with all historical research, the knowledge of what to compare will only come from an in-depth understanding of the particulars of the cases and the theories advanced to explain them.

Gaining Access to Historical Materials

How do sociologists gain access to these kinds of materials? Where might social researchers find the kinds of archival materials that historical researchers use? Gaye Tuchman (1998) offers some useful advice to beginning qualitative historical researchers. You should begin by reading the secondary literature—what other historians and social scientists have said about the topic. This helps you to conceptualize your study and figure out what the main controversies are. Chapter 2 gave you some suggestions for conducting secondary research. You should follow those leads before turning to the primary sources.

Locating primary sources is much more difficult. As Tuchman (1998) argues, locating good primary sources requires a great deal of detective work. It is, essentially, specialized labor. In finding appropriate primary sources, you will need to figure out what kinds of archives may hold particular types of materials. For example, Cornell University's archives are a marvelous source for historical information on sexuality. The Lesbian Herstory Archives in New York are an extraordinarily rich source of primary material on lesbian life. Those who are doing research in the field you are interested in usually know of potential sources, as do good reference librarians. You would be well advised to begin there. You can also search the holdings of many libraries online. If you are restricted in your ability to travel, you may be able to find good archival material close to home. Often, primary source material is available on CD-ROM (sometimes for a fee) or over the Internet.

Evaluating Sources

One of the main challenges in using historical materials is evaluating them. Perhaps more than any other type of data, you need to evaluate historical materials carefully. When you are using secondary sources, you need to be alert to historians' implicit theories and paradigms. History is never simply a recitation of "just the facts." Rather, historians decide what to report, what details to emphasize, and how to interpret events. In the course of their research, historians typically gather thousands of pages of documents. Obviously, they don't simply print these documents verbatim and let the reader decide for her- or himself what they mean. Rather, they compress the huge volume of pages into a more manageable form. How do historians accomplish this? How do they decide what to focus on and what to ignore? They don't usually specify this process in their published works. As a careful reader, you need to try to figure out what the biases and predilections of the historian are. You also need to figure out if the author's viewpoint is well established. Do other historians say similar things? What kinds of evidence do they use? Does their evidence seem credible?

Primary sources require extra care. You need to determine first if the source is *authentic*. That is, was it actually written by the person said to have written it? When was it written? Where? Again, is the document authentic, or merely a clever fake?

You also need to determine if the primary source is *representative*. As we discussed in the section on material artifacts, not all documents survive. In evaluating primary source documents, it's important to consider which people are more likely to have left primary source documents behind. Literate people, for example, obviously are more likely to leave diaries and correspondence than those who cannot write or read. Thus, because African American slaves were forbidden to learn to read and write, they left few letters and other written materials that would document their daily lives. Much of what we know about African American life during slavery comes from oral histories and the testimonies of former slaves collected after the Civil War.

In general, ordinary people tend not to think that their lives are particularly interesting or worth documenting. Ordinary working-class people don't usually donate their private papers to archives or otherwise make their papers accessible to historical researchers. For example, have *you* donated your papers and personal effects to an archive? This fact leads to an inevitable bias in the kinds of personal materials available. Because people such as presidents or famous actors tend to assume that their lives are worth documenting, they are much more likely to preserve their papers. Yet most of us don't live like presidents or movie stars. The kinds of historical materials available tend to make it easier to gain knowledge of famous people's lives than ordinary people's.

In evaluating primary source materials, you need to ask whose perspective they reflect and what kinds of interests the writer had. For example, was the author of a slavery-era document a slaveholder? Someone active in the movement for the abolition of slavery? Each position carries with it a perspective and set of vested interests. A slaveholder who emphasized the good living conditions of slaves would probably not be believable. But if an abolitionist remarked on the quality of slave housing in a particular location, that person might be more credible. Historical records often reflect the interests of those in power. Thus, you need to evaluate materials carefully for bias.

You also need to consider how the document was preserved and how it made its way to an archive (or to your hands through some other means). Do you have access to the whole document, or only a fragment? What didn't survive? Did anyone have an interest in suppressing certain parts of the material? For example, the niece of poet Emily Dickinson censored passionate letters that Dickinson wrote to her sister-in-law, Sue Miller (Miller 1995). Censorship like this has made the study of lesbian and gay history (and, in general, the historical study of sexuality) difficult.

But not all gaps (or "missing data") result from censorship. Sometimes, materials are simply lost or discarded. Other times, despite people's best efforts to save them, materials may be destroyed. This means that historical researchers are inevitably working with fragmentary evidence. Because the "complete" record never survives, the conclusions you make based on such evidence must also be tentative.

Creating Meaning

When evaluating historical materials, you also should pay careful attention to meanings, at both a literal (or surface) level and a deeper one. At the surface level, you need to ask what the document means and what language was used. Sometimes, words change from one period to the next, so you need to be certain that you can understand the literal meaning.

At a deeper level, you need to know something about the conditions under which the document was produced. Again, this involves knowledge of the specific context and time period. Thus, you need to determine what kind of language was common for the time and place and person who created the document. And you need to determine whether other documents support the perspective or whether the document seems to be at odds with what others tend to say.

Doing historical and documentary research can be hard work. Perhaps more than any other type of research, it demands knowledge of the particular, local contexts in which various materials (written and otherwise) are produced, consumed, kept, and discarded. It demands a critical eye and an ability to scrutinize sources carefully. Yet, because of their very specificity, historical methods can provide a richer and more finely nuanced study than many other methods.

QUESTION FOR THOUGHT

What are some of the differences involved in analyzing material artifacts and written documents? What different kinds of information might they give you? Which would you prefer to study? Why?

EXERCISES

1. Look around your own neighborhood. What physical traces might help you figure out what kinds of people live there? (If you're having trouble getting started, try checking cemeteries, names on mailboxes, types of stores and restaurants, and so forth.)

2. How might you study the following things without either interviewing or directly observing people?
   a. Which toys are most popular among children
   b. Whether college students in a particular school exercise frequently
   c. Whether people in a particular neighborhood eat healthy foods

3. Locate some material artifacts that you can analyze. (If you're having trouble thinking of something, remember that material culture is all around you. It can be, literally, just about anything.) The items can be contemporary or historical. Try to find out as much as you can about how the things were produced and for whom. See if you can find out some of the meanings these items may have.

4. Choose a magazine that interests you. Try to step back and look at the magazine as a social analyst, not as a consumer. Then see what you can determine about the audience for the magazine. What does the magazine seem to assume are the interests and preoccupations of its readers?

What can you tell about the biases and interests of those who publish the magazine? (Alternatively, try this exercise using a newspaper, a TV show, or a radio program. If you are choosing a TV show or radio program, you will probably need to watch/listen a number of times.)

5. Investigate what historical materials are available, either in your school library, in a public library near you, in a local historical society, or on the Internet.

6. Choose a Web site of interest to you, and analyze its potential uses for research, using the guidelines for evaluating Web sites in Chapter 2.

SUGGESTIONS FOR FURTHER READING

Hodder, Ian. "The Interpretation of Documents and Material Culture." In Norman K. Denzin and Yvonna S. Lincoln (eds.), *Collecting and Interpreting Qualitative Materials*. Thousand Oaks, CA: Sage, 1998.

Lee, Raymond M. *Unobtrusive Methods in Social Research*. Buckingham, England: Open University Press, 2000.

Neuman, W. Lawrence. *Social Research Methods: Qualitative and Quantitative Approaches*, 2nd ed. Boston: Allyn & Bacon, 1994. Devotes a full chapter (16) to historical-comparative research.

Ragin, Charles C. *Constructing Social Research*. Thousand Oaks, CA: Pine Forge Press, 1994. Gives more on comparative research.

Tuchman, Gaye. "Historical Social Science: Methodologies, Methods, and Meanings." In Norman K. Denzin and Yvonna S. Lincoln (eds.), *Strategies of Qualitative Inquiry*. Thousand Oaks, CA: Sage, 1998.

Walters, Ian. "Vietnam Zippos." *Journal of Material Culture* 2(1): 61–75. 1997. A good example of analysis of material culture.

Webb, Eugene T.; Donald T. Campbell; Richard D. Swartz; and Lee Sechrest. *Unobtrusive Measures*. Thousand Oaks, CA: Sage, 1999.

7

Action Research

Organizing is the active unearthing of people's individual stories,
the collective examination of the meaning of those stories in light of
our shared story, and the opportunity to write new endings to both
our individual and collective stories.

—LARRY MCNEIL (1995)

Who can conduct research? Can only people with Ph.D.'s or other specialists conduct research? Or can ordinary people do it themselves? What should be the relationship between the researcher and those being researched? And what is the purpose of research? To enlighten? To entertain? To create "basic" knowledge that has no particular application (at least not yet)? Or should research end with some form of action or improvement in the lives of people?

THE PURPOSE OF ACTION RESEARCH

Action researchers argue that research should not be aimed solely at creating esoteric knowledge, nor should it be conducted only by people with advanced degrees. The outcome of research should be *useful*, aimed at improving the lives of those who are the subject of research. Research, says Ernest Stringer, should be "organized and conducted in ways that are conducive to the formation of community—the 'common unity' of all participants—and that strengthen the democratic, equitable, liberating, and life-enhancing qualities of social life" (1996, p. 25). Because individuals are the experts on their own lives, action research should involve community members at all levels, including the development of the problem and strategies for researching it.

M. Brinton Lykes (1997), for example, engaged in participatory action research over an extended period in Guatemala, a nation plagued by war for decades. She was invited by a community-based women's association to work with members to respond to and ameliorate the effects of war. One of the projects the women planned was to distribute cameras and film so that women in the community could tell one another their stories of survival. By documenting their lives on film and meeting to discuss the common themes, the women could begin to research the strengths that they had developed and use the information to improve their ongoing programs for children.

Brinton's research is just one example of action research. Others have studied many different settings, including business organizations like Xerox Corporation (Greenwood, Whyte, and Harkavy 1993), Asian nongovernmental organizations (Brown 1993), worker cooperatives in Spain (Greenwood, Whyte, and Harkavy 1993), and older Aboriginal women in Canada (Dickson 2000).

Unlike other forms of data collection discussed in this book, action research doesn't involve a particular strategy. Rather, action researchers may use many different strategies to gather data, both qualitative and quantitative, depending on the problem at hand and their personal preferences. In fact, action researchers are likely to use novel and eclectic approaches to gathering and interpreting data. Action research can be thought of as an approach to doing research, one with a very specific aim—the creation of social change—and one that involves creating particular kinds of relationships among all of those involved in the research process. In these respects, action research turns traditional ways of doing research on its head.

Action researchers believe that the process of research must be open and democratic. Thus, they reject the clear separation between researcher and researched that the positivist tradition mandates. (Remember from Chapter 1?) Instead of viewing the researcher as the only one who can contribute to knowledge, they argue that ordinary people can as well. And instead of treating research participants as passive objects, like bugs under a microscope, they argue that research participants can become active in all phases of the research project, including formulating the problem and collecting and analyzing data. If individuals are the best sources of knowledge about their own lives, then they should become full and equal participants in the research process. Thus, participants are often called coresearchers, to reflect their more active role.

Action researchers focus on both the *process* of conducting research and its *outcome*. Unlike traditional forms of research, in which researchers specify in advance exactly what types of questions they will ask (and the exact procedures for raising them), action research is typically fluid, allowing for changes as coresearchers together define what the problem is and how best to investigate it. The process of conducting research is liberating, as individuals gain knowledge about their own situations. Action researchers see knowledge as power. As individuals gain knowledge about the conditions affecting their own lives, they gain the power to change them.

The outcome of action research is also important. Action research typically begins with an interest in a specific problem of a community or group (Stringer 1996, p. 9). Action research thus tends to be local, specific, and oriented to a particular case (Small 1995). Its aim is always practical: to lead to some kind of change or practical application. For example, one potential outcome of the project that Lykes (1997) described was a photographic exhibit for the community. In this sense, action research is often *applied research*—research with real-world applications.

VARIETIES OF ACTION RESEARCH

An enormous variety of activities can be included under the umbrella term "action research." Action research is often multidisciplinary, bringing together people from diverse social locations and with diverse skills and abilities. While different people involved in action research may bring something different to the project, they all tend to agree that *action*—some kind of outcome—should come about as a result of their work. Research results shouldn't gather dust in the library, to be used only by people with advanced degrees. Research must be relevant to, and thus created by, those who are affected by it. At heart, all action researchers are concerned that research not simply contribute to our knowledge but also lead to positive changes in people's lives.

Participatory Action Research (PAR)

Within action research, there are several different traditions. One tradition, known as *participatory action research* (PAR), emphasizes the active participation of those being researched. One version of PAR was developed in Third World movements for human liberation, drawing on the adult education movement created by Paulo Freire (1970). This version of PAR is explicitly political; it emphasizes the political nature of knowledge production and sees the ultimate aim of research as human liberation. PAR practitioners in this tradition argue that knowledge production has typically been viewed as the province of elites, who use knowledge to control and oppress common people. One objective of PAR, then, is to create knowledge rooted in the lives and perspectives and experiences of ordinary people and directed toward progressive social change. Thus, PAR emphasizes investigation, education, and political action.

The differences between this and other forms of action research are perhaps more of degree than of kind. PAR practitioners see themselves as breaking down the walls between researcher and researched and creating genuinely equal participation. Perhaps more than other action researchers, their goals tend to be overtly political. So, for example, Noel Keough, Emman Carmona, and Linda Grandinetti (1995) describe a collaboration between Canadian and Filipino popular theater and environmental organizations, published in *Convergence*, a journal that focuses explicitly on PAR. Their goal was to improve the organizations' popular theater skills, to create public awareness of environmental issues, and to spur individuals to make changes in the size of their ecological "footprint." They worked collaboratively to disseminate information on sustainable development through theater performances and creation of a video and training manual.

Other practitioners of PAR do not see themselves as having quite so overtly political a purpose. They emphasize the advancement of both basic science and practical knowledge through the common participation of researchers and local communities (Small 1995; Whyte 1991, 1999). To make effective changes, they argue, some basic research is needed, and the results of action research conducted in this tradition are often published in academic journals and disseminated in other ways to reach a more general audience. These researchers often focus on organizations and may include decision makers in their research. For these reasons, the more radical PAR practitioners discussed earlier tend to distance themselves from them.

Some action researchers in this tradition have worked with private industry and organizations (Small 1995). William Foote Whyte (1991) discusses several industry-based action research projects, including a project with Xerox Corporation and the Amalgamated Clothing and Textile Workers Union aimed at finding ways to cut costs without eliminating jobs or sacrificing workers' pay. With David Greenwood, Whyte was also involved in a study of organizational culture at the worker-owned Mondragon Cooperatives in Basque, Spain (Greenwood, Whyte, and Harkavy 1993; Whyte 1995, 1999).

The Mondragon Cooperatives, which have made stoves, refrigerators, and washing machines since the 1950s, are one of the world's largest cooperative economic enterprises. Workers own the industrial plants, a coopera-

tive bank, and other services including research and development and educational services. Whyte and other researchers were interested in how
worker-owned cooperatives could succeed in the long run, for conventional
wisdom had argued that worker-owned cooperatives would inevitably fail
or remain small-scale. They began their PAR at the request of one of the
cooperatives, which asked for assistance in solving some organizational
problems. The academic researchers were initially asked to teach the cooperative members research skills; the research eventually developed into a
large-scale project on organizational culture (Greenwood, Whyte, and
Harkavy 1993).

Feminist Action Research

Feminist researchers also have a long history of doing action research. In
fact, some people argue that feminist research is inherently action-oriented,
because it is aimed at social change. Feminist action researchers date back to
the early twentieth century, when the social sciences were in a state of rapid
development at the University of Chicago (Reinharz 1992). Shulamit Reinharz describes several examples of feminist action research, including the
work of sociologist Crystal Eastman, who, after receiving graduate degrees
in sociology and law in 1907, studied industrial accidents with the goal of
improving work conditions.

Despite their long history of applied and activist research, relatively
few feminist researchers have thought of themselves specifically as action
researchers (Cancian 1996). Although there are similarities between feminist research and action research, including an emphasis on political action
and a critique of models of research that emphasize a hierarchical relationship between the researcher and those being researched, the two approaches have tended to stay distinct (Cancian 1996). More recently,
however, some feminist researchers have begun to incorporate community
participation as an important component of their research (Small 1995).
Nancy A. Naples, for example, describes her experiences in a PAR project
with childhood sexual assault survivors (Naples with Clark 1996). Herself a
survivor of childhood sexual abuse, she had been active in a collective that
tried to create alternative methods for healing. In her PAR, she wanted to
fully involve other survivors and to merge her separate roles of political
activist and researcher. J. K. Gibson-Graham (1994) also provides a recent
example of feminist action research in her work with women in Australian
mining towns. She recruited miners' wives to develop questionnaires and
conduct interviews with other women in mining towns to collect stories

about the women's activism in the Miners' Women's Auxiliaries and other organizations.

Evaluation Research

Sometimes, researchers are invited to evaluate a program or policy. For example, drug counselors might want to see if their treatment program actually helps addicts stop using drugs. Or a group of educators and school administrators might want to find out if their experimental school helps students learn. Or social workers might want to see if their programs are serving those for whom they are designed. Or a legislator might want to know if an agency is providing services in the most efficient way possible. In each case, to do so, they need to conduct an evaluation. Sometimes, the practitioners may decide to conduct the research by themselves; other times, they may decide to bring in the services of an evaluation researcher.

Evaluation researchers can use the same kinds of tools as other qualitative researchers (see Patton 1990 for a classic textbook on qualitative evaluation research; see also Posavac and Carey 1997). They may decide to do interviews or field observations; they may analyze documents or do quantitative analyses. Often, evaluation researchers draw on the same collaborative techniques as other action researchers. They may, for example, work with practitioners to identify the focus and design of their research. When they work more collaboratively in this way, their work can be seen as having much in common with action research.

RESEARCH FOR WHOM?

Action researchers invite us to ask, Who owns the research process? In traditional research, specialized researchers, often connected with a university or educational institution, develop research agendas based on their own interests. They develop the problem statement, figure out what methods to use, conduct the research by themselves or with the help (often purchased) of others, and write up the results. The research participants are typically seen as "subjects," whose sole role is to provide the information the researcher is seeking. Although the research may be either basic (intended to contribute to general knowledge) or applied (intended to serve some practical application), those being researched don't typically have a voice in how the research is done or even how the results are to be used. In this traditional form of research, it might be said that the researcher "owns" the research process.

Action research sets out to democratize the process. How can a strategy for change be effective if it isn't the creation of those who are expected to do the changing? From an action research perspective, knowledge "belongs" to those who create it. If only a specialized researcher is involved in creating that knowledge, then it will not belong to the larger group. The research will not necessarily reflect the aims and priorities of those being researched, and the research participants may have little motivation to effect the kinds of change suggested by the researcher. And the results may not be written in a language that the participants can understand.

You can easily verify this claim. As a college student, you have reading and literacy skills far above those of most of the population. But go to the library and scan just about any academic journal. How much of that journal can you understand? How much do you think a less-educated audience might understand? This is not to imply that technical language is never important or that academics should always write in ways that are accessible to the general public. Much of the writing that academics do is really intended for other academics. But that makes it difficult for practitioners and community activists to use it. Action researchers are committed to making the process and the results more widely available. Ernest Stringer (1996) calls action research "user friendly." Even discussions of the approach are more likely to be presented in terms that laypeople can understand, and the specific methods and techniques for researching and solving problems tend to be ones that ordinary people can learn to use.

In large part, action research involves relinquishing at least some control over the research process. In this respect, it draws on the skills and techniques of both community organizers and social researchers. Because all of those who are affected by the problem should be participants in the process, the researcher is not the only one making decisions. As Stringer (1996) points out, it's a little unsatisfactory to distinguish between "the researcher" and the participants because they are all coresearchers together. But it's often the case that a professional researcher or academic will be the one to facilitate the process. Thus, it makes more sense to think of the researcher as a facilitator or a catalyst. Randy Stoecker (1999) calls this the role of "animator."

EMPOWERMENT

Action researchers believe that the process of conducting research should be empowering for research participants. Through the process of defining the problem and seeking solutions, all participants gain a sense of mastery of their environment. This is empowering—especially for those who are at the bottom of the social hierarchy. Creation of knowledge is powerful, especially for those who are used to having knowledge used against them. For example, Geraldine Dickson (2000) describes some of the effects of participating in an action research project with Aboriginal grandmothers in Canada. The women held weekly get-togethers, sat on community committees (such as police advisory committees), and joined in an array of special events and community activities. By participating in the project, which was focused on health promotion, the women expressed greater pride in their cultural and spiritual identities, acquired the information and skills to obtain needed resources, and expressed a greater willingness to influence the system, among other things.

THE PROCESS OF ACTION RESEARCH: LOOK, THINK, ACT

Ernest Stringer (1996) divides the process of doing action research into three phases: look, think, and act. In the first phase, the goal is to look carefully at the situation and define the problem. The research facilitator must figure out who the stakeholders are and work with them to define the problem. The group must gather the data that will help them to craft a solution. In the second phase, the group needs to think about what they are finding out. They need to interpret and explain what is going on, and why. In the final phase, the group develops a plan for action and puts it into place. Of course, the process is not so neat and linear in practice. For example, the process of thinking about the data might lead a group to redefine the problem and invite new stakeholders to the table. The plan for action might lead the group to reexamine the problem and start anew. The process is more of a spiral (or a Slinky) than a straight line.

Look: Identifying Stakeholders and Formulating a Collective Problem

Identifying the Stakeholders   One of the first things a research facilitator must do is to identify the stakeholders. Who are the people most affected by the problem? Who must be brought to the table to figure out what the parameters of the problem might be and how to research them? Sometimes, a group or community will already be organized and will have brought the researcher in for a specific purpose. Other times, the researcher might join at an earlier stage. At the very beginning of the process, the research facilitator(s) should do what Stringer (1996) calls a "social analysis" of the setting to ensure that all the necessary stakeholders are present.

Let's say that you are interested in facilitating an action research project on the parking problem at school. You know that there is a problem, because you have heard many people complain about not being able to find a parking place, and you yourself have had that experience. The campus paper has published articles on the shortage as well. In this example, who might be the stakeholders? Certainly, anyone who has to park on campus might be a stakeholder. This includes commuter students most obviously, but it may include residential students as well. Faculty also park on campus, as do staff, which includes not only clerical and maintenance workers, cooks, and security guards but also administrators such as deans and provosts and chancellors. People who live nearby may also be stakeholders, as they find it difficult to park on the streets in their own neighborhood.

Which of these groups would you need to invite to the table? Participatory action researchers might argue that you need to invite those who are disadvantaged by the current arrangements. Perhaps faculty and administrators have reserved parking spaces and don't have difficulty finding a spot. If that is the case, then you might want to focus on bringing to the table those who are more severely affected by the problem. (From this perspective, the goal would be to organize the disenfranchised.) Other action researchers might argue that you need to invite all to the table; otherwise, a mutually acceptable solution to the problem won't be found. L. David Brown (1993) describes this as the difference between northern and southern approaches. The southern tradition encourages participation by the poor and dispossessed and excludes participation by elites. The northern tradition may include a more diverse group of participants, including those who have organizational or societal power.

In bringing together the stakeholders, you need to consider if there are any barriers to participation. For example, if you hold meetings at night, commuter students who have children or night jobs may not be able to attend. If you hold meetings during certain parts of the day, perhaps students will be in class and people in the neighborhood will be at work. Are there any language barriers? For example, the stakeholders may not all speak the same language. Are there any barriers of disability? For example, holding a meeting in a building without ramps or elevators will make it difficult for many disabled people to attend. What about social barriers? For example, if you are interested in working with a community group, holding the meeting on campus might be intimidating to members.

You also need to consider whether any particular stakeholders are key (Stringer 1996). Some individuals may be especially influential in a particular setting (just like a gatekeeper in participant observation). It may be that, once one or two key individuals decide to participate, the rest of the community will follow. Without those key individuals, you may not be able to proceed.

Formulating a Collective Problem   Action research is by definition collaborative research. Thus, the research facilitator cannot single-handedly define the research problem. The definition of the problem must arise from the group. Randy Stoeker (1999) argues that community groups need to decide which decisions (such as how to define the question, design the research, and gather the data) to let the researcher make by him- or herself and which to reserve for the group. This can entail a number of challenges. Most importantly, each stakeholder might have a very different understanding of the problem and potential solutions.

To illustrate, let's return to our parking problem example. Students may see the problem as one of distribution. That is, there are plenty of spaces for staff and faculty, but not enough for students. Because they are paying tuition, they may feel that they have a right to a parking space. Administrators may see the problem as a financial one. They'd love to build more parking spaces, but there simply isn't room or money. Or they may see the problem as rooted in students' behavior, arguing that if students took the shuttle bus or if residential students didn't park on campus there wouldn't be a problem. Faculty may view their reserved parking spaces as an employee benefit. Finally, neighborhood groups may see the university as encroaching on their space and taking up valuable neighborhood resources without giving anything in return.

To find out how the different groups see a given problem, the research group needs to gather data. Here, the research facilitator may play a key role in sharing information about specific ways to gather information, but the action group must decide how to gather the information and how to interpret it. At this stage, the group might use any one (or more) of the techniques discussed in this book, such as participant observation, interviews, or documentary research, as well as more novel forms. Sometimes, action research groups use quantitative methods as well, such as surveys. In our parking example, the group may decide to conduct interviews with students, faculty, and staff. It may also decide to observe in parking lots and to conduct documentary research—for example, tracing campus newspaper stories on parking or conducting an analysis of parking tickets issued.

Think: Exploring the Problem

In this phase, the research group works collaboratively to try to figure out what the data it has gathered mean. It's often a good idea to develop a descriptive account first, which defines how the various stakeholders see the process. At this stage, it may be helpful to convene a meeting (or a series of meetings) with groups of stakeholders, so that all have the opportunity to voice their opinions and contribute to the emerging analysis of the data. The research facilitator's role might be to help bring the stakeholders together and create a setting in which they can develop various interpretive accounts. Again, the stakeholders will have to determine which of the tasks they want to retain for themselves and which to leave for the researcher.

In our parking example, perhaps the group convenes a meeting of students, faculty, staff, and community members who are all committed to working on the problem. They might break up into a number of small groups, each consisting of two students, two staff people, two faculty members, and two community representatives. Each small group might be given the task of defining the parking problem in a way that reflects all viewpoints. When the large group reconvenes, each group's work might be displayed. Then the large group might sift through the definitions, looking for commonalities and differences. In general, the process of sorting through the data will require several meetings so that all involved can have input. Groups may adapt any of the analytic strategies we discuss in Chapter 8 for this phase of the project.

Act: Defining an Agenda for Action

Finally, the time comes to craft a solution or an action step that speaks to the problem the group has defined. Clearly, some social problems are much more complex than others. Solving the problem of parking at a small college might be relatively easy compared with, say, solving the problem of access to health care or racism or environmental pollution. Still, at this stage, the group must try to define some action steps that will address the situation. They need to set priorities and figure out a plan of action. As with the other steps, this process should be done in a collaborative way. (This typically means more meetings!) The people who are affected by the problem must be the ones to craft the solution.

The kinds of action steps depend entirely on the nature of the problem and the groups involved in the process. Some action steps are educational—for example, working to inform others about the problem. Often, action research groups devise novel ways of educating those who are affected, such as putting on plays, making videos, or writing comic books. For example, as part of her work with Latina domestic workers, Pierrette Hondagneu-Sotelo helped produce novelas (comic-strip-like booklets) that helped educate domestic workers about their rights (Hondagneu-Sotelo 1996). Some action steps are short-term; others may be long-term. What's most important is that the steps address the problem and implement the solutions articulated by those most affected by the problem.

SHARING THE RESULTS

In traditional research, researchers usually publish their results in an academic journal or book, and they may present them at a conference of academics as well. Typically, however, research results do not make it into the popular press (at least in the social sciences). Often, those who are the subjects of research do not find out what the researcher has said about them. This isn't because researchers don't want to share their results. Rather, it has to do with the structure of academic training and rewards. There aren't many rewards in academe for publishing in popular books or magazines or for presenting one's work on television or radio or via photo exhibitions in indigenous communities. Action researchers usually make a commitment to distribute the results of their work more widely. If they do publish in an academic journal, it is usually as an adjunct to other forms of distribution. Action researchers want to be sure that their work has an impact on the people who are most affected.

SOME PROBLEMS AND OPPORTUNITIES IN ACTION RESEARCH

For those social scientists who were attracted to the field because they want to effect social change, action research may seem to be a perfect solution. It allows them to use their specialized training in the service of social change. It brings with it the possibility of more equal and collaborative relationships than traditional ways of doing research. It allows researchers to develop community organizing skills even while developing research skills. Yet researchers typically aren't trained in those kinds of community organizing and educational skills. If you are interested in conducting participatory action research, you may want to find out more about community organizing. You might want to learn more about the Highlander Center in Tennessee, which has long been involved in education for community change (Gaventa 1991; Greer 1991) or about Saul Alinsky's mode of community organizing (Alinsky 1971; McNeil 1995).

Sharing Power

Action research may also present other difficulties. One of those difficulties centers around the issue of sharing power. To what extent can social researchers, who are often middle class, with highly specialized degrees, really share power with their collaborators, especially when they are from marginalized social groups (Chataway 1997; Lykes 1997)? And it's not clear to what extent marginalized groups are necessarily *interested* in such a sharing. As Cynthia Chataway (1997) notes, more powerful social groups often offer a role in decision making to less powerful groups as a way to co-opt or manipulate them. How can participants be sure that information won't be used against them? Establishing a coequal relationship can take extraordinary time and commitment, and even then it is not assured.

On a practical level, difficulties can arise when a researcher analyzes a problem very differently from participants who are more directly affected by the problem or thinks that a very different solution might be needed. Should the researcher defer to the group? Or the group may express sentiments that seem contrary to the facilitator's values, as M. Brinton Lykes (1997) describes in her research in Guatemala. In one of her projects, she found that being accepted by the mostly male staff meant also being privy to language and jokes that were demeaning to women. She recounts, "I struggled with the unanticipated experience that in order to sustain my status as an 'insider' I was forced to violate my sense of self as a woman" (Lykes 1997, p. 734).

In bringing together groups of stakeholders, a facilitator may have to deal with differences in power. For instance, in our parking example, how can the relative power held by faculty, students, neighborhood residents, and staff be dealt with? Students may see themselves as relatively powerless in relation to faculty. They may not feel free to speak openly in front of those who have the power to grade them. An action research session I was invited to had a similar problem. The goal of the two-day session was to find ways that the community could more effectively meet the needs of youths. Many small groups were established, each containing a few youths, a few community activists, and a few parents and educators. In a brainstorming session, the youths' voices were quashed as the adults became more and more excited with their own vision.

Leading Groups

Action research is hard work. Because it is collaborative in nature, it involves group leadership skills that are typically not taught as part of research methods. Successful action research involves a sensitivity to group dynamics and an ability to work in a respectful way with diverse groups of people (McNicoll 1999). Thus, action researchers need to learn empathy and listening skills. They need to figure out how to balance competing perspectives and to negotiate potential conflicts among the participants (Chataway 1997).

Acting Ethically

Action research also involves several unique ethical issues. As activists, action researchers are especially concerned with creating mutually rewarding, democratic relationships with their participants. Yet action researchers often stand to benefit from the work they do. They can gain status and earn promotions through their publications and grants. One of the issues that action researchers deal with, then, is the potential for exploitation of research subjects (Small 1995). Is it fair for researchers to reap career benefits from the research? Is research that does not seem to benefit those being researched ethical?

In addition, because action research tends to be open-ended, changing in response to the needs and input of the community of researchers, it is difficult to know when (and how) to present action research proposals to institutional review boards (IRBs) (McNicoll 1999). If you make an IRB proposal before contacting community stakeholders, you will have trouble providing a general guide for what you will be studying, given that the problem definition will come from that very contact. But if you wait until after the problem has been defined, you may find yourself holding community members up while the proposal wends its way through IRB channels. As a rule, IRBs are not well set up to deal with open-ended research agendas. If you are planning an action research project at your school, you should consult with your professor or adviser to get additional information about how your IRB will treat such a proposal.

Despite the difficulties involved, action research can be an exciting way to combine an interest in social research with a desire to effect social change. It can be heartening to see your research have a real impact—and to see yourself affected by the research process as well. By working through the research problem as a coequal with others, by listening to their experiences and developing a shared commitment to action, you can be transformed by action research.

QUESTIONS FOR THOUGHT

1. Consider some of the differences between activist research and more traditional forms of researcher-directed research. Which form is more appealing to you? Why?

2. What are some of the difficulties you might encounter in trying to do an action research project? What strategies can you think of to overcome those difficulties?

3. What kind of a role do you think researchers should play in creating political change? Do you think creating political change should be a goal of research? Why or why not?

EXERCISES

1. Consider a group that you might like to conduct activist research with. Outline a strategy that you might use to begin your research. How might you identify stakeholders? How might you get the process started while still allowing participation by the coresearchers? What strategies can you think of to ensure full participation?

2. Interview a community organizer. Find out what kinds of skills are needed for that work. What does she or he do on a daily basis? Then consider: How is that work different from and similar to action research?

SUGGESTIONS FOR FURTHER READING

For descriptions of participatory action research projects, see the journal *Convergence*, which is published by the International Council for Adult Education.

Cancian, Francesca M. "Participatory Research and Alternative Strategies for Activist Sociology." In *Feminism and Social Change: Bridging Theory and Practice*, edited by Heidi Gottfried. Urbana and Chicago: University of Illinois Press, 1996.

Patton, Michael Quinn. *Qualitative Evaluation and Research Methods,* 2nd ed. Newbury Park, CA: Sage, 1990.

Posavac, Emil J., and Raymond G. Carey. *Program Evaluation: Methods and Case Studies,* 5th ed. Upper Saddle River, NJ: Prentice Hall, 1997.

Reinharz, Shulamit. *Feminist Methods in Social Research.* New York: Oxford University Press, 1992. Focuses on feminist action research in Chapter 10.

Small, Stephen A. "Action-Oriented Research: Models and Methods." *Journal of Marriage and the Family* 57:941–956.

Stringer, Ernest T. *Action Research: A Handbook for Practitioners.* Thousand Oaks, CA: Sage, 1996.

8

Making Sense of Data

The ultimate goal is to produce a coherent, focused analysis of
some aspect of the social life that has been observed and recorded,
an analysis that is comprehensible to readers who are not directly
acquainted with the social world at issue.
— EMERSON, FRETZ, AND SHAW (1995, p. 142)

Help! You've collected pages and pages of field notes and interview transcripts. You have gathered a number of documents. You seem to be swimming in a pool of paper. What do you do? How can you begin to make sense of this mass of materials you have collected? How can you begin to transform it into something coherent? How can you develop some kind of an analysis?

In previous chapters, we focused on the process of collecting data. Now it's time to consider what to do with the data once you've gathered them. For many researchers, beginning data analysis can be difficult. The process of gathering data has its own rhythms, and it may seem hard to begin analyzing at the same time. Still, ideally, you should begin data analysis in the field or in the process of gathering data. If you wait until you have finished the last interview or left the field completely, you won't be able to go back and ask clarifying questions. You won't be able to tailor your observations or your interviews as you make discoveries. Waiting until the papers pile up may also make the process of analysis more daunting. If you have been putting off trying to make sense of your data until everything has been collected—and in a qualitative research project "everything" can run to hundreds of pages— the process will be harder than necessary.

Analyzing qualitative data generally involves several stages. First, you have to find some way to physically manage or organize the data: Put it into three-ring binders or files, enter it into the computer, or develop some other technique. Then you need to immerse yourself in the data and become familiar with what you have gathered. As you become increasingly intimate with the data, you will begin to generate themes or categories or identify patterns in the data. Finally, you will need to find ways to present the analysis to others.

MAKING MEANING OUT OF QUALITATIVE DATA

In qualitative research, data analysis is a process of making meaning. It is a creative process, not a mechanical one (Denzin 1989). It's not as if all the meanings are embedded in your field notes or interview transcripts or documents, and your job, as researcher, is to "uncover" them. Rather, your job is to actively create meaning out of your raw materials. Two researchers, encountering the same data, may analyze them very differently. This is to be expected, given that you bring to the process different skills, emphases, and theoretical orientations.

At the same time, the different ways of analyzing the data should at least be plausible. Consider the process of creating something out of a set of raw materials. For example, given a bolt of fabric and some notions (thread, zippers, buttons, and so forth), different people might end up making very different kinds of creations. One person might make a dress, another a Halloween costume, and a third a tent. But what they come up with must at least be plausibly created from the raw materials. It would be awfully difficult to make a working motorcycle or an edible meal out of a bolt of fabric.

Here's another example: My office is a terrible mess right now. There are books and journals scattered all over—in piles on the floor; on bookshelves, and so on. There are several filing cabinets of different colors. On one of the two desks are a few coffee cups and a plate. There are pens, pencils, reams of paper, and a box of Kleenex. Running clothes hang on a hook on a wall, and a shirt is draped over one of the chairs. There is a computer, a printer, and lots of standard office supplies, like rulers, scissors, tape, and computer disks.

Suppose I ask you to organize my office. You might do so in any number of ways. You might lump all the books and journals together as "things to read." You might place the desks and chairs in the category of furniture. You might place the pens, pencils, and computer together as things to write with. But clearly this is only one way to organize my mess. You could also categorize things by color: all the beige things (computer, printer, one of the

filing cabinets), all the black things (tape dispenser, calculator, the other filing cabinet, some books), all the colorful printed things (running shorts,
plate, Kleenex box, some books), and so on. Or you could divide them into
two categories: things to throw out and things to keep. How you decide to
organize the objects depends very much on your purpose in categorizing
them. If you are planning a yard sale, arranging them by color won't do you
much good. You'll want to know what should be kept and what should be
gotten rid of. But if you are trying to make sense of how I use this office and
the things in it, arranging the things by function (things to write with, things
to read, things to use for running) might be helpful. Or, if you want to distinguish among things that I use often and things that I don't use, you might
want to arrange things spatially. Items on the tops of piles or near my computer are things that I use often. Books on shelves are less often used than
books on the floor. Pencils left on top of the desk are favored over those that
are in a drawer. Again, your purpose in analyzing the materials will suggest a
strategy.

One of the difficulties in analyzing qualitative data is that there is no
single method for making sense of what you have found. Just as there is no
single "right" way to organize my messy office, so there is no single "right"
way to organize and analyze qualitative data.

MANAGING DATA

As you begin the process of analyzing qualitative data, your first task is to
arrange or organize your data so that you can begin to make sense of it. Margaret LeCompte and Jean Schensul (1999b) call this process "tidying up."
That is, you have to do some "serious housekeeping" before you can begin
the analysis. You need to make sure that all of your taped interviews are
transcribed and that your field notes are together and complete. You need to
label the computer disks or the audiotapes so that you know what is contained on each. You need to make a comprehensive list of all the materials
you have gathered. At one level, this is a fairly mechanical process of gathering all your materials and devising a filing system or other way of organizing them so that you can easily access them. Yet even at this level you can go
in various directions.

Separating Different Types of Data

You may want to keep different types of data separate. For example, you
may choose to separate transcripts of interviews from your field notes. I

usually assign each interview a code number as I conduct the interview. Then, as interviews are transcribed, I put a copy of each transcript in a file folder along with a copy of the face sheet and any field notes relating to the interview. I also store any correspondence or other materials relating to that interviewee in that file. And I usually keep these files separate from my field notes, which are organized chronologically, and other documents.

Keeping Data in Chronological Order

Some materials, like field notes, should be kept in chronological order. I usually type up full field notes on my computer and print out copies during the course of my observations. In a three-ring binder, I place all my field notes chronologically. I also sometimes put into this binder copies of any documents I have collected during the course of my research. (It's best to do this while you are in the field; on the day you collect a document, write the date on it and put it into the binder.) If I am collecting a series of documents, such as a set of newsletters, I'll usually keep these in a separate file, organized chronologically or, for undated materials, alphabetically.

If you are keeping a personal journal for the research, you may want to place copies of the dated entries in the same binder as your field notes, again organized chronologically. Some people like to keep these separate; the choice is yours. As you are generating these materials, be sure to label them clearly. For example, write "FIELD NOTES" or "PERSONAL JOURNAL" at the top of the page. I often keep original documents (including handwritten scratch notes) in a separate file. You don't need to use a binder (or multiple binders for a big research project) if you don't find it helpful. A file box will work, too. Whatever system you use, make sure you devise a system for keeping the papers together and in order.

Organizing by Topic or Document Type

You may want to organize some of your materials according to a specific topic. For example, if you have collected a number of written documents, you can organize them by topic rather than by chronological order. Suppose you are studying a mothers' organization. During the course of your field research, you collect a number of miscellaneous documents. You might have a number of handouts and magazine or newspaper articles about different topics: methods of discipline, arts and crafts activities, and stories about mothering. You could organize these according to topic. Or you might have several types of materials: meeting agendas, newsletters published by the group, newspaper clippings, and flyers advertising the group. You could arrange these according to type of document.

Making a List or Logbook

However you decide to arrange your materials, it's a good idea to make a comprehensive list of everything you have gathered. For interviews, you might want to include the dates that the interviews were conducted and transcribed, as shown here:

Interview	Date Conducted	Date Transcribed
001	2/15/99	3/1/99
002	2/15/99	3/4/99
003	2/19/99	3/5/99

For documents, you might want to include the title of the document, its date, and a short description of it, as shown here:

List of Documents

1. *Working Mother Forum* (photocopied newsletter)
   April 1999
   May 1999
   July 1999
   August 1999
   September 1999
   October 1999
   January 1999
   February 2000
   March 2000
   April 2000
   May 2000
   June 2000

2. Meeting agendas and minutes
   April 1999 through April 2000. December 1999 missing notes and agenda because meeting was canceled.

3. Miscellaneous documents
   a. Mission statement and bylaws of group
   b. Handout on birth order given out at April 1999 meeting

c. Mother's Lament—poem e-mailed to me by "Roz" May 1999

d. Handout on finding day care given out at June 1999 meeting

Some researchers like to keep track of their materials in a computer database; others like to use index cards. You should use whatever system is most comfortable for you.

Choosing Between Computer and Hard Copy

If you use a software program for qualitative data analysis, you need to enter your data in a form that the program can use (we'll discuss qualitative analysis programs later in this chapter). Many qualitative researchers find that a basic word processing program works fine. Even if you are going to be doing most of your analysis directly on the computer, it's still a good idea to print out a hard copy (and often two or three copies) of all your materials.

Keeping Multiple Copies

Make sure you keep multiple backup copies of all your materials. Hard drives can fail, computer viruses can erase files, and accidents can happen. I usually make several backup disks of the interview transcripts and keep one at my home office and the other at my school office. I know one researcher who had just returned from the field and hadn't yet had a chance to make copies of much of the material. During a routine fire drill, he carried all of his data outside with him "just in case." Most researchers have heard horror stories (whether true or not) about researchers who lost all of their data to a catastrophic fire or a stolen car or a flooded office. The moral of the story? Make multiple copies of your field notes, interview tapes, transcripts, and other data, and keep them in different places. You should keep one copy as a "master" file and two or three other copies for different kinds of analyses (Patton 1990).

Some people—those who are organized—have an easier time with this stage of the research process than others. If you are good at keeping things filed and in order, this stage will be much more pleasant than if you tend to be disorganized and hate to put things away.* Still, the process of gathering your materials together and organizing them is important. You can't analyze

---

*If you are a compulsive organizer, you may enjoy reading Werner and Schoepfle's 1987 book *Systematic Fieldwork*, Volume 2. If you are considerably less organized, you may want to stay away from it!

data that you can't find. Whatever method you choose, be sure that you assemble all of your data and can find what you need, when you need it. And be sure to keep multiple copies of everything.

GETTING INTIMATE WITH YOUR DATA

The next stage involves getting intimate with your data. Maybe some time has elapsed between when you gathered your data and when you're ready to begin the analysis. Even if you have been keeping up, some time has probably passed since you began the research project, and interviews and observations from the beginning of the project may have faded from your memory. The goal at this stage is to immerse yourself in the data. Read over your field notes from beginning to end—several times. Do the same with interview transcripts and any documents you have collected. If you learn better by hearing than by reading, you might find it helpful to listen to the interview tapes—several times if necessary. Some people like to listen to their interview tapes in the car. As you review your materials, take notes if you find it helpful. But don't worry at this stage if it feels as if you will never be able to make sense of all of your materials. Your main object is to try to load up your memory with all your data. You should think about it while you're driving and while you're eating and while you're running and whenever you have a spare moment.

CODING

Once you begin to immerse yourself in the data, how do you make sense of them? How do you identify what is most important? How do you figure out what to leave alone? How can you develop a sense of which themes are recurrent? How can you reduce the sheer volume of material to a more manageable quantity?

The first step in making sense of your data is coding. You might already have some ideas about coding based on quantitative methods. In quantitative methods, the goal is to come up with a small number of categories so that you can manipulate the data on the computer. You begin with a set of categories and assign numbers to cases. For example, if you asked interviewees how much education they had, you might get a variety of responses worded in various ways. One person might say that she had a college education; another might say that he graduated from high school; another might say that she had an associate's degree. In quantitative coding, you would assign each one a number—for example, a "1" for less than a high school education, a "2" for a high school diploma, a "3" for some college education, and so forth. The process is mainly a procedure for counting how many people had each level of education (Coffey and Atkinson 1996).

In qualitative analysis, the goal is not to assign numbers to cases. Rather, the goal is to begin to focus on the potential meanings of your data. Amanda Coffey and Paul Atkinson suggest that qualitative coding entails three basic procedures: "(a) noticing relevant phenomena, (b) collecting examples of those phenomena, and (c) analyzing those phenomena in order to find commonalities, differences, patterns, and structures" (1996, p. 29).

Especially at the beginning of the process, you don't want to limit potential insights by rigidly applying preestablished codes to your data. Instead, you want to use the process of coding to begin to reveal potential meanings. My students often find that initial bouts of coding add more complexity rather than simplify things. They sometimes despair that they'll never figure out what their data mean. This is to be expected. What you want to do at this first stage is to begin to develop hunches and ideas about what is going on in your data. Later, as you refine your codes and develop basic themes, the meanings will become clearer.

Open Coding

Many researchers use some version of grounded theory to work with their data and develop meanings (Strauss and Corbin 1990). Essentially, this method involves a two-stage process of coding. In the initial stage, called *open coding*, you work intensively with your data, line by line, identifying themes and categories that seem of interest. In this early stage, you should remain open to whatever you see in the data. Thus, you shouldn't hesitate to note categories or themes that may not seem relevant to your original research problem.

In open coding, you don't use someone else's preestablished codes, or even your own. Rather, your goal is to see what is going on in your data. If you develop codes in advance, you will impose your own sense of what *ought* to be there in the data and may very well miss what *is* there. In developing open codes, it's important to make sure that you understand the particular themes and categories you see in the data. As you work through your data intensively, don't worry if you see somewhat different things and use different labels for your themes. As you become more familiar with your data, you will naturally begin to see patterns and commonalities and develop a focus.

You can do open coding in a number of ways. For example, you can simply write your codes in the margins. If you like working directly on the computer, you can use the comment function of a word processing program to insert codes. Some people like to use multicolored highlighters or pens to note key phrases in conjunction with marginal notes; others like to use colored Post-it notes. You should try a few different strategies to see what works best for you.

Figure 8.1 shows an example of open coding based on a short segment of an interview conducted with a mother who was juggling paid work and household work. In this segment, she talks about what that juggling was like for her. A number of themes seem prominent: finding day care providers, assessing the quality of day care providers, leaving her son, and so forth.

Development of Themes

After you have done open coding for a while, some recurring themes should begin to emerge. Maybe some categories show up in case after case (in interviews) or over an extended period (in field notes). Maybe some themes seem especially interesting or relevant. At this time, you need to work more intensively with your codes to see what kinds of themes you might develop. Out of all the various codes you have created, which ones might be most helpful in shaping your analysis?

How will you know when to do this? There's no single "right" time, and you can repeat this process as often as you like. It's usually helpful to have done open coding on more than one case (for example, if you are coding interview transcripts, it's helpful to have gone through several different interviews) or a number of days' worth of field notes. When you begin seeing the same codes over and over and don't seem to be seeing quite as many new themes or creating many new codes, this should suggest potential themes.

There are any number of "tricks" you might use to develop themes. Which ones you use will depend in part on what kind of learner you are. Some people like to see things visually; others like to physically manipulate things. Some people work best on a computer; others do best on the floor surrounded by their materials. You should probably try several different approaches until you figure out what works best for you.

Some analysts like to physically sort through the categories they are developing. As they are doing their open coding, they create a series of index cards. Each index card contains the relevant line or portion from the interview or field note on one side and the code on the other. They make sure to note exactly where each piece of the data is from (for example, the

K: Can you talk a little about what it was like for you when you were both working, and with your son, when you were trying to balance that. What was that like?

finding day care

R: First of all, finding day care was very very difficult for me. I interviewed a dozen people. Um. Most of them were young, young ladies with new babies themselves. And it was very

day care providers

leaving son - hard

stressful to think about leaving my son, whom I wanted to have a child, leaving him to be raised with somebody else. I ended up

finding day care provider - mature

finding a day care person who was in her mid 50s. She was really a nice woman and I felt very comfortable with her. And the whole

day care provider - nice

surrounding. And my husband would drop him off in the morning so I didn't have to deal with that separation thing, which was kind of nice. And then I would pick him up at night, so I got that

separation

opportunity. The day care woman was really nice, she very rarely called me for any trivial things. I kind of wish she would have—

day care provider - didn't call

you know, you hear now about day care people keeping logs, you know, about what they ate or how many times their diaper was changed or whatever. So I don't really have a history from, you know, I went back to work when he was 3 months and I quit when he was 9 months. So there's a whole 6 month gap there. It was

missing kid's history

hard there, it really was.

feelings abt day care - hard

day care providers - young

son raised by someone else

day care provider - feelings about drop off

pick up

day care provider - nice

kid's day - getting info abt

missing kid's history

quitting work

FIGURE 8.1   Open Coding

interview number and page number). Then, when they have done a signifi-cant amount of open coding and have a number of cards, they sort them into piles to see which codes emerge most frequently. They might sort them a number of different ways to see if the same kinds of themes seem to emerge. Each time they sort the cards, they keep track of which categories they created. (There are also computer programs for creating and sorting index cards that can be very helpful.)

Instead of making index cards, some researchers literally cut up a copy of the interview transcript or their field notes into pieces, each with a relevant line or segment marked with a code. Again, they carefully note where each slip comes from so that they can refer back to it. Then, they sort the slips into piles, often multiple times, to see what themes seem to emerge. And, again, they keep track of the outcome of each sorting.

Focused Coding

Once you begin to identify several key recurring themes, you can do focused coding (Coffey and Atkinson 1996). Like open coding, *focused coding* entails going through your data line by line, but this time you focus on those key themes you identified during open coding. So, for example, in the open coding segment in Figure 8.1, I might decide to focus on two themes: day care providers and separations. I would then go through a copy of each of the transcripts and field notes, line by line, noting those categories. Of course, if you were doing open coding on a longer section of data (as you should), you would probably develop more and perhaps different themes.

As with open coding, you can use any technique you like for focused coding. Again, some people like to write directly on the text; others like to work on the computer. There are a number of software programs for qualitative analysis that can help you store and retrieve codes; you may also choose to use an ordinary word processing program. If you are working with word processing software, it's often helpful to do a computerized search for key words or phrases. You may need to check your searches carefully, however. Sometimes, people use somewhat different words to describe similar things, and unless you search for all the possibilities, you may miss important sections of the text. For example, if I were looking for passages relating to day care providers, I would probably need to search a number of different words: "day care provider," "child care provider," "baby-sitter," the name of the specific provider mentioned by the respondent, and so on.

If it's available, some people like to work with a clean copy of the data in this stage. I sometimes find it helpful to create a long word processing document with all the quotes I've identified for each code, as in this example (with all my transcripts and notes already on the computer it's a fairly easy process):

Day Care Providers—Feelings About

"She was a really nice woman and I felt very comfortable with her."
(001, p. 4)

"The day care woman was really nice, she very rarely called me for any trivial thing." (006, p. 4)

"I was so angry with [my day care provider]. When my daughter got bit by her cat, I was out of there. I couldn't believe that she wouldn't just lock the cats up." (009, p. 6)

"I really like how [my day care provider] is so calm and patient with Zoe. She's terrific with her. I always lose patience." (010, p. 15)

Thus, if one of my codes is "feelings about day care providers," I might create a word processing document that contains each quote that relates to the code. (I'd be sure to indicate the interview number and page number so I could find it easily.) I might then break that down into further categories: positive feelings, neutral feelings, and negative feelings, or perhaps strong feelings and weak feelings. When I was ready to write up the analysis, I would already have the quotes in one place. Other researchers might make index cards or use other techniques.

You are probably getting the impression that coding is a laborious, time-consuming process. It is. But in qualitative analysis, there really are no shortcuts in analyzing your data. While the computer programs available for data analysis can help you manage data and reduce the amount of time you spend retyping and rewriting things (such as making index cards), they can't do the analysis for you. *You* still have to develop the codes and themes yourself. *You* still have to make the decisions about what is important and what is not. At the same time, there are many different techniques you can use; there is no one single way to analyze qualitative data. This leaves you free to develop the methods that make the most sense for your particular situation.

Maps and Diagrams

Many researchers like to use visual techniques in working with their data. For example, you might look at the themes you have developed and create a map or diagram that shows how the themes seem to relate to one another. There are any number of ways you can create diagrams or maps. You might, for example, map how individuals or groups relate to one another. This means identifying the various groups in a social setting and determining whether members of one group are also members of another. For example, can you be both a student and an employee at the same time? Do some individuals serve to "connect" groups or bring them together?

You may want to diagram the structure of events in a sequence of action. For example, consider children's birthday parties. What are the vari-

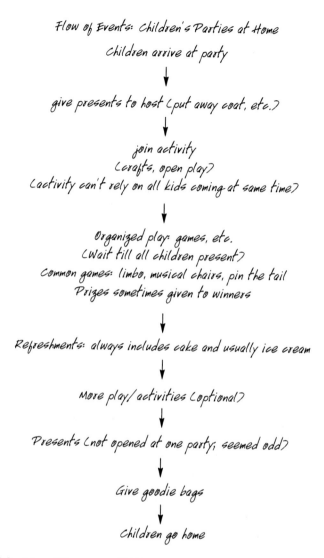

Flow of Events: Children's Parties at Home

Children arrive at party

↓

give presents to host (put away coat, etc.)

↓

join activity
(crafts, open play)
(activity can't rely on all kids coming at same time)

↓

Organized play: games, etc.
(wait till all children present)
Common games: limbo, musical chairs, pin the tail
Prizes sometimes given to winners

↓

Refreshments: always includes cake and usually ice cream

↓

More play/activities (optional)

↓

Presents (not opened at one party; seemed odd)

↓

Give goodie bags

↓

Children go home

FIGURE 8.2   Map of Events at a Children's Birthday Party

ous events in a birthday party? What are the things that *must* be present in order for one to consider it a birthday party? There are usually games, things to eat, birthday cake, "goodie" bags, and presents, among other things. But would it still be a birthday party without a cake? What about a party without the guest of honor—the child who is having the birthday? Is there a specific order in which events happen? Or are there several possible orderings of events? Figure 8.2 shows a map of events at a typical children's

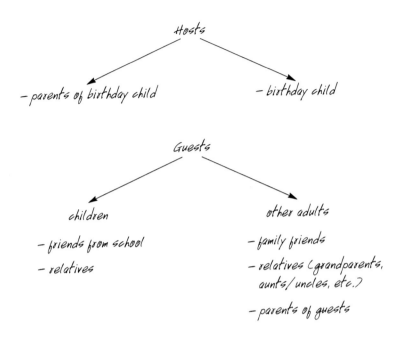

FIGURE 8.3   **Map of the Relationships Among Attendees at Birthday Party**

birthday party; Figure 8.3 shows a map of the relationships among party attendees. Creating a diagram of the flow of events can help you figure out if you have included all the steps in an event or process and if you understand the process fully.

MEMOS

At each step of the way, it's helpful to write up memos. Writing is a process of making meaning. Writing memos helps you shape your thoughts about the emerging analysis and provides a record of your progress. Thus, through the process of writing about your findings, you develop your analysis a bit further. Think of memos as letters or notes to yourself to help you understand your data. They are written for you, not for a teacher or an outside reader. Thus, you can use whatever format you like and feel most comfortable with. Whatever format you use, however, it's important to date your memos so you know when you created them.

Procedural Memos

You can use memos in a number of ways. First, you can write up *procedural memos* to help you remember how you did your coding, what kinds of categories you created, and so forth. (Strauss and Corbin [1990] call these code memos.) Procedural memos focus on the nuts and bolts of your research. They summarize exactly what you did—what codes and categories you created, what they included, what codes you rejected and why, and so on. These memos are important for they help you keep track of what you have done. (They are also useful for creating a description of how you analyzed your data, which you will need to include in your write-up.) Some people like to keep a separate logbook of their memos, which helps them keep a running record of all the steps they took. Others prefer to keep their memos with their field notes. I find it helpful to give each memo a title so that I can keep track of it. The following memo distinguishes between two codes:

Procedural Memo: Feelings About Day Care Providers and Pick-ups and Drop-offs

The code "feelings about day care providers" includes any kind of emotion word or evaluation that interviewees use to refer to their day care providers. These include things like the provider was "nice" or that the respondent "liked" her, and so forth. It applies to feelings about the provider as a person (or as a provider). It does not include feelings the interviewee might have about placing her child in day care or feelings about pick-ups and drop-offs.

The code "pick-ups and drop-offs" includes anything the respondent says about picking up or dropping off her child at day care. Ex: "I was always glad to let my partner do the drop-off" or "I liked to go in a few minutes early to see how my daughter was playing with the other kids."

Analytic Memos

You can also write *analytic memos* that help you think about the categories and themes you are developing. In these memos, you focus on what's important in your data and make connections between cases. If you're following the advice I gave in Chapter 4, you've already been writing this kind of memo while doing field work. These memos contain your hunches and ideas and best guesses about what you should be thinking about. As you develop your coding further, these memos should get more and more detailed. Ideally, you should be able to draw on these memos in your final write-up. Here's an example of an analytic memo:

> ### Analytic Memo: Drop-offs
>
> It seems like the drop-offs are very charged for some of the mothers I've been interviewing. Some of the parents seem to have a hard time with it—I think they feel guilty about leaving their kids in day care (maybe they feel like bad mothers?) and the drop-off then becomes difficult. This was definitely the case with Roz and Lee ("I can't stand it when she cries 'Mommy stay, Mommy stay.' Every morning I wonder if I'm doing the right thing"). Not all the mothers find it hard, though. Leah said: "I love to see Zoe [her daughter] throw herself in Callie's [the day care provider] arms. She really loves it there."
>
> Does it have to do with the quality of the day care provider? The parents' own feelings about their mothering? The parents' feelings about their work? Maybe mothers who enjoy their work more or need the money more feel less ambivalent about the drop-off. [I'll need to check this out in field notes too. Do I notice the same kinds of difficulties?]

ASKING QUESTIONS

Coding is not the end of your analysis, however. It's more like a beginning. In the initial stages, the coding opens you up to the possibilities of your data; it makes it more complex. Coding thus serves the purpose of what Amanda Coffey and Paul Atkinson (1996) call "data complication." At the same time, focused coding helps you to reduce the data—to bring it down to size and make it more manageable. Yet this data reduction, by itself, is not the finished analysis. You still have to answer what I think of as the "so what" question: So what? What do these data mean? You still have to figure out what the themes and categories that you are identifying might mean in conjunction with one another.

At this stage, as you are working intensively with your data, it's helpful to ask a number of questions (Emerson, Fretz, and Shaw 1995; Patton 1990). And you can focus your questions in a number of directions:

Questions about events:
   What happened?
   Who was involved?
   How did the event begin?
   How did it end?

Questions about chronology:
   What happened first? Next? Then?

Questions about the setting:
   What is this place like?
   What does it look like?

Questions about people:
   Who are the people involved?
   What are they like?

Questions about processes:
   What are people trying to accomplish?
   How do they do this?

Questions about issues:
   What are the key issues for these people?
   What is important to them?
   How do they describe what is important?
   What language do they use?

Answering these kinds of questions can alert you to different facets of the analysis and help you describe an event or a group of people. For example, if you have been observing at mothers' play groups, you might want to describe what happens at a typical group meeting. This kind of descriptive writing is important, as we'll discuss further in Chapter 10, for it helps you to set the scene. Part of a good qualitative analysis entails describing to others what you have observed.

Answering these questions can also lead you to make interpretations about the meanings of things. For example, you may want to interpret what the play groups mean to the women involved in organizing them. Perhaps they serve as a way for the mothers to provide friends and playmates for their children or as a source of support for the women. Perhaps they help solidify the women's identities as "good" mothers. These are all interpretations—arguments about what the play groups mean. These kinds of interpretations must be grounded in the data—hence the laborious process of working intensively, line by line, with the data.

Some scholars argue that *all* writing is interpretive. That is, even when you are describing something, you can only present your interpretation of what you saw. Regardless of where you come down on this issue, you should always think about how you can orient yourself in terms of two modes of inquiry: (1) how to describe events or people or cases to others and (2) how to interpret (or make your best argument about) what those things might mean.

DEVELOPING AN ANALYSIS

Developing a qualitative analysis may seem like a mystical process. As I keep emphasizing, the activities you engage in throughout data analysis are not mechanical ones. But there are several methods of analyzing data that may be of use to you. These activities generally include looking for patterns in the data (similarities and differences), comparing cases, building typologies, and conducting a content analysis. In Chapter 9, we will consider the process of constructing narrative accounts or stories.

Looking for Patterns

One of the first things you can do in your coding is to look for patterns in the data. Different interviewees might deal with the same kinds of issues or handle different issues in similar ways. The same kinds of events might occur over and over, or similar patterns might occur among different events. The coding that you do should help alert you to these kinds of patterns. For example, in the analysis of working mothers, a researcher might find that women give similar accounts of leaving their children with the day care provider. Perhaps all of the women describe a process of dropping their children off in the morning and picking them up at the end of the day.

Comparing Cases

Once you have identified a few patterns, you may want to compare cases more systematically. What is a case? It all depends on your research. If you have primarily conducted interviews, you might want to compare individual interviewees. Each person you interviewed might be a case. You might also compare events, like birthday parties. Each birthday party might be a case. Or you might consider cases on a larger scale: organizations (like universities or colleges), neighborhoods, and so forth.

	Pick-up	Drop-off
Self does	001, 002, 007, 008, 012, 013, 014	001, 002, 005, 006, 008, 011, 015
Partner does	003, 005, 006, 011	003, 007, 012, 013, 014
No partner (interviewee does both)	004, 009, 010	004, 009, 010

FIGURE 8.4   Chart for Comparing Cases

For example, let's say you have interviewed fifteen mothers who work outside the home. You may want to systematically compare them on a variety of dimensions: whether they tell pick-up/drop-off stories, whether their spouse or partner shares the work of picking up and dropping off, and so forth. You could create a grid or chart like the one in Figure 8.4 to help you compare. Here, you're simply comparing the cases in terms of who picks up and drops off children at day care. For example, your first interviewee (001) does both the pick-up and drop-off. Interviewee 3 does neither—her partner does both. Interviewee 7 does the pick-ups and her partner does the drop-offs. The single parents in the sample (004, 009, 010) naturally do both because they don't have a partner to share the work with. Comparing the cases in this way may help you think about other ways that you can compare the cases. For example, some of the women who have partners are like the single parents—they do all the work of picking up and dropping off. Are they similar in other ways as well? Different?

Building Typologies

One relatively simple analysis involves the construction of a *typology*, which is simply a system for categorizing types of things. So, in our day care example, you might notice while coding that some of the women seem to share picking up and dropping off their kids at daycare with a partner and others do not. Maybe you notice that some of the women seem to share the work of child care more generally with their partners and others do not. You might want to create a typology: equal sharers and unequal sharers. If you look at the grid in Figure 8.4, you can see that in three cases the woman does both pick-up and drop-off (001, 002, 008) and in one of the cases her partner does both (003). You can call this group the unequal sharers. In seven of the cases, the woman and her partner split up the picking up and dropping off equally (005, 006, 007, 011, 012, 013, 014). These are the equal sharers. In three of the cases, the woman doesn't have a partner, so you might make them either a third category (single parents) or leave them out of the typology.

Obviously, this is a very simple typology. Sharing pick-up and drop-off might not say much about whether the women's partners share in other activities, such as staying home with a sick child, supervising homework, feeding and bathing the children, and putting them to bed. But it might help you think about ways to make sense of the data. If some partners share this task equally, do they share other tasks as well? You might go back through your interview transcripts and field notes to find out. And how do people feel about the tasks that they share—or, perhaps more tellingly, don't share?*

Getting Stuck and Unstuck

It can be very easy to feel "stuck" while you are attempting to analyze the data. Maybe you have been coding for a while and haven't "come up for air" to look at the general patterns. Then, when you do, it's hard to get ahold of them. Maybe you're having trouble telling others what you think you are finding. If you do feel stuck, here are a few tricks that may help you become "unstuck."

First, you might try making analogies of the form "this phenomenon I am studying is like X, and unlike Y." For our birthday party example, you might say, "Children's birthday parties are like adult birthday parties in that the person whose birthday it is usually gets presents and friends are invited to come celebrate. Children's birthdays are unlike adult birthdays in that children are often happy to get a year older; but adults often are not." If you are really stuck, you might try coming up with analogies that seem ridiculous.

Second, you might try choosing different words for your key concepts or codes (Lofland and Lofland 1995). Sometimes, the way things are phrased obscures meaning. For example, if you have been studying peer pressure, try saying "pressuring peers," "influence," "force," "fads," "crazes," "role modeling," or "following the crowd." Each way of wording gives you a slightly different spin on the concept.

Third, try talking about your developing analysis with friends and fellow students. They can often help you clarify what you are seeing or stimulate new ways of thinking about your topic. Listening to others talk about how

---

*If you're interested in "equal sharers," you might enjoy Francine Deutsch's 1999 interview study of parents who share the work equally, called *Halving It All*.

they are dealing with a particular data analysis problem might give you some ideas as well. It's often helpful to think about how you might explain your developing analysis to someone who knows nothing about your topic. I sometimes suggest that students think about how they would describe their study to a 12-year-old child, an older relative, or a being who has just arrived from outer space and knows nothing about their topic or the culture.

CONTENT ANALYSIS

One technique that can be used to analyze any kind of text is *content analysis*, which generally involves a systematic analysis of texts. *Texts* include any kind of written material, such as books, magazines, diaries, letters, minutes of meetings, transcripts of TV programs, interview transcripts, and field notes. Often in content analysis, quantitative scholars count the frequency with which specific words or themes appear in the texts and then conduct statistical analyses on those frequencies.

Qualitative scholars may use content analysis as well. Sometimes, simple counting is useful. For example, if you want to know how often men and women appear in textbooks, you might simply count how many photos there are of each. This strategy is sometimes used by people who want to document discrimination against particular groups or by those who want to see if stereotyped images are improving over time (see, for example, Clark, Lennon, and Morris 1991). You may want to use this kind of simple counting in your field notes or interview transcripts. For example, it might be helpful to count how often a particular theme is mentioned by your interviewees. Suppose you want to gain more understanding of pick-ups and drop-offs at day care. You might count how often each interviewee mentions a pick-up or drop-off and, for each case, decide whether the event is negative, positive, or emotionally neutral. You can then get a sense of whether, overall, the interviewee sees each event as positive or negative.

At other times, you may want to focus more on the meanings of texts. For example, Ralph LaRossa and his colleagues wanted to understand how fathers have been portrayed in the media and whether the cultural meanings of fatherhood have changed over time (LaRossa, Jaret, Gadgil, and Wynn 2000). Thus, they decided to conduct a content analysis of Father's Day and Mother's Day cartoon strips published between 1940 and 1999. They found that the cultural meanings of fatherhood had changed over time, but not in a straightforward way. Depictions of nurturing fathers, for example, were more likely to appear in the late 1940s and early 1950s, as well as in the 1990s.

What should you count? It all depends on your research topic. (See Carley 1993 for a discussion of some of the choices you must make in content analysis.) Some content analysts count specific words (Ryan and Weisner 1996). Others might count every time a theme—for example, feeling positive about one's work—appears in a phrase or a sentence or, more rarely, a paragraph (Berg 2001). Still others count individuals—for example, whether an article is authored by a male or female or whether photos include Asian Americans or African Americans or European Americans. Still others might count concepts, things that can't be observed directly, such as "guilt" or "deviance."

Researchers who use content analysis may focus on several different levels. At the simplest level, researchers stick to relatively straightforward content—words that appear in the text directly or pictures or objects that can be counted directly. This is sometimes referred to as *manifest content*. Others try to conduct a more interpretive analysis, focusing more on the underlying meanings in the text. This is known as *latent content*. Still others focus on the linguistic or semantic properties of the text itself (Franzosi 1990a, 1990b). They argue that the way in which things are expressed also gives insight into the meanings of texts.

SEMIOTIC ANALYSIS

Researchers sometimes use *semiotic analysis*, the study of signs (Manning and Cullum-Swan 1998). A *sign* is simply something that stands for something else. So, for example, a rainbow flag might symbolize the lesbian/gay/bisexual movement, the ☮ symbol peace, and the Star of David (✡) Judaism. A sign consists of two parts: (1) the sign itself (such as the flag or the star or the peace sign) and (2) the content with which it is associated. Semiotics is based on language, but there are other semiotic systems as well. Thus, mathematics is a semiotic system, as are highway signs and systems of etiquette, which might include things like shaking hands or bowing to greet someone (Manning and Cullum-Swan 1998, p. 252).

By themselves, signs don't mean anything. They only take on meaning within a particular social context and when interpreted by someone within that context. Signs thus can take on many different meanings and may be connected in a number of different semiotic systems. In semiotics, the analyst tries to "unpack" the meanings of the signs. These meanings may be multiple and layered.

You "read" signs all the time even though you may not be aware of it. For example, I dropped my daughter off at kindergarten this morning. All the children were wearing uniforms: white blouses and shirts, blue plaid skirts and navy slacks. The youngest children were in matching navy blue sweat suits with the school logo printed on the front. The school logo itself is a sign that symbolizes the school. The uniform symbolizes order and uniformity, as well as perhaps a desire to level class differences in the school. Uniforms may be associated with parochial schools or with public charter schools that emphasize the qualities of discipline and order of a parochial school. In a public charter school, then, the uniform might be a sign of a sign.

In addition, all the children in my daughter's school wore backpacks or carried bags with logos indicating particular brand names (signs of social class) or characters like Winnie the Pooh, Tigger, Barbie, and the Powerpuff Girls. Each of these characters can also be analyzed: Winnie the Pooh stands for childhood and innocence, Barbie can be analyzed in terms of race and class, the Powerpuff Girls symbolize girl power, and so on.

Parochial schools themselves can take on many different meanings. They may signify religious faith and the desire to inculcate certain religious values in children. They may signify educational quality. In neighborhoods with inferior public schools, parochial schools may signify a neighborhood-based alternative. They may also signify class distinctions between those who can afford private schools and those who cannot.

There are many different ways to conduct a semiotic analysis and a number of different theoretical traditions that shape the kind of analysis you might do. Readings in semiotics are often very difficult. Many who do this kind of work have been trained in literary criticism or cultural studies. If you are interested in finding out more about semiotics, you may want to see the article by Peter Manning and Betsy Cullum-Swan listed at the end of this chapter for a relatively accessible introduction.

GROUNDING THE ANALYSIS

Let's say you've gone through several stages of coding and writing memos and analyzing. You have worked to try to see how the various codes you developed might relate to one another. You have drawn maps and diagrams and feel you have developed what seems to be a sound analysis of your data. Perhaps you have conducted a semiotic analysis as well. What next? How do you verify that your interpretation of the data is actually a good one? Before you finish your analysis, you will need to examine your work carefully against the data you have gathered. You want to make sure that the analysis you've developed is actually supported by the data.

Shortcomings in the Research

Michael Huberman and Matthew Miles list a number of "shortcomings" in qualitative research (1998, pp. 198–199). First, researchers may gather too much data, or too much of a certain kind of data, so that they fail to see patterns or "skew" the analysis in one direction or another. You need to consider carefully whether you've collected the right kinds of data or whether you're missing crucial information.

Second, first impressions tend to be more intense than later ones. You may weigh initial impressions more heavily than you should. The same is true for more recent impressions. Often, you tend to remember the most recent events, not the overall pattern. In conducting your analysis, you need to pay attention to events taken from the whole time span. After you have completed an initial analysis, you need to check to make sure you have done so.

Third, people tend to see things that occur at the same time as related when it may simply be coincidence. For example, suppose that every morning when you get up you see your neighbor leave in her car, presumably to go to work. Does your getting up have anything to do with your neighbor? Of course not. Sometimes, qualitative researchers see related patterns when none, in fact, exist.

Fourth, the information may not be reliable. Perhaps an interviewee didn't tell the truth or exaggerated. Perhaps you didn't take good field notes and don't have a good record of what you saw. Perhaps you didn't interview the right people. You need to think about what kinds of shortcomings you have in your data.

Some of these shortcomings are fixable. If you are still in the field, you can gather more data. If you have field notes spanning a long period, you can try to focus especially carefully on the middle events. Sometimes, simply knowing that people have a tendency to make unrelated events seem related can cause you to scrutinize your interpretations more carefully. Sometimes, however, shortcomings in the data or the analysis aren't fixable. If you've already left the field and cannot go back, you cannot patch the holes in your field notes or interview more informants. In these cases, it is better to be honest in your write-up about the problems you have discovered.

Negative Cases

One of the first things you can do to ground your analysis more carefully in the data is look for *negative cases*. In creating your argument, you probably amassed positive examples (evidence) that support your case. For example, if I believe that women's identities as mothers is implicated in the difficulty or ease with which they drop their children off at day care, I need to look for positive cases in which mothers express both difficulty with drop-off and guilt about their mothering role. Having found those cases, however, I also need to look for evidence that disconfirms my interpretation. For example, if I find a series of cases in which the mothers express great difficulty with drop-offs but also express satisfaction with their mothering role in general, I probably need to think again about the analysis I created. If you are still collecting data while you are conducting your analysis, you can specifically seek out negative cases. Regardless, you should always search through your data for negative cases after you complete the initial analysis.

The Null Hypothesis Trick

Howard Becker (1998) suggests that you should initially assume that there is no pattern or relationship in the data. Then, you need to tease out the conditions under which the pattern you observed might develop. He calls this the "null hypothesis trick" because in quantitative research researchers are always trying to support the *null hypothesis*, the hypothesis that two events or variables are not related. In a qualitative analysis, you might want to do something similar by assuming initially that there is no pattern in the data. You then have to amass the evidence, based on examples, to show that there is a pattern. So, for example, the null hypothesis in our child care research might be that there's no relationship between dropping off one's child at day care and how one feels about oneself as a mother. In order to feel reasonably secure in the interpretation that there is such a relationship, you would need to come up with clear evidence, based on examples from the data, that there is one. In doing so, we would need to sort through the selection processes that lead people to end up in various social groups. (Becker's book, *Tricks of the Trade*, offers many useful examples of how you can work with your data.)

Here's a simple example. Let's say you want to understand the process of how some parents come to be full-time parents after the birth of a child while others return to the workplace relatively quickly. The null hypothesis assumes that there really aren't any differences between the two groups. Looking over your data carefully, however, you notice that men are more likely than women to return to the workplace quickly, though many women do as well. You might focus your attention, then, on the question of *why?* You might notice that women are more likely to have access to paid maternity leaves than men, who have very little access to paid parenting leaves. You might notice that men often get paid more than women, so that it costs a family more to lose the man's income. You might notice that some women and men enjoy their jobs very much, and others don't. You might also look at the kinds of social messages about parenting and work that men and women receive. By paying attention to the social processes that treat men and women as very different sorts of parents, you can begin to understand some of the differences you observed between the two groups.

Triangulation

Triangulation is often used to mean bringing different kinds of evidence to bear on a problem (Denzin 1989). Thus, if you have access to interview data, observational data, and historical documents, your analysis is likely to be much sounder than if you rely on only one source of evidence. This is because each kind of evidence has its own strengths and weaknesses. With observation, you can actually see how people behave; it allows you to see a whole process unfold over time. With interviews, you can gain insight into their feelings or reasons for behaving in a certain way. Using multiple kinds of data allows you to balance the strengths and weaknesses of each. So, for example, if you want to know about the social messages that male and female parents receive, you might want to analyze the media. Yet this kind of analysis will tell you relatively little about how individual women and men feel about those messages or whether they take them into account when making decisions about their own lives. Triangulation—using different types of evidence—will help.

Some researchers also use the term to refer to the findings of different researchers (Huberman and Miles 1998). Thus, if you come to a similar conclusion as other researchers, you can feel more confident of your findings. If you come to a very different conclusion, it doesn't mean that your analysis is wrong. It may mean that you used different kinds of evidence, perhaps from different historical periods. Maybe you emphasized very different themes or were informed by very different theoretical traditions. You may want to examine the methods others used in conducting their research to give you insight into any differences you find.

COMPUTER-ASSISTED DATA ANALYSIS

Just about all qualitative researchers use computers for at least some aspect of their field research. While there still may be a few who use typewriters to write up field notes and transcribe interview tapes (or who write up all their notes by hand), these are surely a distinct (and dwindling) minority. Most researchers at least use word processing software to transcribe interview tapes and write up full field notes. Many will use simple search capabilities or sorting procedures. In that sense, computers are used widely throughout qualitative research. Yet relatively few qualitative researchers use software that is specifically designed for qualitative data analysis (Richards and Richards 1998). But that situation may be slowly changing, as a growing number of computer programs have been developed especially to assist in qualitative data analysis.

Why haven't qualitative researchers been faster to incorporate the computer into their procedures for analyzing data? Probably most importantly, the computer can't solve easily the kinds of problems that qualitative researchers confront. Qualitative researchers work with texts (words), not numbers, and computers can't "crunch" texts as easily as they can numbers. Qualitative analysts rely on their own judgment, which can't be wholly mechanized. Thus, you already have to know what you want to do with your data before using a qualitative data analysis program. Dedicated programs for qualitative data analysis can also be expensive and difficult to learn. For these reasons, I often recommend that beginning researchers work with their texts by hand or on word processors before attempting to use a qualitative data analysis program. That way, you can develop a feel for what it is that you want automated and whether a data analysis program might help.

That said, computers (and qualitative data analysis programs) can be extremely useful. They can do the kinds of mechanical storage and retrieval tasks that we often do by hand. Computers have far better memories than humans do, as well as greater capacities for storing texts. Used well, computers can offset some of the shortcomings involved in qualitative data analysis, such as relying more heavily on later field notes than on earlier ones (Dohan and Sanchez-Jankowski 1998).

Qualitative data analysis typically involves (1) recognizing patterns (or categories) in the data, (2) generating ideas about what these patterns might mean, and (3) exploring potential meanings in the data. Computer software programs can help in this process in several ways (see Dohan and Sanchez-Jankowski 1998; and Richards and Richards 1998 for useful overviews). There are numerous software programs available (Dohan and Sanchez-Jankowski count over twenty). None, however, is dominant, and the availability of programs changes rapidly. To figure out which program you might want to use, you need to identify your purpose and try out a variety of programs.

BOX 8.1   Web Sites for Computer-Assisted Qualitative Data Analysis

CAQDAS Network (a general site for computer-assisted qualitative data analysis)
   http://caqdas.soc.surrey.ac.uk/

ATLAS.ti
   www.atlasti.de/

The Ethnograph
   www.qualisresearch.com

HyperRESEARCH
   www.researchware.com

NVivo and NUD*IST
   www.qsr.com.au or www.scolari.com

First, qualitative data analysis programs can help researchers search and retrieve chunks of text. Basic word processing programs like WordPerfect and Microsoft Word can facilitate this task. A number of other programs are also designed to help in searching and retrieving chunks of text; they go beyond word processing programs by storing the number of "hits" or conducting a quantitative content analysis.

Other software programs help you organize your data, code and retrieve text, create a structure for manipulating the data, and annotate the data. Popular programs that accomplish these tasks include The Ethnograph and QUALPRO. Some software programs go further in helping you develop theory. These kinds of programs, like NUD*IST or HyperRESEARCH, allow you to look at relationships among codes or to create hierarchical relationships between codes. They can also aid you in making maps of relationships. Finally, some programs, such as ATLAS.ti and NVivo, enable researchers to incorporate sound, graphics, and audio data in their analyses.

If you are interested in learning more about a specific qualitative data analysis program, you can find out more by searching on the Internet or by reading a recent review of the program. Some useful sites are listed in Box 8.1. Many software developers will let you try out the program (or at least portions of it) at those sites. As with any computer software, however, changes come rapidly. By the time this book is published, any general review of software programs will be out of date.

Whether you choose to use a qualitative data analysis program or analyze your data by hand, try to "play" with your data. Be creative. Experiment. Explore your data from numerous perspectives. This is, after all, the purpose behind all the work you have gone through to collect the data: to see what kinds of meanings you can create.

QUESTION FOR THOUGHT

Think about what kind of a learner you are. Do you learn best when things are presented visually? Orally? Or do you learn best when you can manipulate things? Consider which strategies for data analysis will best suit your learning style.

EXERCISES

1. The purpose of this exercise is to give you practice in categorizing things. Select an assortment of 10–20 things (or, better yet, ask a friend to do it for you). Simply select the first 10 or 20 things you come across. Don't try to pick the things with any order in mind. Then classify what you have found into a smaller number of categories in as many different ways as you can (say, three to five categories each time you sort). Each time you sort the items, you must find a category for each item, leaving at most only one item uncategorized.

2. If you conducted one or more interviews or did participant observation as part of this class, try analyzing the interview transcripts or your field notes using the methods outlined in this chapter. If you do not have access to these materials, you can search the Internet for copies of oral histories or other materials that you might want to analyze.

3. Choose a popular magazine or newspaper and conduct a content analysis to help you determine the most frequent themes. What unit should you count? Then obtain a series of at least five to ten issues of the same magazine or newspaper and conduct another content analysis.

4. Take that same magazine or newspaper and conduct a semiotic analysis. You may want to pay special attention to the advertisements. What signs do you identify?

5. Locate at least one of the qualitative data analysis sites on the Internet. See what you can find out about at least one of the programs. Try it out if you are able.

SUGGESTIONS FOR FURTHER READING

Becker, Howard, S. *Tricks of the Trade: How to Think About Your Research While You're Doing It.* Chicago: University of Chicago Press, 1998.

Coffey, Amanda, and Paul Atkinson. *Making Sense of Qualitative Data.* Thousand Oaks, CA: Sage, 1996.

Dohan, Daniel, and Martin Sanchez-Jankowski. "Using Computers to Analyze Ethnographic Field Data: Theoretical and Practical Considerations." *Annual Review of Sociology* 24:477–498.

Manning, Peter, K., and Betsy Cullum-Swan. "Narrative, Content, and Semiotic Analysis." Pp. 246–273 in *Collecting and Interpreting Qualitative Materials,* edited by Norman K. Denzin and Yvonna S. Lincoln. Thousand Oaks, CA: Sage, 1998. See especially their semiotic analysis of MacDonald's.

Miles, Matthew B., and A. Michael Huberman. *Qualitative Data Analysis: An Expanded Sourcebook.* Thousand Oaks, CA: Sage, 1994.

Strauss, Anselm, and Juliet Corbin. *Basics of Qualitative Research: Grounded Theory Procedures and Techniques.* Newbury Park, CA: Sage, 1990.

9

Narrative Analysis

People tell and retell stories: stories about the first day of classes, stories about how they dealt with adversity, stories about how they came to see themselves in a particular light. People tell coming-out stories and growing-up stories and stories about how they dealt with oppression. People tell stories to describe or make sense of their experiences. Stories are one of the ways in which we produce and reproduce social knowledge—and try to make sense of our place in the social world.

Qualitative data are typically full of narratives and stories. Sometimes, data collection efforts are explicitly aimed at gathering life stories, as when interviewers collect oral histories or conduct biographical interviews (Anderson, Armitage, Jack, and Wittner 1990; Denzin 1989; Smith 1998). Other times, stories can be recorded in ethnographic field notes or in the process of conducting semistructured or unstructured interviews. Texts and documents, like diaries and first-person accounts, may contain stories. Robert Franzosi (1998) reminds us that even advertisements may contain stories that can be analyzed.

The method for analyzing these kinds of stories is called *narrative analysis*. Drawing on the same kinds of techniques for interpretation and analysis of texts that literary scholars use, narrative analysis encourages social researchers to pay attention to the language used to describe experiences and to focus on the structure of stories. Rather than viewing the language that people use as unimportant, narrative analysis assumes that language conveys meaning and that *how* a story is told is as important as what is said. This type of analysis is relatively new within sociology; it is more firmly established in anthropology and education.

Unlike the methods for analyzing data discussed in Chapter 8, narrative analysis provides techniques for looking at stories as a whole. Chapter 8 focused on breaking down materials (including stories) into smaller pieces, or themes, for analysis. Sometimes, however, we might want to understand the various elements of the story and how it is told. We might want to analyze the audiences for a particular story, the kinds of cultural resources that are available for telling stories, or the kinds of social contexts that surround particular types of stories.

WHAT IS A NARRATIVE?

Scholars in a variety of fields, ranging from literary criticism to folklore to nursing to law to business, use narrative analysis in a number of ways. (See Riessman 1993 for a good discussion of the varieties of narrative analysis.) There is also disagreement about what a narrative is. Some people argue that narratives and stories are distinct. The story is what happened, according to Franzosi (1998), and the narrative is the telling of it. For our purposes (and following Coffey and Atkinson 1996), we won't worry too much about the distinctions between stories and narratives. Nor will we worry about some of the more complex methods of literary analysis. Instead, we'll use a relatively simple version.

We can think of a *narrative* as a kind of story told by someone (a "narrator") with a beginning, a middle, and an end. Usually, a story has some kind of plot, or action. In Western traditions, stories are often told chronologically, but this isn't the only way that stories may be structured (Riessman 1993). Nor can all kinds of talk be considered a story. For example, in a typical semistructured interview, you might move back and forth between relatively brief questions and answers, asking interviewees how they feel or what they think. But people can discuss their feelings or describe something without necessarily telling a story.

Let's return to our campus parking example. Perhaps you're interested in how students think about the parking problem at your university, so you interview students about their experiences trying to park their cars and their feelings about it. In the following extract, notice that the student is talking about how she feels. She is not telling a story, although we could imagine this extract appearing within a narrative.

INTERVIEWER: Do you ever park your car on campus?

STUDENT: Yes.

INTERVIEWER: What do you think about the parking problem on this campus?

STUDENT: I hate trying to park on this campus, I really do. It seems like there are lots of parking spaces for faculty and staff, and none for students.

In the preceding extract, notice that there is no *action*—and hence, no story.

Yet interviews can also encourage people to tell stories. By asking open-ended questions about people's experiences, you can often elicit a story in response. In the next extract, notice how the interviewee tells a story about parking on campus with a beginning, a middle, and an end.

INTERVIEWER: Tell me about your experiences parking on campus.

STUDENT: The last time—I was so mad. I was late to class, and I drove to the A lot where there are sometimes a few spaces. I circled around. Nothing. So I went to the B lot. There was a space—not really a space, not a regular space with a line—but a little bit of space where I could squeeze in. I didn't want to miss class, so I just parked. When I came back, my car had been towed. It cost me 50 bucks to get the car back. I was so pissed off.

Notice how in this extract something happened: She went to park her car, there weren't any legal spaces, she parked anyway, and her car was towed.

THE STRUCTURE OF STORIES

Stories have a kind of structure or logic to them. One of the most widely used models for understanding the structure of stories comes from the sociolinguist William Labov (1978; see Coffey and Atkinson 1996, pp. 57–58, for a good summary). Labov argues that all stories have a similar structure. There are six basic elements to a story, which Labov says occur in sequence: abstract, orientation, complication, evaluation, results, and coda (or finish narrative). All stories do not have every single element, but a story must at least have some action. Something must happen in order for a story to occur.

The first element, the *abstract*, provides an introduction to the story. It signals that a story is about to begin. People might introduce the beginning of a story in a variety of ways. "Once upon a time" is a classic way of opening a fairy tale, for example. You know when you hear or read that opener that a particular kind of story is about to follow. Conversation analysts (sociologists who study the structure of conversation) like Harvey Sacks (1974) note that there are some standard ways to "properly" begin a story. Storytellers have to establish, first, that they have the floor, or the right to speak. Small children often begin stories by prefacing them with "You know what?" The typical response, "What?" gives them permission to begin. If you think about it, you can probably come up with a number of ways in which people signal a story. (For starters, how about "You'll never guess what happened to me" or "You won't believe what just happened.")

The second element, the *orientation*, provides basic information: Who was involved? What happened? When? Where? The orientation provides enough information for the listener to figure out the setting and the main actors in the story. Then comes the *complication*: What happened next? How did events become complicated? The complication is a necessary part of stories; without it, there is no way for the story line to advance.

The *evaluation* answers the "so what" question: Why is this important? It helps the listener establish why she or he should hear the storyteller out. Perhaps the story is a cautionary tale or a success story. Or perhaps it is a tale of conversion: I used to be an active drunk, but now I am sober.

The *results* tell what happened at the end—the punch line. Usually, stories resolve in one way or another. A common element of stories is a surprise ending or a twist in the plot, but not all stories have this kind of resolution. Finally, the *coda*, or conclusion, wraps up and lets the listener (or reader) know that the story has ended.

In our parking story, notice the following elements: The abstract is provided in part by the interviewer, who asks the student to tell about her experiences parking on campus. The student signals that she is ready to begin the story by stating, "The last time—I was so mad." The next few lines provide the orientation, in which the student tells how she was late to class and couldn't find a parking space. Then, in the complication, she discusses how she drove to another lot, still couldn't find a legal space, and parked anyway. In the evaluation, she notes that she didn't want to be late to class, implying that looking for a legal space would cause her to be even later. In the results, we find that her car was towed. And in the coda, she lets the interviewee know that her story is finished by closing with, "I was so pissed off."

Abstract: [*Interviewer:* Tell me about your experiences parking on campus.] The last time—I was so mad.

Orientation: I was late to class, and I drove to the A lot where there are sometimes a few spaces. I circled around. Nothing.

Complication: So I went to the B lot. There was a space—not really a space, not a regular space with a line—but a little bit of space where I could squeeze in.

Evaluation: I didn't want to miss class, so I just parked.

Results: When I came back, my car had been towed. It cost me 50 bucks to get the car back.

Coda: I was so pissed off.

Sometimes, storytellers will move back and forth among the various elements before closing. Other times, storytellers will edit their stories (Gubrium and Holstein 1998), changing their perspective and their position within the story. For example, in our parking narrative, the storyteller might draw out the narrative.

> STUDENT: The last time—I was so mad. I was late to class, and I drove to the A lot where there are sometimes a few spaces. I circled around. Nothing. So I went to the B lot. There was a space—not really a space, not a regular space with a line—but a little bit of space where I could squeeze in. I didn't want to miss class, so I just parked. When I came back, my car had been towed. It cost me 50 bucks to get the car back. I was so pissed off. *Now, I know I shouldn't park in spaces like that. Usually, I don't. When people block others from getting in, they really should get towed. But I didn't really think I was in the way.*

In this telling of the story, notice in the italicized sentences how the storyteller shifts perspective. On the one hand, she's angry that she was towed. She didn't want to be late for class, so she squeezed into an illegal space. She invokes a sense of herself as a good student—one who is not late for class—even as she admits to shady parking practices. But as the story continues, notice that she doesn't justify all illegal parking. In fact, she admits that maybe she shouldn't have parked where she did, but she didn't see herself as being "really in the way." Those who are "really in the way" deserve to be towed. In this way, the storyteller shifts her perspective and invites the listener to pay attention to multiple aspects of the parking problem.

OTHER STRUCTURES OF STORIES

Some narrative analysts find the chronological ordering of Labov's model too restrictive (Becker 1999; Gee 1991; Riessman 1993). Rather than simply locating the abstract, orientation, and so forth, they suggest that analysts try to organize the narratives into stanzas, like poems, or try alternative ways for presenting and analyzing the story line.

For example, Bettina Becker (1999) wanted to understand the experiences of older people with chronic pain. She found that the attempt to force some of the narratives of research participants into a strict chronological order made the stories seem less coherent. One research participant in particular, Mrs. Green, seemed to talk in circles and repeat herself. Becker found that transcribing the narrative into stanzas, like a poem, enabled her to capture more clearly the circularity and repetition of the narrative. She also found that the form, because it was unusual (at least within sociology and the social sciences), encouraged a critical reading (Becker 1999), a point that others have argued as well (Richardson 1992; Riessman 1993). It enabled readers to identify with the narrator, Mrs. Green, in a way that more traditional analyses would not. Becker called her transcription of Mrs. Green's story "PAIN STORY: 'Nothing Much'." In the story, Mrs. Green talks about having had arthritis since her thirties. Now in her eighties, she needs a walker (which she calls a "frame") to walk around. She connects her arthritis with her childhood experiences of repeatedly getting wet with her father.

> "Oh no, oh I can't tell you much but,
> I had it since I was about, well thirty I suppose,
> being better getting worse and worse.
>
> "But I mean before that,
> I used to go out and on the rounds with my father
> and get wet, and dry and wet and dry,
> and that's how I think I got it.
>
> "You know all this arthritis and that,
> before I used to get myself wet,
> and then it would dry on me,
> day after day probably,
> when I was out with my father.
>
> "And, it's not until this last year or so,
> that I've been like I am now,
> I could move about more you know,
> and it didn't ache so much.
>
> "But now, it takes me a long time to get around
> and you know, I use this frame now,
> so that's about, you know, all there is really,
> nothing much." (Becker 1999, pp. 77–78)

Notice how placing the story into poetic form creates a very different feel than the more structured narrative of student parking. Mrs. Green's story doesn't lend itself to a chronological analysis. The stanzas seem to contain relatively complete thoughts that give readers insight into Mrs. Green's experience of pain.

Some analysts, such as Laurel Richardson (1992) and Susan Krieger (1991), argue that using fictional devices or poetry may provide greater insight into respondents' life stories than more traditional methods of analysis. Phil Smith (1999) also has explored poetry as an analytic form. He wanted to explore alternative ways of talking about disability, ones that included the voices of disabled people themselves and that broke stereotyped ways of discussing disability. How, he wondered, could he tell people in a more authentic way about the men with developmental disabilities whom he had come to know? He searched for a variety of forms, including fiction, poetry, and songs. Eventually, he came to a story about one of the men, who calls himself Food Truck, which he presented in an article called "Food Truck's Party Hat" (Smith 1999). Smith presents the story in this way: "So here's a story I got from Food Truck. I couldn't help writing it; it wouldn't let me go. It's his story, his words. It's my story, my words. None of it is fiction. It's all fiction" (Smith 1999, p. 248).

The story begins:

> "He looks me square in the face, square as a man can whose head
> doesn't ever stop bobbing and weaving, swooping and diving.
> His head is a butterfly looking for nectar in a field of flowers,
> a swallow in the darkening sky searching out mosquitoes,
> a surfer climbing up and down green waves under a setting sun.
> Food Truck's blue eyes look for mine
> while his smile and almost-white hair slide and weave and float in the
> air in front of me.
> *Boy use jug*
> he says, and grins, and puts the frayed corner of his jacket collar
> into his mouth." (Smith 1999, pp. 248–249)

In this analysis, the line between fact and fiction, and between researcher and researched, is blurred. The resulting story provides far more powerful insight into Food Truck's—and Smith's—reality than could be achieved using other means.

STRUCTURE, STORY, AND SOCIAL CONTEXT

Narrative analysts pay attention to the structure of stories: the way an individual's story is constructed (chronologically or otherwise), the language used, even the pauses and false starts in the narrative. Narrative analysts also pay attention to the story itself—to what is said—and to the social contexts in which the story occurs. Jaber Gubrium and James Holstein (1998) argue that it is difficult to pay attention to all aspects at once. Thus, they outline a technique they call "analytic bracketing" that enables us to focus on one thing at a time. Sometimes, they suggest, we should stop thinking about the story itself (what is being said) and focus on the structure of the story. Other times, we may want to focus more directly on the social contexts in which the story is told.

A Focus on Structure

Again, suppose you're interested in exploring students' stories about parking on campus. Perhaps you have collected a small number of narratives from students. At one level, you might want to focus on the structure of the stories, as we did earlier in this chapter. You might want to identify how the stories begin and how the plot moves forward. In analyzing the stories, you might want to see if the stories unfold in similar ways. Do the students structure their stories similarly? Do they open their stories or end them in a small number of ways? Do they tend to use the same devices for telling the stories? Do they use similar language?

Perhaps there are a relatively few *types* of stories. For example, you may identify a series of narratives about being towed. The stories all center around making a decision to park illegally in a particular place and then returning to the parking lot to find the car towed. Maybe each narrator ends with a variation of "I won't park *there* again." You might read these accounts as *cautionary tales*, stories that warn potential parkers about the consequences of particular courses of action. They may not necessarily serve to warn parkers about all illegal parking, but only certain kinds of illegal parking, such as parking in handicapped spots or in the dean's reserved parking space. You might also identify a series of success stories, stories in which students find a parking spot or avoid getting a ticket. By paying attention to the structure of the stories, you might see that they serve similar purposes.

The Social Contexts of Stories

You might also temporarily bracket, or set aside, concerns with the structure of the stories to focus on the social context. Let's consider again students' stories of parking on campus. Suppose the stories are all collected at a large, geographically dispersed state university campus in which many of the students commute to school. Many students also work at jobs off campus and have families to care for. Thus, their schedules are extremely tight. In this social context, stories about parking take on a different meaning than they might in a small, residential campus in which few students work off campus or have family responsibilities.

In this case, paying attention to the social context will lead you to think about the economy and the students' places within it. The students have to work; otherwise, they can't afford to go to school. Nor can they afford to live on campus. Perhaps there isn't much family housing on campus. Thus, these students need to worry about transportation in ways that residential students might not. Again shifting to the social context, you might focus on the public transportation system in and the layout of the community. What kinds of public transportation are available? Does public transportation run where students need to get? What kind of neighborhood is the university situated in? Where do most of the students live in relation to the school? How does that affect their reliance on the parking lots?

Paying attention to the social contexts in which stories are told can help you frame the stories differently. Two students in different situations might tell exactly the same story of getting towed, but the social contexts in which they tell the stories might differ. For example, one student's parking difficulties might be placed in the context of balancing work and school and family. The story of getting towed reads very differently for this student than for the student who lives on campus and has few other responsibilities. In addition, male and female students might respond differently to the experience of parking in a deserted lot at night. The fear of rape or sexual violence provides a different framing for the women's stories. Again, you have to understand the different social contexts in which narrators construct their particular stories.

You might also think of narrators as drawing on particular *cultural resources* in telling their stories. For example, in my research on lesbian and bisexual women's identity accounts, I found that women told very similar coming-out stories, or stories about how they came to think of themselves as lesbian or bisexual (Esterberg 1997; see also Plummer 1995). In telling their stories, they drew on the culturally available language of "the closet." In modern Western cultures, coming out of the closet has become the predominant way of thinking about developing a lesbian or gay identity. In the particular community I studied, a number of cultural resources were available for organizing lesbian experiences, including coming-out support groups, political action and social groups, and books and newspapers. Women drew on these cultural resources in telling their own stories of becoming lesbian or bisexual.

Another cultural resource that narrators may draw on is a particular form of storytelling. One particularly compelling narrative form in modern

Western culture is the *conversion narrative*, which tells how an individual changes or how one became something else. Marjorie Garber (1995) argues that conversion narratives are particularly appealing because they are so very clear: "I was this, but now I'm that. I was blind, but now I see" (p. 345). Conversion narratives are frequently invoked in evangelical contexts (especially with the context of being "born again"), but they are also invoked in circumstances such as becoming sober or coming out as lesbian or gay. When analyzing stories, you may need to consider whether they fall into a particular form: conversion, success, caution, and so forth.

The Story Itself

Sometimes, you need to pay attention to the stories themselves. This means you bracket thinking about structure and context and focus on the individual's narrative. What is the narrator saying? What is his or her particular story? Even though individuals may use similar narrative structures for telling their stories and may be embedded in similar social contexts, their stories are still, ultimately, their own. Individuals may draw on particular cultural resources for telling stories, yet they do not do so unreflectively. At some level, the stories are personal and individual.

Back to our parking example. Imagine two students, Melody and J. T., who both tell tales of getting towed. Each tale is a cautionary tale; that is, each tale is structured as a kind of warning about parking in a certain kind of place. But the two students choose to emphasize very different aspects of their experience. They use different language and ultimately tell their own individual accounts.

Let's look at Melody's narrative:

"Umm . . . This is so embarrassing, you know? I mean, I don't usually *do* this kind of thing. I mean, I was in the National Honor Society, Miss Goody-Two-Shoes, and all that. I don't even jaywalk! But . . . I was driving to school and I had my friend Karen with me, and we were both going to East Campus. I don't usually park there, you know? S-o-o-o I don't know the rules over there . . . that much. She told me that it was okay to park in the 15-minute spots—you know, the spots, um, for dropping people off and picking them up in front of the library. She said she never gets tickets there. I knew we were going to be gone a couple of hours, but she said it was okay. So when I came back, I was shocked. My car wasn't there. I thought it, it was stolen. But it had been towed. I could have *killed* her. It cost me a ton of money to get the car back, and then I was late for work. I'm never going to listen to her again. Not when she tells me to park in a loading zone."

Notice that Melody opens by stressing how she doesn't usually break the law. Even though she is telling a cautionary tale about parking illegally and getting towed, she stresses how doing "this kind of thing" is out of character for her. She emphasizes that her main mistake was listening to her friend and not paying attention to her own instincts, which would normally lead her to park legally. It's simply not the kind of person she *is*.

In the next narrative, notice that J. T. sees himself as a consumer, and one who is badly served. In his cautionary tale, the main problem is parking in a handicapped spot and "pushing his luck." Getting towed doesn't reflect on the kind of person he is at all.

"Well, if it looks like a spot I'll just park in it. You know, sometimes there are spots that you can fit your car in. There aren't painted lines or anything like that. But you can just kind of squeeze in. Or sometimes, like, I'll park on the grass. Like today, I'm on the grass beside Lot Z. I figure I'm, I'm *paying* for this, you know? I *pay* for my school, so why shouldn't I have a place to park? If there were legal spaces, I'd park there. But . . . you know, it's like they, they don't want you to come to class or something. You can, you can never find a space when you need one.

"One day I was in a *big* hurry. I had a, a test, and I didn't want to be, like, late. So I parked in a handicapped spot. *Big* mistake. I knew that a handicapped spot was kinda pushing it, pushing my luck. They—they towed me. And it took me like two days to get the car back. Next time I guess—hmm, I guess I'll just miss the test."

This narrative only serves to warn drivers not to park in a handicapped spot; it says nothing about not parking in other illegal spots (like on the grass) that, presumably, would entail less risk of getting towed.

In both cases, the students draw on similar cultural resources for storytelling. The contexts in which they need to find a place to park are very similar. But they tell their stories in their own, individual ways. They draw on these resources differently. Melody sees parking as reflecting on the kind of person she is—a "goody-two-shoes," someone who obeys the law and doesn't get into trouble. Getting towed is an embarrassment, an indication that she is not the kind of person she maintains she is. It violates her sense of identity as a law-abiding person. J. T., in contrast, views parking more pragmatically.

Getting towed does not reflect on his conception of himself. Rather, it is an inconvenience, at most an affront to his status as a consumer.

Telling the Story in Other Ways

Of course, stories can be told in a number of different ways. In different contexts, with different audiences, perhaps these students would tell very different parking stories. For example, if J. T. were telling his story to campus police with the hopes that they would forgive his ticket, he might stress how he is normally a law-abiding student. Maybe he would emphasize how sorry he is. If he were telling the story to a group of friends, all of whom shared similar stories, he might emphasize his daring in parking illegally. Thus, the kind of story you tell and the way you tell it depends, in part, on your audience. In that sense, stories are not wholly individual—the property of the story teller (Gubrium and Holstein 1998; Schegloff 1997). They are the products of social interaction.

SOME PRACTICAL ADVICE

To this point, the chapter has offered very little advice on how, practically speaking, you might conduct a narrative analysis. What do you actually do that might be different from, say, the kinds of methods described in Chapter 8? First, you need to identify the beginning and end of the story. This may seem a relatively simple task, but it can be tricky. Sometimes, a story is spread throughout a long interview transcript or is told over a series of interviews held on different days. Choosing different beginnings and endings might lead you to make very different kinds of analyses. For example, go back to J. T.'s parking story. If you see the story as beginning at "One day I was in a big hurry," instead of at "Well, if it looks like a spot I'll just park in it," you will miss important information about how J. T. interprets parking. Is either interpretation necessarily wrong? No. But each will lead you to think in somewhat different ways about J. T.'s parking story.

If you are working with interview transcripts, how you transcribe the tapes is important (Mishler 1991). Catherine Riessman (1993) describes a process of retranscribing narratives for analysis. After going through interview transcripts, she picks out the boundaries of the segments she wants to analyze. She retranscribes those portions of the tape in a special, detailed way. First, she numbers the lines and makes sure that short pauses, utterances of the interviewer (for example, saying "uh huh"), and word repetitions are included in the transcript. Then she works through each clause to see what function it plays—for example to orient the listener to the story or to complicate the events (tell what happened next). This helps her to see the structure of the narrative more clearly.

In the following excerpt, pauses are noted by ellipses (. . .). Each clause begins a new line, and each element has been labeled: "a" for abstract, "o" for orientation, "ca" for complication, "e" for evaluation, "r" for results, and "co" for coda. Notice that there are subtle differences between the earlier excerpt and this one. This one, for example, includes the pauses, repetitions, and interviewer's comments.

1   *Melody:* Umm . . . This is so embarrassing, you know? [a]
2   *Interviewer:* Um hmm.
3   *Melody:* I mean, I don't usually *do* this kind of thing. [o]
4   Umm. I mean, I was in the National Honor Society, [o]
5   Miss Goody-Two-Shoes, and all that. [o]
6   I don't even jaywalk! [o]
7   But . . . I was driving to school [ca]
8   and I had my friend Karen with me, [ca]
9   and we were both going to East Campus. [ca]
10 I don't usually park there, you know? [o]
11 S-o-o-o . . . I don't know the rules over there . . . that much. [o]
12 She told me that it was okay to park in the 15-minute spots— [ca]
13 you know, the spots, um, for dropping people off and picking them up [o]
14 in front of the library. [o]
15 *Interviewer:* Yes.
16 *Melody:* She said she never gets tickets there. [ca]
17 I knew we were going to be gone a couple of hours, [ca]
18 but she said it was okay. [ca]
19 So when I came back, I was shocked. [e]
20 My car wasn't there. [r]
21 I thought it, it was, it was stolen. [r]
22 But . . . it had been towed. [r]
23 I could have *killed* her. [e]
24 It cost me a ton of money to get the car back, [r]

25   and then I was late for work. [r]
26   I'm never going to listen to her again. [co]
27   Not when she tells me to park in a loading zone. [co]

In conducting an analysis of the transcript, you might want to ask your-self a series of questions (Riessman 1993, pp. 60–61):

◆ How is this story told? What is the structure of this story?

◆ What is the story being told? What is the plot? What happened?

◆ Who are the listeners of the story? Why did the storyteller choose to tell the story in this particular way to this particular audience?

◆ How might the story be told differently?

◆ Whose perspectives are privileged in the story? Whose perspectives are left out?

◆ What is the social context in which this story is told? What kinds of social and cultural resources might the storyteller have access to?

◆ What are the potential meanings of this story?

After examining the structure of the narrative, you might also compare a few narratives. In general, narrative analysis is very detail-oriented, painstaking work. Thus, narrative analysts tend to focus on a relatively small number of narratives (rather than, say, hundreds or thousands). Some ana-lysts work with only one or a very few storytellers (see, for example, Lem-pert 1994; Rosie 1993). Still, you may want to compare across narratives. Do all the storytellers tell a similar type of story? For example, are many of the stories about student parking framed as cautionary tales? Are they suc-cess stories? You can ask what kind of function these stories might serve within the particular group.

You should pay particular attention to the power dynamics involved in particular storytelling contexts. For example, Jaber Gubrium and James Holstein (1998) demonstrate how particular social arrangements constrain the kinds of stories that can be told. Job interviews, therapy sessions, and court proceedings are just three of the settings they cite. In court proceed-ings, for example, court officials have the power to determine what is an appropriate story. They can determine whether a speaker is off the subject or can continue speaking, and they can stop a speaker from continuing in a particular direction. In these kinds of situations, a narrative analyst would need to pay attention to the power issues involved.

EVALUATING NARRATIVES

How can you tell whether a particular narrative analysis is a "good" one? On what grounds might you decide whether an analysis is useful? Should narratives establish some overarching "truth"? Or do you simply hope that a particular narrative is logical or coherent or plausible? What if subjects lie? In the telling of stories, which are often intended to amuse or entertain, what constitutes a lie, anyway? Is exaggerating the size of a fish in a fishing story lying? And, even if exaggerated, how might the stories tell you something useful about the social world?

First, stories always presuppose a point of view, or perspective. Because stories are the products of an interaction between storyteller and audience (even if that audience is an interviewer), they always involve a selection or sifting of the facts as the storyteller sees them. With other audiences, at other times, the storyteller might emphasize very different events. Clearly, other storytellers will tell somewhat different stories, based on their different experiences. You can never hope, then, that any particular story or narrative (or any analysis of it) will tell "the" one truth. In conducting a narrative analysis, your goal is to try to interpret the possible meanings of the narrative. Thus, you hope that the analysis is plausible.

Catherine Riessman (1993) suggests that we evaluate narrative analyses in terms of (1) whether they are persuasive, (2) whether they correspond to research participants' understandings of events, (3) whether they are coherent, and (4) whether they are useful. In terms of the first dimension, you might ask whether the narrative analysis seems plausible or convincing or reasonable (Riessman 1993, p. 65). A more plausible analysis would be grounded, for example, in the storyteller's own words. If you are making a case that a narrative has a particular meaning, you might want to show how you considered (and rejected) other interpretations. You might provide a documentation of how you conducted the analysis so that others can determine whether your analysis is reasonable. For Riessman, this involves making the transcripts available to other researchers. (Some scholars might include the transcripts, or at least portions of them, as an appendix to the analysis.)

Second, you might evaluate narrative analyses in terms of whether they correspond to the storytellers' understandings of events. You might want to present your analyses to your research participants to see if they, too, find your interpretations plausible. These kinds of "member checks" are increasingly common. Still, Riessman (1993) cautions that sometimes participants won't agree with your interpretations. Maybe the context shifts; maybe their understandings change. If participants disagree with your analyses, it may not signal that the interpretation is necessarily a bad one. But it should at least spark a reconsideration.

Third, you might ask if an analysis is logical or coherent. Does it seem internally consistent? Does it seem consistent with the storyteller's aims? What did the storyteller hope to accomplish by telling the story?

Finally, you might ask if the analysis is useful. Does it help you understand social life in a particular way? Might the research help others understand a particular social process? What does this story help you see about the individual and the social world?

QUESTIONS FOR THOUGHT

1. Think of something that has happened to you recently. Imagine how you would go about telling the story of what happened to a friend of yours. Now imagine telling the story to a parent, to a teacher, to a police officer, and to a small child. How would the story change for these different audiences?

2. Think of some experiences that you share in common with other students (living on campus, eating in the cafeterias, going to class, and so forth).How might the social context in which you do this activity be different from that of other students? In what ways are you similar? How might your stories be different, based on your different life situations?

EXERCISES

1. Select an interview that you have conducted or a portion of your field notes. (If you don't have access to either, interview a fellow student and transcribe the interview.) Find the beginning and end of a story. Retranscribe the selected portion, making sure that all pauses, repetitions, and so forth are included. Try to identify the structure of the story using the elements on pages 183–184.

2. Look through one or more magazines or newspapers. See if you can identify a cautionary tale and a success story.

3. Go back to the narrative you analyzed in Exercise 1. Analyze the social context surrounding the story. What kinds of cultural resources does the storyteller bring to the telling?

4. Again use the narrative you analyzed in Exercise 1. Try presenting it in different forms—for example, in stanzas. Do you have a different interpretation or see different things in the story when it is presented in this way?

SUGGESTIONS FOR FURTHER READING

Becker, Bettina. "Narratives of Pain in Later Life and Conventions of Storytelling." *Journal of Aging Studies* 13(1):73–87.

Coffey, Amanda, and Paul Atkinson. "Narratives and Stories." Chapter 3 in *Making Sense of Qualitative Data: Complementary Research Strategies.* Thousand Oaks, CA: Sage, 1996.

McAdams, Dan. P. *The Stories We Live By: Personal Myths and the Making of the Self.* New York: Guilford Press, 1993.

Riessman, Catherine Kohler. *Narrative Analysis.* Thousand Oaks, CA: Sage, 1993.

Smith, Phil. "Food Truck's Party Hat." *Qualitative Inquiry* 5(2):244–261.

10

Writing About Research

As I sit upstairs in my office, thinking about how to begin a chapter on writing research reports, my daughter Katie Ren sits downstairs learning to write. She painstakingly forms the letters in her 5-year-old's handwriting. After a while, she proudly brings her work up to me. "Read it," she says. "It's a shopping list." Much of it is unintelligible (ELMY, CILUGH), but other words are apparent: BOY, KEY, ROSE, DOG, CAT. Some of it I think I can read if I stretch my imagination: TOOFFU is probably TOFU. Other words she probably got help with or copied from somewhere: FIRE CHIEF. A shopping list. We should go to a store and buy these things.

Of course, her list is not really intelligible as a shopping list, a list of things that one could really buy from a store. She laughs at the absurdity of buying a boy at the store, although she also thinks that buying a rose (with a vase) is an excellent idea. She loves the idea of slipping in a dog (preferably a poodle) with the rest of the groceries. But what does her list have to do with "real" shopping lists, which include things like milk and tofu and eggs and rice and green beans on them? Simply, making a list is one of the things that you *do* with words. Calling a bunch of seemingly unrelated words a shopping list gives them some kind of meaning in relation to one another.

In a similar way, you have probably learned a formula for writing up research reports—another way of giving words meaning. Somewhere in your schooling, you learned how to write an essay with an introduction and a conclusion. Using a variety of techniques, you learned more or less successfully how to research an idea and present it in a way acceptable to a teacher. But writing isn't merely a way of presenting what you already know. It is also way of creating meaning. It's a way of developing—figuring out—what you think.

This chapter focuses on some ways to think about your writing and present your qualitative research. But it won't provide a formula, a format that you can "pour" the contents into. There are some standard conventions for writing about qualitative research, which we will discuss in this chapter, but there is also much greater flexibility than in many other kinds of social science writing.

WRITING AS A PROCESS

By now, you have probably done a great deal of work on a research project. You have collected data and written field notes and interviewed individuals and examined texts. If you've been following my suggestions, you have done a fair amount of writing already, including notes and memos and beginning drafts of an analysis. Writing up a final report isn't a wholly new and separate activity, then; it's more a matter of sifting through and extending the writing you've already done.

It's helpful to think of writing as a process. (This is nothing new—most composition texts present it in this way, too.) Despite what you may think, even experienced writers don't write perfect drafts the first time. Writers typically go through many drafts. They may begin with scratched notes or a rough idea of what they want to say and then create a series of increasingly polished drafts. For example, by the time you read this chapter, it will have gone through at least four drafts. Every writer's process is different. One of the things I'll do in this chapter is describe how *I* go about writing. My aim is not for you to emulate my own way of writing, but for you to think about your own habits and how you can develop your own writing process.

One of the hardest things about writing a qualitative research report for many of my students is that they can't do it in one night, in one draft. My guess is that many of you became accustomed during high school (and maybe even college) to beginning a draft of a paper the night before it was due. Once finished, you simply turned the draft in. Some of you may have done a quick proofread or edit, but others may not have bothered to read the complete draft before handing it in. This simply won't work for a longer paper. I remember vividly the first time I had to write a longer paper—something like ten or twelve pages—and I realized that a single all-night session wasn't going to be enough. When you write a long paper like a research report, you need to begin much earlier than you may think. The Sociology Writing Group at UCLA (1991) suggests that about 50 percent of your time in a qualitative field project will be spent in writing up analyses, and that about 30 percent of your time will be spent writing up the final report. The rest of your time is spent collecting data. Think about how much time that may be in a semester or quarter. And you will need to go through multiple drafts before you have a draft that is polished and ready to turn in.

Sitting Down to Write: Just Do It

Most people think that professional writers write effortlessly, and maybe some do. I remember hearing that romance novelist Barbara Cartland used to dictate her stories to a secretary while she was lying in bed. The secretary would type up the final—and only—draft. But even if that's an accurate description of her writing style (which at least some observers doubt), most of us have to work through a much more labored process. Most of us have to slog through bad days in which writing a paragraph, let alone a whole essay, is a chore. Most of us have to work through multiple drafts before we can come up with something that feels finished. Even published writers think about how to make their work happen—how to set aside the time and space to write.

You may find it helpful to think about physical routines you can develop to help you get started and to create a more productive work environment. Also, consider the different places where and times when you have tried to write papers. Where do you seem best able to write—at the kitchen table, or in the library, or in your dormitory room? What is the best time for you to write—late at night, after everyone else has gone to sleep, or early in the morning? What do you need to do to begin—clean off your desk, or organize your sock drawers, or simply plunge right in? If you can figure out when your best time and place for writing is, try to consistently block out that time for your writing.

I usually write best in my office at home. My desk faces the window, which I like to look out of when I'm stuck. My desk is a kitchen countertop plopped on top of two file cabinets. The best thing about it, though, is that it's the right height. I have a "real" desk, but I can't write at it because it's too high. Although I can, if I have to, write in a library, libraries tend to be too self-consciously quiet for me to write well in them. Also, I often like to move around and read what I've written out loud. (You might want to try this; it helps you hear the rhythm of your writing.) Doing that at the library might bother other people, though, or make them think that I'm peculiar. I don't like to write at my office at school. I can't look out the window there, and I'm more likely to be interrupted by the phone or by visitors, which makes it harder for me to concentrate.

Why should you care about how I write? You shouldn't. My routines aren't very interesting. (Now, if I had to stand on my head and eat four red M&Ms, that might be interesting!) My goal in writing about them is to help you to think about how you can structure your own environment so that it facilitates your writing. Do you need bright lights? Dim lighting? A stash of Skittles or a good cup of coffee? Can you turn your pager or cell phone off? For most writers, finding places where other people won't distract them is important. For many of us, this means getting up early or staying up late or finding odd places to write in.

Also think about the things you do to avoid writing. Do you compulsively check your e-mail, or run a virus scan on your hard drive, or turn on the television merely to see what you're missing? Do you clean out the cat box or wash the kitchen floor? Try to be aware of what stops you from getting your work done. As much as you physically can, pamper yourself while you're writing. Try to give yourself whatever you need to make your environment facilitate your writing.

Beginning Writing

For many writers, the hardest thing is simply beginning to write—actually sitting down and putting the first few words on the page or on the screen. This difficulty might be compounded by the feeling that you don't know what to say, that you can't begin writing until you know exactly what you want to say. If you think of writing as a process of discovery—a way of making meaning—it may take some of the pressure off. You don't need to know exactly what you want to say before you begin. You'll discover it as you go along.

Jotting Notes

I often find it useful to begin by jotting down some notes about my topic. I might jot down some key ideas or merely write about how I don't want to be writing about what I'm supposed to be writing about. If I'm stuck, I might write, "This section is about . . ." and try to go from there. My only goal is to get myself started thinking and writing about the topic. At that stage, I am not looking to write something polished. I don't pay any attention to spelling or even paragraphing, and I sometimes write in incomplete sentences. After I've written a bunch of notes, I step back and try to create a kind of rough outline for the section.

Finding Direction: Making a Writing Plan

At this stage, I like to develop a rough sense of where the report is going. Usually, I make a plan for my writing. I estimate how many sections I'll need, and I give them titles. I also estimate how many pages I'll need for each section. Of course, I can always ditch the plan if it isn't working, and I often change things as I go along. A writing plan isn't the same thing as a formal outline, with numbered and lettered headings and subheadings. That kind of outline feels *too* restrictive for me. Still, I find it helpful to establish some direction for my writing. Especially if I'm working on a long report, having a plan helps me break it down into more manageable sections. The thought of writing a whole report (never mind a book!) might feel intimidating. Writing a brief section of a page or two may seem more doable. (Other writers find any kind of outline too restricting; you should experiment and see what works for you.)

Writing a First Draft

After I have a rough sense of where the report is going, I try to write relatively complete (though not polished) paragraphs. Sometimes, I start at the beginning; other times, I start in the middle or with whichever section seems least daunting. At this stage, everything is still changeable. My main goal is to get a more or less complete (though rough) draft done. I try not to focus too much on the niceties of language. When I get stuck, I read over what I've already written from the start, adding more as I go along. In this way, my drafts grow incrementally. When my first draft is complete, the beginning of it is usually pretty polished. (It should be—I've usually gone over it a number of times.) But the end is generally much rougher.

Revising and Editing

Revising doesn't mean simply fixing punctuation and spelling errors and typos. It means, literally, reseeing what you've written. Revising entails reading what you've written looking for the logic of your argument. It may mean adding sections, taking sections out, and reorganizing. I usually go through two or more revisions before deciding I'm done.

After you have completed an initial draft, you may find it helpful to put it down for a little while. Leave it overnight if you can, or go for a cup of coffee or a run or whatever helps to clear your head. Then read it carefully (I often find it helpful to read it out loud). It may also help to have someone else read it and give you feedback. First, check the logic or structure of your paper. Does the overall organization make sense? Is it logical? Are all the parts in order? You might find it helpful to write an "after the fact" outline. That is, outline what you wrote. Make a heading for each major section and for each paragraph in the section. This can help you make sure that the organization of the paragraphs makes sense.

Only after you've worked on the overall organization does it make sense to look at the level of the paragraph and then at the sentence. At the paragraph level, check to make sure that you've provided adequate support for your argument. If you make a claim, you need to provide evidence to back it up. Also check that you have the right amount of information in each paragraph. Sometimes, people try to pack too many topics in one paragraph. If that's the case, you may need to take some out or to break the paragraph up into two shorter paragraphs.

Finally, work at the sentence level. Check to make sure the grammar and mechanics are correct. Check spelling, usage, and your citations. Especially if you know you have a problem (for example, with spelling), have a friend or tutor read your work and help you edit. Many schools provide writing tutors. But even if your school doesn't, you can find a friend or family member to serve as an editor. An editor can help you spot problems with spelling and grammar and logic. More importantly, an editor can help ensure that what you meant to say is what you actually said. Be sure to pick an editor who will give you helpful feedback. Sometimes, friends or family members are afraid to be critical. It's not very helpful to have a friend read over your work quickly and tell you it's fine if it really needs some work.

One of the biggest problems my students have is wordiness—using too many words (or too many unnecessary big words) so that the writing seems bloated. One exercise you may find useful is to take a pen and see how many words you can delete. You'd be surprised at how many words you can get rid of without changing your meaning.

As a final step in this stage, I recommend that you read the report out loud. How does it sound? Does it have a rhythm? Does it sound wordy or awkward? Does one section seem to flow smoothly into the next? Do you find yourself tripping over your words? Do you need to revise to make it sound better?

Proofreading

After revising and editing, I do a final check for typos, spelling and grammar errors, and so forth. How many drafts should you work through? It depends on your own writing process. I strongly recommend you work through at least two drafts: an initial rough draft and a revised and more polished one. Box 10.1 gives a revision checklist.

BOX 10.1 Revision Checklist

I. The Big Picture
  1. Is the structure of your argument logical?
  2. Is your paper well organized?
  3. Have you provided enough evidence? Is your argument believable?
  4. Is your paper interesting?
  5. Is your paper written at the appropriate level for your audience?
  6. Do you include all the necessary sections?
  7. Have you included all appendixes?

II. Some Writing Issues
  1. Do you use a consistent voice throughout the paper? If there are different voices in the paper, do they work with each other or against each other?
  2. Is the paragraphing appropriate (usually one topic per paragraph)?
  3. Are there appropriate transitions between and within paragraphs? Do you use transition words and phrases to help readers follow your argument?

III. Grammar, Mechanics, Spelling, and Punctuation
  1. Have you proofread the paper for grammar and mechanics—for things like complete sentences, subject-verb agreement, and comma usage?
  2. Have you spell-checked the paper?
  3. Are your citations in appropriate form? Are all paraphrases and direct quotations appropriately credited? Have you double-checked to make sure that all necessary references are included?
  4. If you included appendixes, have you mentioned them in the body of the paper?

AUDIENCES AND VENUES

Writing is not only a process of discovering (or developing) what you think but also a means of communication. Although some writing is personal, intended only for your own use, a qualitative research report usually will be read by others. After all, you have done all that work of collecting and analyzing qualitative data. You now have to think about how to share your work with others. In doing so, you need to think about who your audience or your intended readers are.

There are many different audiences you might consider. Often, academics are a major audience for qualitative research. A great deal of qualitative research is written with them in mind. But practitioners (such as social workers or educators) and the general public are also potential audiences. For example, if you have been studying workers in a homeless shelter, the shelter staff may be very interested in what you found. Perhaps you have been studying personal networks among international students (Sia 2000). If so, the international student office at your school might be interested in the results. Perhaps you have been conducting an evaluation of a program or doing participatory action research with a group of activists. If you have received sponsorship from a particular group or organization, they will probably expect a report. In all of these cases, you need to consider how to frame your results in ways that are useful to those audiences.

If you are writing for other academics, there are a number of venues in which you may present your work. Academics present their research at professional conferences (like the annual meetings of the American Sociological Association and the Midwest Sociological Society), in scholarly journals, and in books. As a rule (though there are exceptions), academic writing tends to be more formal than writing for a general audience. In academic writing, you usually need to include information about the methods and theories you used. In writing aimed at a general audience, you generally write more informally and include less information about your methodology. (You might notice, for example, that some books based on ethnographic or interview data include a section on methods in the appendix; that way, the more academically inclined reader can find out more and the general reader can ignore it.) If you are writing for practitioners or a business audience, you may find that you need to write more concisely. Practitioners tend to be very busy people, without a lot of time to waste. Thus, your main findings should be condensed.

This chapter focuses primarily on writing for an academic audience. If you are writing a paper for a class, it may help to imagine an audience that consists of other beginning social science researchers, like yourself. Assume that your audience doesn't know very much about your particular topic but does know a little bit about the process of conducting social research. Thus, your audience will want information about the specific methods and procedures you used but will not need to be told, for example, specifically what a focus group or an interview or a participant observation is.

You should also assume that your reader is a bit skeptical. Your reader doesn't believe anything on faith, but instead wants to see enough of your data and methodology to come to her own conclusions about your findings.

Thus, you will need to document your assertions with evidence and ground your research in the larger body of social research.

USEFUL WAYS TO STRUCTURE QUALITATIVE RESEARCH

Qualitative research reports traditionally have been more flexible than reports of quantitative research. This is, in part, a product of necessity. Because qualitative researchers cannot fall back on tables or numbers or charts to present their data, their words have to convey the analysis. Thus, qualitative researchers have to think more carefully about how they say things than quantitative researchers do. They have to pay attention to language.

In recent years qualitative researchers have begun to present their work in more creative formats (Richardson 2000). Some qualitative researchers have begun to experiment with fiction and poetry (for example, Denzin 2000; Krieger 1991). Others have experimented with dialogue and personal narratives (Denzin 1998; Ellis 1998; Ellis and Bochner 2000; Ronai 1992). These innovative ways of presenting research are often depicted as an alternative to the traditional research report. And they are. But it still helps to have a sense of what a traditional research report looks like.

A traditional research report typically has these parts: title (don't forget to make a title page), abstract, introduction, review of the literature, data and methods section, findings, and conclusion. References are usually included in a separate list of works cited. Sometimes, appendixes will present additional information at the end of the paper.

Title and Abstract

The title should give a good sense of what the paper is about. Ideally, it should be catchy as well, inviting the reader to pick up the report and jump in. You might want to scan the titles in the references of this book. Which ones seem to give you a good idea of what the article or book is about? Which ones are more obscure?

The *abstract* is a brief description (less than 250 words) of the main points of the paper. It should include a summary of the most important things you found, the evidence you cite, and an indication of how you analyzed the data. Essentially, an abstract should give a potential reader just enough information to decide whether to read the paper.

In very traditional academic writing, authors are counseled not to use personal pronouns (like "I" or "we") in abstracts (or, indeed, throughout the body of the paper). This has led to a tendency to write abstracts in the passive voice ("It was found that . . ."). The use of the passive voice tends to imply that no one actually did the research; it somehow merely appeared or "was found." But I strongly recommend writing in the active voice. It's better to use "we" or "I" to show that a real person did the research.

The following is an abstract of an article that appeared in the journal *Gender & Society.* Although a little unwieldy, the title describes what the article is going to talk about: "Gender and Emotion in the Advocacy for Breast Cancer Informed Consent Legislation." The abstract is short—less than 150 words—and gives a summary of the full article.

This is a qualitative study of the role of gender and emotion in a political setting. The data are from interviews of activists and legislators, as well as from archival accounts of the debates in state legislatures about breast cancer informed consent legislation. I found that proponents for and against the legislation shared the belief that women are more emotional than men. This social belief shaped the political strategies the activists adopted and initially contributed to their effectiveness; however, their opponents claimed that the women activists should be dismissed because their emotionalism made them irrational. I close by discussing Western cultural beliefs about emotions, social stereotypes regarding women, and their consequences for women activists in political arenas. (Montini 1996, p. 9)

Notice how the author includes a brief description of the approach she has taken to her topic (the focus on the role of emotions and gender). She describes her data sources (interviews and archival research) and sketches out her main finding: that beliefs about women's greater emotionalism both helped and hindered the movement for legislation.

Introduction

Just as its name implies, the *introduction* should introduce readers to your topic. It should give them a hint about what is to follow and entice them to continue. You might want to think of an introduction as a slippery banana peel. You want readers to "slip" on your introduction and "fall into" the next section.

In qualitative research, you have a number of options for your introduction. Beginning writers are often counseled to begin with a general statement and move to the specific. In the introduction, this might take the form of documenting why the topic of your paper is of general interest and then moving on to the specifics of your study. You can use this kind of standard opener for a qualitative research report, but you have other, more creative options available as well. For example, you might begin with a specific case or a story about a research participant that illustrates the main points you will be discussing. You might begin with a story about how you entered the field or encountered the problem. Or you might begin by setting the scene: describing your field setting.

Notice how Joshua Gamson begins his study of tabloid television talk shows:

> Let's begin here: talk shows are bad for you, so bad you could catch a cold. Turn them off, a women's magazine suggested in 1995, and turn on Mother Teresa, since watching her 'caring feelings' radiate from the screen, according to psychologist Dr. David McClelland of Harvard, has been shown to raise the level of an antibody that fights colds. (1998, p. 3)

Notice how this beginning pulls us in. We want to know whether Gamson really means this. It also sets up a discussion of his aims, which he outlines in his opening chapter.

Josepha Schiffman uses a slightly different technique in her study of grassroots peace organizations. She begins with a scene from her field site:

> It's a rainy San Francisco night, and an affinity group of Bay Area Peace Test (BAPT) is meeting to plan an upcoming act of civil disobedience. One woman volunteers to facilitate, and the group collectively constructs an agenda. First they deliberate alternative actions, making sure that everyone has a chance to express an opinion. They also discuss how they're going to maintain a sense of community in the Nevada desert, how they will support each other through the various hardships they're likely to encounter: radioactive dust, dehydration, possible police brutality. The meeting ends with an evaluation of the group's process, and finally, holding hands, they sing a freedom song. (1991, p. 58)

This introduction gives us a sense of the group. Schiffman then moves on to a description of the second organization she is studying, followed by a more theoretical description of her aims in the article.

Compare these introductions to Theresa Montini's introduction to her article on breast cancer informed consent legislation:

> This article is a qualitative study of the role of gender and emotion in a political setting, taking as a case example women's activism for

breast cancer informed consent laws. I studied former breast cancer patients who worked for the passage of breast cancer informed consent legislation in their state legislatures during the decade of the 1980s. A breast cancer informed consent law specifies that after a woman is diagnosed with cancer, but before she is treated for cancer, her practitioner will give her information regarding the various treatments that are available and appropriate to treat her cancer and gain her specific consent for the administration of the treatment. The procedure may sound like standard protocol in any practitioner-patient encounter, but it is not. Public concern prompted legislation to be introduced in 22 states and passed in 15 during the 1980s. (1996, p. 9)

Which introduction is best? It depends on a number of factors, including individual preferences in writing style, the audience, and the kinds of data that follow. If you have been conducting participant observation, for example, a personal account of how you first encountered the group may be more fitting. If you have been conducting a textual analysis, that kind of personal story may not feel appropriate.

Literature Review

At some point in your report, you have to link your work to the broader research on your topic. In more traditionally organized papers, the literature review is included as a separate section, usually near the beginning. In this section, you outline the main controversies in the literature. You note the main questions other researchers have asked, the theories and methodologies they used, and the results they obtained. Your goal is to show how your work fits into the larger body of research. You need to think about how your work relates to the main controversies and debates in the field. Does it challenge existing ways of thinking about the topic? Does it extend previous studies? Does it try out a new methodology? Does it use a new field setting or source of data? When well done, a literature review section leads readers to think that your work is a natural and logical step in research about the topic.

I strongly recommend that you organize your literature review thematically—that is, according to the main themes or debates within the literature. For example, you might open with "There are three main controversies in this field: A, B, and C." You can then discuss how each of the studies you've found relates to A, B, and C. You may want to be critical. For example, if some of the research is badly done, explain the shortcomings. If some studies seem to contradict others, try to resolve the seeming contradiction. Perhaps a new theory or new technique will solve some of the pressing problems identified in the literature.

Sometimes, qualitative researchers use the literature review section to outline a theoretical perspective. Because qualitative research typically focuses on a small number of cases or on a unique field setting, there may not be a large body of research on exactly the same topic to draw on. A researcher might want to explore how a particular theoretical perspective might help shed light on her or his case. For example, Theresa Montini (1996) was interested in using a sociology-of-emotions perspective to understand a particular social movement: the movement to gain informed consent laws for breast cancer patients.

The literature review should help your readers understand the context for your research. A badly written literature review can be the most boring section of the report. No one wants to read through pages and pages of sentences that all sound something like "Author X found Y; then author Z found Q. Author A found B, and author C found D." Here's a hint: If you are bored writing this section, then your readers will be bored reading it.

Sources of Data and Methodology

The next section of the paper typically deals with the question of methods. This section should include a description of the field setting, if you did an ethnographic study, or whatever other data source you used. Methodologists sometimes say that this section should provide enough information that someone else, armed with your report, could replicate your research. Of course, in qualitative research, this clearly isn't possible. If you observed in a field setting during a particular time and place, that time has passed already. A new researcher entering the field will encounter a changed setting, even if the only apparent change was the entrance (and exit) of the former researcher. In addition, observational research depends on the personal relationships between the researcher and those being researched. In this sense, qualitative research cannot be replicated. You cannot duplicate the exact relationships and events that occurred. Still, you should give enough information in your methods section that another researcher could *try* to approximate what you accomplished. In general, you need to discuss the particular methodological choices you made and the reasons you made them. If there were particular issues related to confidentiality or protection of the research participants, you should describe these as well.

Sources of Data   First, you need to discuss the source of your data. If you conducted interviews, you should specify how you located interviewees, how many interviews you conducted, with whom, and under what circumstances. You should also specify where the interviews were conducted, how long they lasted, how structured they were, and whether they were taped and transcribed. When it's relevant, you should also include demographic information about the interviewees: age, sex, race, and so forth.

If you analyzed documents or other material artifacts, you should state what kinds of documents or artifacts you used and address issues of data collection. How did you find these artifacts for analysis? Are there any particular problems with the artifacts? For example, are parts missing? Are there problems of authenticity? If you are using a series of magazines or newspapers or other published materials, you should include information on the issues selected. Why did you select the particular issues you did? Are there missing issues? Why?

If you conducted observational research, you should include a description of your setting and how you gained access to it. You should specify for how long a period you observed and during what specific times. You should include basic information about what you did during the period of observation. For example, if you observed in a public place, did you openly take notes?

Methods of Analysis   You should also describe the procedures you used for analyzing the data. Did you conduct a content analysis, or analyze your interviews for the main themes, or use a grounded theory approach? In comparison to quantitative researchers, qualitative researchers tend to give much less information about how they analyzed their data. Still, you should at least mention any specific procedures you used. If you used a software program for qualitative data analysis, you should mention the name of the program and any related details that seem helpful. Again, keep in mind that your main goal is to help other researchers understand what you did.

How much detail is enough? How much is too much? You might find it helpful to imagine potential readers for your research. In general, you can assume that your readers are much like yourself. They have a basic understanding of qualitative methods, just as you do. They don't need to be told, then, exactly what participant observation is or what an interview is. You can assume that they know. But because there are different kinds of interviews, they need to know what kind you used. They don't need to be told what observation *is;* they need to know how you accomplished it within a particular context.

The Main Body: Findings

The main body of your report should focus on your findings. This section should be the heart of your paper. It's what you've spent most of your time trying to figure out, after all.

The main body can be structured in a variety of ways, depending on your research. Sometimes, researchers organize this section according to the main themes they found in their analysis. Let's say, for example, that you found two distinct styles of leadership in your observation of a student organization. You might want to organize your findings around the two different styles you found. Or suppose that, in your analysis of the image of teenagers in the news media, you found four main ways that teenagers are portrayed. You might want to organize your findings around those four ways.

Another way you might organize your findings is as a narrative, especially if you have been conducting participant observation. In this case, your main goal is to tell an ethnographic story. You might choose, for example, to tell the story of one of your research participants, or you might tell the story of a specific event. The story serves to highlight something important you discovered in the field. If you choose this strategy, ask yourself: What is the most important story I want to tell? How can I tell it in a way that will be believable? If you organize your results as a narrative, you may find yourself weaving your analysis of it into the story. (Remember, the analysis is the "so what" part; it tells why this story is important.) Or you might decide to place your analysis in a separate section, following the story itself.

However you organize this section, remember to include support for your analysis. This support should be in the form of examples from your research, including quotations from your interviews or field notes and excerpts from your documents. How many examples is enough? How many are too much? There are no magic numbers. You need to include enough examples so that your analysis is believable. But you don't want to include so many that readers will get bored or lose the thread of your story.

As you're writing this section, you need to think about levels of generality. At the broadest level, you can make *universal statements*, statements that are meant to be about "human nature." As a rule, most qualitative researchers hesitate to make these kinds of claims—and for good reason. We simply don't have the kind of data (or maybe the chutzpah) to make such claims. At the other end of the spectrum, you can make very specific statements about a particular incident or a particular person. In qualitative writing, you typically have to move back and forth between different levels of generality. You can use specific statements about incidents or persons to try to back up broader theoretical claims. And you can use the insights from the data you collected to reflect on (or at least generate ideas about) larger groups of people.

Because the main body is usually the longest section of your report, you may want to create headings to divide the different parts within it. Headings help readers figure out where your argument is going. They're like street signs: although you may be able to figure out where you are without them, it's much easier if you have them.

Summary and Conclusion

The summary and conclusion should, just as the name implies, briefly summarize your most important points. You don't need to discuss *everything* you found, just the most important points. In this section, you might also discuss the implications of your research. Are there any policy implications? Is further research indicated? What next steps might researchers want to take?

List of References and Appendixes

At the end of your report, you should include a list of references, providing publication information for all works cited in the text. Different academic disciplines have different styles for referencing others' work. Most journals and publishers have specific guidelines for the format of citations. In general, sociologists tend to use parenthetical style rather than footnotes. That is, they include the author and the year (and page number, if they are quoting directly or paraphrasing) within the body of the text and provide the full citation in a separate section at the end of the report. I strongly recommend that you consult a writing handbook or style guide to make sure you use the correct format. Sociology students may want to obtain a copy of the *Style Guide of the American Sociological Association*, which is available from the American Sociological Association (www.asanet.org).

What should you reference in the text? In general, you need to provide citations to acknowledge the work of other authors. If you use someone else's written ideas in your own report without acknowledging the source, that is *plagiarism*—whether you intended to plagiarize or not. You should always include a citation when you make a direct quotation from someone else's work. You should also include a citation when you paraphrase another author (that is, restate their idea in your own words). Consider these examples:

> Direct quote: "Careful citation is important because plagiarism is burglary—cheating which presents another writer's words or ideas as if they were your own" (Sociology Writing Group 1991, p. 45).

Paraphrase: According to the Sociology Writing Group (1991, p. 45), plagiarism can be considered a form of burglary or theft because it involves passing someone else's words off as your own. To avoid plagiarism, writers should be careful in their citations.

When in doubt, it's a good idea to err on the side of inclusion. That is, it's better to provide a citation that you may not really need than to omit one that you do.

After the list of references, you may want to provide various appendixes to your report. These may include, for example, a map of your field site, a list of questions or topics covered in interviews, photographs from a magazine or other text you have been analyzing, or any other supplemental information that might be of use to your readers. You don't want to include too much, however. For example, you probably shouldn't provide complete transcripts of all your interviews, although you might want to include portions. (If you are doing a narrative analysis, you should probably include portions of the transcripts.)

MAKING WRITING VIVID

The best qualitative writing is vivid. It tells a gripping story; it provides an insightful analysis; it tells us something vital. The best qualitative writing is like a good story, a page turner you have to stay up all night to finish. Why, then, as Laurel Richardson (2000) asks, is so much qualitative writing so boring? Partly, she answers, because we have not "put ourselves in our own texts" (p. 925). We have not developed our own voices but have, instead, relied on formulaic and scientized ways of writing.

One of the challenges of qualitative writing is trying to tell the story in your own words. How can you find an authentic voice of your own in which to write? This is a tricky proposition, of course, for you may have been taught over the years *not* to do this. Thus, many students (and professional sociologists as well) avoid using "I" or "we." They use too much jargon and inaccessible language, thinking that this will make them sound more "educated." They "puff up" their writing with extraneous words. Many use the passive voice (for example, "It was found that . . .") in order to make their work seem more "objective." These are all things you should avoid.

The only way you can develop your own voice is to write a lot. (Reading a lot helps, too.) Practically speaking, you may find that keeping a journal is one way to get that kind of practice. You should also try to avoid jargon. If you can use a short word, why use a longer one? If the longer word is more precise, then by all means use it. But if the short word serves just as well, use it. It will make your writing leaner and help readers move through it faster. My guess is, as well, that you are more likely to speak and think in shorter words; they may be closer to your own personal voice. It may also help to refer to yourself in the first person ("I" or, if appropriate, "we"). It sounds awkward and a little arrogant to refer to yourself as "this author."

Another way to make your report more compelling is to tell the story in your research participants' own words. Often, a direct quotation or story will make the point better than you could otherwise. Susan Krieger (1983), for example, chose to structure her book-length exploration of identity in a lesbian community using only the voices of her research participants. Except for the first chapter, her entire book consists of carefully selected quotations and paraphrases from the interviews she conducted. Although this is an unusual strategy (most researchers speak in their own voices as well), it highlights the possibilities for creating an analysis out of the participants' own words. Whether you attempt a more experimental or more traditional text, try to weave the voices of your participants into your writing. See if you can make your research participants visible throughout the text.

OTHER GENRES OF QUALITATIVE RESEARCH

Certainly, there are other ways to write qualitative research. As I have mentioned at various points, some qualitative scholars have experimented with fiction, poetry, dialogue, and a variety of other styles. Critics of more conventional techniques argue that traditional scientific writing is dry and dull and that it takes the person out of the research (Ellis and Bochner 2000). These critics argue that the new techniques for presenting qualitative research, like autoethnography, poetry, and fiction, are a way to "merge art and science" (Ellis and Bochner 2000, p. 761). Some critics, like Norman Denzin (2000), maintain that the boundaries between fiction and nonfiction, ethnography and story, and poetry and performance art are artificial—they are all social and political constructions (p. 899).

Qualitative scholars still debate the place of fiction, poetry, and autobiography in qualitative research (see, for example, Gans 1999; Karp 1999; Plummer 1999; Whyte 1996). In general, those who are more comfortable with a postmodern perspective have been more open to and willing to embrace fictional techniques. From their perspective, there is no single "right" story, but merely a number of different stories that might be told. Fiction provides a useful adjunct for these scholars. For others, especially those who are working within a positivist tradition, the use of fiction violates the tenet that in studying the empirical world researchers should be objective and ground their studies in the "real" world. You will have to figure out for yourself where you stand in this debate. Whatever decisions you make, remember that writing is a process of discovery. Writing helps you figure out what you think. It is also a method for communicating what you think to others.

QUESTIONS FOR THOUGHT

1. Think about your own writing routines. Where and when do you do your best writing? What kinds of routines do you have for beginning writing? How can you try to establish good work habits for your writing?

2. What kind of advice have you been given about writing? Have you been told, for example, to "write from your experience"? Or have you been encouraged to use "big words" to sound more "academic"? How might the advice you have been given aid you in or discourage you from developing your own voice?

EXERCISES

1. Write an introductory paragraph to a qualitative study. Then try rewriting it using a different technique. For example, if you used a standard opening ("This paper is about . . .") for the first version, try using a description of an important event or key research participant for the second version. Which version do you like better? Why?

2. Write a paragraph that describes what your research is about. First, try writing it without using the personal pronoun "I." Then rewrite the paragraph in your own voice. Compare the two versions. Which version do you like better? Why?

3. For one of the paragraphs you wrote in Exercises 1 and 2, count the number of words you used. Then take a pencil and see how many words you can delete without changing your meaning. Again, count how many words you used. What is the smallest number of words you can get by with?

4. Find a piece of writing that you think is interesting and well written. It can be fiction or nonfiction. What makes it well written? Can you emulate some of those qualities in your own writing?

5. This exercise assumes that you have been assigned to write a paper for your class. Take a first draft of your paper and switch copies with a classmate. Act as an editor for your classmate, and have your classmate do the same for you. After you have read the paper, answer these questions:
   a. What is the author's main argument(s)? Your goal here is not to criticize but to restate the author's points. (This will help your classmate evaluate whether his or her argument is effective.)
   b. What evidence does the author use to support his or her argument? (Be specific.)
   c. Does the author's main argument seem well considered and credible? Why or why not? How might the argument be improved?
   d. What are the greatest strengths of the paper?
   e. What are the greatest weaknesses of the paper?
   f. What suggestions do you have for improvement?

6. After you have received your classmate's feedback on your paper, make a revision plan. Try to answer these questions:
   a. After you completed the first draft of your paper, what did you feel you had accomplished well? What did you feel needed more work?
   b. Overall, what did the feedback indicate? What were the major strengths and weaknesses?
   c. What are the most important changes you need to make for the final draft?
   d. How are you going to accomplish those changes?

7. Take an excerpt from your paper that presents an analysis or description. (This should be part of the findings or main body.) Rewrite the excerpt in the form of a dialogue between two people. Then, rewrite it in the form of a poem or fictionalized story. What are some of the differences among the three forms? Which do you like better? Why?

SUGGESTIONS FOR FURTHER READING

American Sociological Association. *Style Guide*, 2nd ed. Washington, DC: American Sociological Association, 1997.
Becker, Howard. *Writing for Social Scientists: How to Start and Finish Your Thesis, Book, or Article*. Chicago: University of Chicago Press, 1986. One of the standard guides—and an excellent model for writing.
Janesick, Valerie J. *"Stretching" Exercises for Qualitative Researchers*. Thousand Oaks, CA: Sage, 1998. Contains many exercises that help you focus on writing as a method of analysis.

Lamott, Anne. *Bird by Bird: Some Instructions on Writing and Life*. New York: Anchor, 1995. A general (and very well written) self-help book on writing.

Richardson, Laurel. "Writing: A Method of Inquiry." Pp. 923–948 in *Handbook of Qualitative Research*, 2nd ed., edited by Norman K. Denzin and Yvonna S. Lincoln. Thousand Oaks, CA: Sage, 2000. Includes a number of useful suggestions for making your writing more interesting and provides some exercises to help you experiment with more novel methods of data presentation.

Sociology Writing Group. *A Guide to Writing Sociology Papers*. New York: St. Martin's Press, 1991. A good, basic guide for undergraduate students.

Wolcott, Harry F. *Writing Up Qualitative Research*. Newbury Park, CA: Sage, 1990. A short, chatty monograph that provides practical advice for writing up an ethnographic project.

Appendix A
American Sociological Association Code of Ethics

The American Sociological Association's (ASA's) Code of Ethics sets forth the principles and ethical standards that underlie sociologists' professional responsibilities and conduct. These principles and standards should be used as guidelines when examining everyday professional activities. They constitute normative statements for sociologists and provide guidance on issues that sociologists may encounter in their professional work.

ASA's Code of Ethics consists of an Introduction, a Preamble, five General Principles, and specific Ethical Standards. This Code is also accompanied by the Rules and Procedures of the ASA Committee on Professional Ethics which describe the procedures for filing, investigating, and resolving complaints of unethical conduct.

The Preamble and General Principles of the Code are aspirational goals to guide sociologists toward the highest ideals of sociology. Although the Preamble and General Principles are not enforceable rules, they should be considered by sociologists in arriving at an ethical course of action and may be considered by ethics bodies in interpreting the Ethical Standards.

The Ethical Standards set forth enforceable rules for conduct by sociologists. Most of the Ethical Standards are written broadly in order to apply to sociologists in varied roles, and the application of an Ethical Standard may vary depending on the context. The Ethical Standards are not exhaustive. Any conduct that is not specifically addressed by this Code of Ethics is not necessarily ethical or unethical.

Membership in the ASA commits members to adhere to the ASA Code of Ethics and to the Policies and Procedures of the ASA Committee on Professional Ethics. Members are advised of this obligation upon joining the Association and that violations of the Code may lead to the imposition of sanctions, including termination of membership. ASA members subject to the Code of Ethics may be reviewed under these Ethical Standards only if the activity is part of or affects their work-related functions, or if the activity is sociological in nature. Personal activities having no connection to or effect on sociologists' performance of their professional roles are not subject to the Code of Ethics.

PREAMBLE

This Code of Ethics articulates a common set of values upon which sociologists build their professional and scientific work. The Code is intended to provide both the general principles and the rules to cover professional situations encountered by sociologists. It has as its primary goal the welfare and protection of the individuals and groups with whom sociologists work. It is the individual responsibility of each sociologist to aspire to the highest possible standards of conduct in research, teaching, practice, and service.

The development of a dynamic set of ethical standards for a sociologist's work-related conduct requires a personal commitment to a lifelong effort to act ethically; to encourage ethical behavior by students, supervisors, supervisees, employers, employees, and colleagues; and to consult with others as needed concerning ethical problems. Each sociologist supplements, but does not violate, the values and rules specified in the Code of Ethics based on guidance drawn from personal values, culture, and experience.

GENERAL PRINCIPLES

The following General Principles are aspirational and serve as a guide for sociologists in determining ethical courses of action in various contexts. They exemplify the highest ideals of professional conduct.

Principle A: Professional Competence

Sociologists strive to maintain the highest levels of competence in their work; they recognize the limitations of their expertise; and they undertake only those tasks for which they are qualified by education, training, or experience. They recognize the need for ongoing education in order to remain professionally competent; and they utilize the appropriate scientific, professional, technical, and administrative resources needed to ensure competence in their professional activities. They consult with other professionals when necessary for the benefit of their students, research participants, and clients.

Principle B: Integrity

Sociologists are honest, fair, and respectful of others in their professional activities—in research, teaching, practice, and service. Sociologists do not knowingly act in ways that jeopardize either their own or others' professional welfare. Sociologists conduct their affairs in ways that inspire trust and confidence; they do not knowingly make statements that are false, misleading, or deceptive.

Principle C: Professional and Scientific Responsibility

Sociologists adhere to the highest scientific and professional standards and accept responsibility for their work. Sociologists understand that they form a community and show respect for other sociologists even when they disagree on theoretical, methodological, or personal approaches to professional activities. Sociologists value the public trust in sociology and are concerned about their ethical behavior and that of other sociologists that might compromise that trust. While endeavoring always to be collegial, sociologists must never let the desire to be collegial outweigh their shared responsibility for ethical behavior. When appropriate, they consult with colleagues in order to prevent or avoid unethical conduct.

Principle D: Respect for People's Rights, Dignity, and Diversity

Sociologists respect the rights, dignity, and worth of all people. They strive to eliminate bias in their professional activities, and they do not tolerate any forms of discrimination based on age; gender; race; ethnicity; national origin; religion; sexual orientation; disability; health conditions; or marital, domestic, or parental status. They are sensitive to cultural, individual, and role differences in serving, teaching, and studying groups of people with distinctive characteristics. In all of their work-related activities, sociologists acknowledge the rights of others to hold values, attitudes, and opinions that differ from their own.

Principle E: Social Responsibility

Sociologists are aware of their professional and scientific responsibility to the communities and societies in which they live and work. They apply and make public their knowledge in order to contribute to the public good. When undertaking research, they strive to advance the science of sociology and to serve the public good.

ETHICAL STANDARDS

1. Professional and Scientific Standards

Sociologists adhere to the highest possible technical standards that are reasonable and responsible in their research, teaching, practice, and service activities. They rely on scientifically and professionally derived knowledge; act with honesty and integrity; and avoid untrue, deceptive, or undocumented statements in undertaking work-related functions or activities.

2. Competence

(a) Sociologists conduct research, teach, practice, and provide service only within the boundaries of their competence, based on their education, training, supervised experience, or appropriate professional experience.

(b) Sociologists conduct research, teach, practice, and provide service in new areas or involving new techniques only after they have taken reasonable steps to ensure the competence of their work in these areas.

(c) Sociologists who engage in research, teaching, practice, or service maintain awareness of current scientific and professional information in their fields of activity, and undertake continuing efforts to maintain competence in the skills they use.

(d) Sociologists refrain from undertaking an activity when their personal circumstances may interfere with their professional work or lead to harm for a student, supervisee, human subject, client, colleague, or other person to whom they have a scientific, teaching, consulting, or other professional obligation.

3. Representation and Misuse of Expertise

(a) In research, teaching, practice, service, or other situations where sociologists render professional judgments or present their expertise, they accurately and fairly represent their areas and degrees of expertise.

(b) Sociologists do not accept grants, contracts, consultation, or work assignments from individual or organizational clients or sponsors that appear likely to require violation of the standards in this Code of Ethics. Sociologists dissociate themselves from such activities when they discover a violation and are unable to achieve its correction.

(c) Because sociologists' scientific and professional judgments and actions may affect the lives of others, they are alert to and guard against personal, financial, social, organizational, or political factors that might lead to misuse of their knowledge, expertise, or influence.

(d) If sociologists learn of misuse or misrepresentation of their work, they take reasonable steps to correct or minimize the misuse or misrepresentation.

4. Delegation and Supervision

(a) Sociologists provide proper training and supervision to their students, supervisees, or employees and take reasonable steps to see that such persons perform services responsibly, competently, and ethically.

(b) Sociologists delegate to their students, supervisees, or employees only those responsibilities that such persons, based on their education, training, or experience, can reasonably be expected to perform either independently or with the level of supervision provided.

5. Nondiscrimination

Sociologists do not engage in discrimination in their work based on age; gender; race; ethnicity; national origin; religion; sexual orientation; disability; health conditions; marital, domestic, or parental status; or any other applicable basis proscribed by law.

6. Non-exploitation

(a) Whether for personal, economic, or professional advantage, sociologists do not exploit persons over whom they have direct or indirect supervisory, evaluative, or other authority such as students, supervisees, employees, or research participants.

(b) Sociologists do not directly supervise or exercise evaluative authority over any person with whom they have a sexual relationship, including students, supervisees, employees, or research participants.

7. Harassment

Sociologists do not engage in harassment of any person, including students, supervisees, employees, or research participants. Harassment consists of a single intense and severe act or of multiple persistent or pervasive acts which are demeaning, abusive, offensive, or create a hostile professional or workplace environment. Sexual harassment may include sexual solicitation, physical advance, or verbal or non-verbal conduct that is sexual in nature. Racial harassment may include unnecessary, exaggerated, or unwarranted attention or attack, whether verbal or non-verbal, because of a person's race or ethnicity.

· · ·

11. Confidentiality

Sociologists have an obligation to ensure that confidential information is protected. They do so to ensure the integrity of research and the open communication with research participants and to protect sensitive information obtained in research, teaching, practice, and service. When gathering confidential information, sociologists should take into account the long-term uses of the information, including its potential placement in public archives or the examination of the information by other researchers or practitioners.

11.01 Maintaining Confidentiality

(a) Sociologists take reasonable precautions to protect the confidentiality rights of research participants, students, employees, clients, or others.

(b) Confidential information provided by research participants, students, employees, clients, or others is treated as such by sociologists even if there is no legal protection or privilege to do so. Sociologists have an obligation to protect confidential information, and not allow information gained in confidence from being used in ways that would unfairly compromise research participants, students, employees, clients, or others.

(c) Information provided under an understanding of confidentiality is treated as such even after the death of those providing that information.

(d) Sociologists maintain the integrity of confidential deliberations, activities, or roles, including, where applicable, that of professional committees, review panels, or advisory groups (e.g., the ASA Committee on Professional Ethics).

(e) Sociologists, to the extent possible, protect the confidentiality of student records, performance data, and personal information, whether verbal or written, given in the context of academic consultation, supervision, or advising.

(f) The obligation to maintain confidentiality extends to members of research or training teams and collaborating organizations who have access to the information. To ensure that access to confidential information is restricted, it is the responsibility of researchers, administrators, and principal investigators to instruct staff to take the steps necessary to protect confidentiality.

(g) When using private information about individuals collected by other persons or institutions, sociologists protect the confidentiality of individually identifiable information. Information is private when an individual can reasonably expect that the information will not be made public with personal identifiers (e.g., medical or employment records).

11.02 Limits of Confidentiality

(a) Sociologists inform themselves fully about all laws and rules which may limit or alter guarantees of confidentiality. They determine their ability to guarantee absolute confidentiality and, as appropriate, inform research participants, students, employees, clients, or others of any limitations to this guarantee at the outset consistent with ethical standards set forth in 11.02(b).

(b) Sociologists may confront unanticipated circumstances where they become aware of information that is clearly health- or life-threatening to research participants, students, employees, clients, or others. In these cases, sociologists balance the importance of guarantees of confidentiality with other principles in this Code of Ethics, standards of conduct, and applicable law.

(c) Confidentiality is not required with respect to observations in public places, activities conducted in public, or other settings where no rules of privacy are provided by law or custom. Similarly, confidentiality is not required in the case of information available from public records.

11.03 Discussing Confidentiality and Its Limits

(a) When sociologists establish a scientific or professional relationship with persons, they discuss (1) the relevant limitations on confidentiality, and (2) the foreseeable uses of the information generated through their professional work.

(b) Unless it is not feasible or is counter-productive, the discussion of confidentiality occurs at the outset of the relationship and thereafter as new circumstances may warrant.

11.04 Anticipation of Possible Uses of Information

(a) When research requires maintaining personal identifiers in data bases or systems of records, sociologists delete such identifiers before the information is made publicly available.

(b) When confidential information concerning research participants, clients, or other recipients of service is entered into databases or systems of records available to persons without the prior consent of the relevant parties, sociologists protect anonymity by not including personal identifiers or by employing other techniques that mask or control disclosure of individual identities.

(c) When deletion of personal identifiers is not feasible, sociologists take reasonable steps to determine that appropriate consent of personally-identifiable individuals has been obtained before they transfer such data to others or review such data collected by others.

11.05 Electronic Transmission of Confidential Information

Sociologists use extreme care in delivering or transferring any confidential data, information, or communication over public computer networks. Sociologists are attentive to the problems of maintaining confidentiality and control over sensitive material and data when use of technological innovations, such as public computer networks, may open their professional and scientific communication to unauthorized persons.

11.06 Anonymity of Sources

(a) Sociologists do not disclose in their writings, lectures, or other public media confidential, personally identifiable information concerning their research participants, students, individual or organizational clients, or other recipients of their service which is obtained during the course of their work, unless consent from individuals or their legal representatives has been obtained.

(b) When confidential information is used in scientific and professional presentations, sociologists disguise the identity of research participants, students, individual or organizational clients, or other recipients of their service.

11.07 Minimizing Intrusions on Privacy

(a) To minimize intrusions on privacy, sociologists include in written and oral reports, consultations, and public communications only information germane to the purpose for which the communication is made.

(b) Sociologists discuss confidential information or evaluative data concerning research participants, students, supervisees, employees, and individual or organizational clients only for appropriate scientific or professional purposes and only with persons clearly concerned with such matters.

11.08 Preservation of Confidential Information

(a) Sociologists take reasonable steps to ensure that records, data, or information are preserved in a confidential manner consistent with the requirements of this Code of Ethics, recognizing that ownership of records, data, or information may also be governed by law or institutional principles.

(b) Sociologists plan so that confidentiality of records, data, or information is protected in the event of the sociologist's death, incapacity, or withdrawal from the position or practice.

(c) When sociologists transfer confidential records, data, or information to other persons or organizations, they obtain assurances that the recipients of the records, data, or information will employ measures to protect confidentiality at least equal to those originally pledged.

12. Informed Consent

Informed consent is a basic ethical tenet of scientific research on human populations. Sociologists do not involve a human being as a subject in research without the informed consent of the subject or the subject's legally authorized representative, except as otherwise specified in this Code. Sociologists recognize the possibility of undue influence or subtle pressures on subjects that may derive from researchers' expertise or authority, and they take this into account in designing informed consent procedures.

12.01 Scope of Informed Consent

(a) Sociologists conducting research obtain consent from research participants or their legally authorized representatives (1) when data are collected from research participants through any form of communication, interaction, or intervention; or (2) when behavior of research participants occurs in a private context where an individual can reasonably expect that no observation or reporting is taking place.

(b) Despite the paramount importance of consent, sociologists may seek waivers of this standard when (1) the research involves no more than minimal risk for research participants, and (2) the research could not practicably be carried out were informed consent to be required. Sociologists recognize that waivers of consent require approval from institutional review boards or, in the absence of such boards, from another authoritative body with expertise on the ethics of research. Under such circumstances, the confidentiality of any personally identifiable information must be maintained unless otherwise set forth in 11.02(b).

(c) Sociologists may conduct research in public places or use publicly available information about individuals (e.g., naturalistic observations in public places, analysis of public records, or archival research) without obtaining consent. If, under such circumstances, sociologists have any doubt whatsoever about the need for informed consent, they consult with institutional review boards or, in the absence of such boards, with another authoritative body with expertise on the ethics of research before proceeding with such research.

(d) In undertaking research with vulnerable populations (e.g., youth, recent immigrant populations, the mentally ill), sociologists take special care to ensure that the voluntary nature of the research is understood and that consent is not coerced. In all other respects, sociologists adhere to the principles set forth in 12.01(a)–(c).

(e) Sociologists are familiar with and conform to applicable state and federal regulations and, where applicable, institutional review board requirements for obtaining informed consent for research.

12.02 Informed Consent Process

(a) When informed consent is required, sociologists enter into an agreement with research participants or their legal representatives that clarifies the nature of the research and the responsibilities of the investigator prior to conducting the research.

(b) When informed consent is required, sociologists use language that is understandable to and respectful of research participants or their legal representatives.

(c) When informed consent is required, sociologists provide research participants or their legal representatives with the opportunity to ask questions about any aspect of the research, at any time during or after their participation in the research.

(d) When informed consent is required, sociologists inform research participants or their legal representatives of the nature of the research; they indicate to participants that their participation or continued participation is voluntary; they inform participants of significant factors that may be expected to influence their willingness to participate (e.g., possible risks and benefits of their participation); and they explain other aspects of the research and respond to questions from prospective participants. Also, if relevant, sociologists explain that refusal to participate or withdrawal from participation in the research involves no penalty, and they explain any foreseeable consequences of declining or withdrawing. Sociologists explicitly discuss confidentiality and, if applicable, the extent to which confidentiality may be limited as set forth in 11.02(b).

(e) When informed consent is required, sociologists keep records regarding said consent. They recognize that consent is a process that involves oral and/or written consent.

(f) Sociologists honor all commitments they have made to research participants as part of the informed consent process except where unanticipated circumstances demand otherwise as set forth in 11.02(b).

12.03 Informed Consent of Students and Subordinates

When undertaking research at their own institutions or organizations with research participants who are students or subordinates, sociologists take special care to protect the prospective subjects from adverse consequences of declining or withdrawing from participation.

12.04 Informed Consent with Children

(a) In undertaking research with children, sociologists obtain the consent of children to participate, to the extent that they are capable of providing such consent, except under circumstances where consent may not be required as set forth in 12.01(b).

(b) In undertaking research with children, sociologists obtain the consent of a parent or a legally authorized guardian. Sociologists may seek waivers of parental or guardian consent when (1) the research involves no more than minimal risk for the research participants, and (2) the research could not practicably be carried out were consent to be required, or (3) the consent of a parent or guardian is not a reasonable requirement to protect the child (e.g., neglected or abused children).

(c) Sociologists recognize that waivers of consent from a child and a parent or guardian require approval from institutional review boards or, in the absence of such boards, from another authoritative body with expertise on the ethics of research. Under such circumstances, the confidentiality of any personally identifiable information must be maintained unless otherwise set forth in 11.02(b).

12.05 Use of Deception in Research

(a) Sociologists do not use deceptive techniques (1) unless they have determined that their use will not be harmful to research participants; is justified by the study's prospective scientific, educational, or applied value; and that equally effective alternative procedures that do not use deception are not feasible, and (2) unless they have obtained the approval of institutional review boards or, in the absence of such boards, with another authoritative body with expertise on the ethics of research.

(b) Sociologists never deceive research participants about significant aspects of the research that would affect their willingness to participate, such as physical risks, discomfort, or unpleasant emotional experiences.

(c) When deception is an integral feature of the design and conduct of research, sociologists attempt to correct any misconception that research participants may have no later than at the conclusion of the research.

(d) On rare occasions, sociologists may need to conceal their identity in order to undertake research that could not practicably be carried out were they to be known as researchers. Under such circumstances, sociologists undertake the research if it involves no more than minimal risk for the research participants and if they have obtained approval to proceed in this manner from an institutional review board or, in the absence of such boards, from another authoritative body with expertise on the ethics of research. Under such circumstances, confidentiality must be maintained unless otherwise set forth in 11.02(b).

12.06 Use of Recording Technology

Sociologists obtain informed consent from research participants, students, employees, clients, or others prior to videotaping, filming, or recording them in any form, unless these activities involve simply naturalistic observations in public places and it is not anticipated that the recording will be used in a manner that could cause personal identification or harm.

13. Research Planning, Implementation, and Dissemination

Sociologists have an obligation to promote the integrity of research and to ensure that they comply with the ethical tenets of science in the planning, implementation, and dissemination of research. They do so in order to advance knowledge, to minimize the possibility that results will be misleading, and to protect the rights of research participants.

13.01 Planning and Implementation

(a) In planning and implementing research, sociologists minimize the possibility that results will be misleading.

(b) Sociologists take steps to implement protections for the rights and welfare of research participants and other persons affected by the research.

(c) In their research, sociologists do not encourage activities or themselves behave in ways that are health- or life-threatening to research participants or others.

(d) In planning and implementing research, sociologists consult those with expertise concerning any special population under investigation or likely to be affected.

(e) In planning and implementing research, sociologists consider its ethical acceptability as set forth in the Code of Ethics. If the best ethical practice is unclear, sociologists consult with institutional review boards or, in the absence of such review processes, with another authoritative body with expertise on the ethics of research.

(f) Sociologists are responsible for the ethical conduct of research conducted by them or by others under their supervision or authority.

13.02 Unanticipated Research Opportunities

If during the course of teaching, practice, service, or non-professional activities, sociologists determine that they wish to undertake research that was not previously anticipated, they make known their intentions and take steps to ensure that the research can be undertaken consonant with ethical principles, especially those relating to confidentiality and informed consent. Under such circumstances, sociologists seek the approval of institutional review boards or, in the absence of such review processes, another authoritative body with expertise on the ethics of research.

13.03 Offering Inducements for Research Participants

Sociologists do not offer excessive or inappropriate financial or other inducements to obtain the participation of research participants, particularly when it might coerce participation. Sociologists may provide incentives to the extent that resources are available and appropriate.

13.04 Reporting on Research

(a) Sociologists disseminate their research findings except where unanticipated circumstances (e.g., the health of the researcher) or proprietary agreements with employers, contractors, or clients preclude such dissemination.

(b) Sociologists do not fabricate data or falsify results in their publications or presentations.

(c) In presenting their work, sociologists report their findings fully and do not omit relevant data. They report results whether they support or contradict the expected outcomes.

(d) Sociologists take particular care to state all relevant qualifications on the findings and interpretation of their research. Sociologists also disclose underlying assumptions, theories, methods, measures, and research designs that might bear upon findings and interpretations of their work.

(e) Consistent with the spirit of full disclosure of methods and analyses, once findings are publicly disseminated, sociologists permit their open assessment and verification by other responsible researchers with appropriate safeguards, where applicable, to protect the anonymity of research participants.

(f) If sociologists discover significant errors in their publication or presentation of data, they take reasonable steps to correct such errors in a correction, a retraction, published errata, or other public fora as appropriate.

(g) Sociologists report sources of financial support in their written papers and note any special relations to any sponsor. In special circumstances, sociologists may withhold the names of specific sponsors if they provide an adequate and full description of the nature and interest of the sponsor.

(h) Sociologists take special care to report accurately the results of others' scholarship by using correct information and citations when presenting the work of others in publications, teaching, practice, and service settings.

13.05 Data Sharing

(a) Sociologists share data and pertinent documentation as a regular practice. Sociologists make their data available after completion of the project or its major publications, except where proprietary agreements with employers, contractors, or clients preclude such accessibility or when it is impossible to share data and protect the confidentiality of the data or the anonymity of research participants (e.g., raw field notes or detailed information from ethnographic interviews).

(b) Sociologists anticipate data sharing as an integral part of a research plan whenever data sharing is feasible.

(c) Sociologists share data in a form that is consonant with research participants' interests and protect the confidentiality of the information they have been given. They maintain the confidentiality of data, whether legally required or not; remove personal identifiers before data are shared; and if necessary use other disclosure avoidance techniques.

(d) Sociologists who do not otherwise place data in public archives keep data available and retain documentation relating to the research for a reasonable period of time after publication or dissemination of results.

(e) Sociologists may ask persons who request their data for further analysis to bear the associated incremental costs, if necessary.

(f) Sociologists who use data from others for further analyses explicitly acknowledge the contribution of the initial researchers.

14. Plagiarism

(a) In publications, presentations, teaching, practice, and service, sociologists explicitly identify, credit, and reference the author when they take data or material verbatim from another person's written work, whether it is published, unpublished, or electronically available.

(b) In their publications, presentations, teaching, practice, and service, sociologists provide acknowledgment of and reference to the use of others' work, even if the work is not quoted verbatim or paraphrased, and they do not present others' work as their own whether it is published, unpublished, or electronically available. . . .

Appendix B
Sample Informed Consent Form

Kristin G. Esterberg, Ph.D.
Department of Sociology
University of Massachusetts Lowell

A Study of Mothers, Identity, and Social Support

Purpose of study: You are being asked to participate in a study of mothers. The research seeks to understand how women think about what it means to be a mother and the kinds of social supports available to mothers.

Procedure and duration: You are being asked to participate in an interview. The interview will take approximately two hours; it will take place at your home or at another location convenient for you. You are also asked to fill out a brief questionnaire.

With your permission, the interview will be audio taped. The tape will be transcribed; your name or other identifying information will **not** be included on the transcript. At the end of the research project, the audio tapes will be destroyed.

Your participation is completely voluntary. You may stop participating in this research at any time or choose not to answer any question, without penalty.

Although disclosure of your identity is a possible risk, every precaution will be taken to protect your privacy and the confidentiality of any records generated by this research. Only the principal investigator (Kristin Esterberg) and her research staff will have access to the audio tapes of the interviews and the transcripts. The audio tapes will be kept in a locked file; at the end of the research project, the tapes will be destroyed. Your name and any other identifying information will not appear in any reports or documents that are published as a result of this research project.

If you do not understand any portion of what you are being asked to do, or the contents of this form, the researchers are available to provide a complete explanation. Questions are welcome at any time. Please direct them to Kristin Esterberg at the address at the top of this form.

I have been informed of any and all possible risks or discomforts.

I have read the statements contained herein, have had the opportunity to fully discuss my concerns and questions, and fully understand the nature and character of my involvement in this research program as a human subject, and the attendant risks and consequences.

I give my permission to audio tape this interview.   ____Yes   ____No

_____

Research Participant   Date

_____

Researcher   Date

References

Acker, Joan; Kate Barry; and Joke Esseveld. 1996. "Objectivity and Truth: Problems in Doing Feminist Research." Pp. 60–87 in *Feminism and Social Change: Bridging Theory and Practice*. Urbana and Chicago: University of Illinois Press.

Adler, Patricia A. 1985. *Wheeling and Dealing*. New York: Columbia University Press.

Adler, Patricia A., and Peter Adler. 1991. "Stability and Flexibility: Maintaining Relations within Organized and Unorganized Groups." Pp. 173–183 in *Experiencing Fieldwork: An Inside View of Qualitative Research*. Newbury Park, CA: Sage.

Adler, Patricia A., and Peter Adler. 1994. "Social Reproduction and the Corporate Other: The Institutionalization of Afterschool Activities." *Sociological Quarterly* 35:309–328.

Alinsky, Saul David. 1971. *Rules for Radicals: A Practical Primer for Realistic Radicals*. New York: Random House.

Altheide, David L., and R. Sam Michalowski. 1999. "Fear in the News: A Discourse of Control." *The Sociological Quarterly* 40:475–503.

American Sociological Association. 1997. *Style Guide*, 2nd ed. Washington, DC: American Sociological Association.

Anderson, Kathryn; Susan Armitage; Dana Jack; and Judith Wittner. 1990. "Beginning Where We Are: Feminist Methodology in Oral History." Pp. 94–112 in *Feminist Research Methods: Exemplary Readings in the Social Sciences*, edited by Joyce McCarl Nielsen. Boulder, CO: Westview Press.

Atkinson, Paul, and Martyn Hammersley. 1998. "Ethnography and Participant Observation." Pp. 110–136 in *Strategies of Qualitative Inquiry*, edited by Norman K. Denzin and Yvonna S. Lincoln. Thousand Oaks, CA: Sage.

Babbie, Earl. 1990. *Survey Research Methods*. Belmont, CA: Wadsworth.

Barthel, Diane. 1988. *Putting on Appearances: Gender and Advertising*. Philadelphia: Temple University Press.

Becker, Bettina. 1999. "Narratives of Pain in Later Life and Conventions of Storytelling." *Journal of Aging Studies* 13:73–87.

Becker, Howard S. 1963. *Outsiders: Studies in the Sociology of Deviance.* New York: Free Press.

Becker, Howard S. 1986. *Writing for Social Scientists: How to Start and Finish Your Thesis, Book, or Article.* Chicago: University of Chicago Press.

Becker, Howard S. 1998. *Tricks of the Trade: How to Think About Your Research While You're Doing It.* Chicago: University of Chicago Press.

Becker, Howard; Blanche Geer; Everett Hughes; and Anselm Strauss. 1977 [1961]. *Boys in White: Student Culture in Medical School.* New Brunswick, NJ: Transaction.

Belgrave, Linda Liska, and Kenneth J. Smith. "Negotiated Validity in Collaborative Ethnography." *Qualitative Inquiry* 1:69–87.

Berg, Bruce L. 2001. *Qualitative Research Methods for the Social Sciences.* Boston: Allyn & Bacon.

Berns, Nancy. 1999. "'My Problem and How I Solved It': Domestic Violence in Women's Magazines." *The Sociological Quarterly* 40:85–108.

Biernacki, Patrick, and Dan Waldorf. 1981. "Snowball Sampling: Problems and Techniques of Chain Referral Sampling." *Sociological Methods and Research* 10:141–163.

Binik, Yitzchak M.; Kenneth Mah; and Sara Kiesler. 1999. "Ethical Issues in Conducting Sex Research on the Internet." *Journal of Sex Research* 36:82–91.

Blee, Kathleen. 1996. "Becoming a Racist: Women in Contemporary Ku Klux Klan and Neo-Nazi Groups." *Gender & Society* 10: 680–703.

Blumer, Herbert. 1969. *Symbolic Interactionism: Perspective and Method.* Berkeley: University of California Press.

Britton, Dana M. 1999. "Cat Fights and Gang Fights: Preference for Work in a Male-Dominated Organization." *Sociological Quarterly* 40:455–474.

Brown, L. David. 1993. "Social Change Through Collective Reflection with Asian Nongovernmental Development Organizations." *Human Relations* 46:249–274.

Burawoy, Michael, et al. 1991. *Ethnography Unbound.* Berkeley: University of California Press.

Cancian, Francesca. 1996. "Participatory Research and Alternative Strategies for Activist Sociology." Pp. 187–205 in *Feminism and Social Change: Bridging Theory and Practice,* edited by Heidi Gottfried. Urbana: University of Illinois Press.

Cannon, Lynne Weber; Elizabeth Higginbotham; and Marianne L.A. Leung. 1991. "Race and Class Bias in Qualitative Research on Women." Pp. 107–118 in *Beyond Methodology: Feminist Scholarship as Lived Research,* edited by Mary Margaret Fonow and Judith A. Cook. Bloomington: Indiana University Press.

Caplan, Arthur L. 1992. "When Evil Intrudes." *Hastings Center Report* 22:29–32.

Chapkis, Wendy. 1997. *Live Sex Acts: Women Performing Erotic Labor.* New York: Routledge.

Charmaz, Kathy. 2000. "Grounded Theory: Objectivist and Constructivist Methods." Pp. 509–536 in *Handbook of Qualitative Research,* 2nd ed., edited by Norman K. Denzin and Yvonna S. Lincoln. Thousand Oaks, CA: Sage.

Chataway, Cynthia. 1997. "An Examination of the Constraints on Mutual Inquiry in a Participatory Action Research Project." *Journal of Social Issues* 53:747–765.

Clark, Roger; Rachel Lennon; and Leanna Morris. 1993. "Of Caldecotts and Kings: Gendered Images in Recent American Children's Books by Black and Non-Black Illustrators." *Gender & Society* 7:227–245.

Coffey, Amanda, and Paul Atkinson. 1996. *Making Sense of Qualitative Data: Complementary Research Strategies.* Thousand Oaks, CA: Sage.

Cole, Caroline. 1991. "Oh Wise Women of the Stalls." *Discourse and Society* 2:401–411.

Collins, Patricia Hill. 1990. *Black Feminist Thought: Knowledge, Consciousness, and the Politics of Empowerment.* New York: Routledge.

Corsaro, William A., and Luisa Molinari. 2000. "Priming Events and Italian Children's Transition from Preschool to Elementary School: Representations and Actions." *Social Psychology Quarterly* 63:16–33.

Coy, Patrick G. 1999. "Participant Observation, Shared Risks, and the Search for the Research Self Amidst Political Violence." Paper presented at the American Sociological Association annual meeting, Chicago.

Davidman, Lynn. 1999. "The Personal, the Sociological, and the Intersection of the Two." Pp. 70–87 in *Qualitative Sociology as Everyday Life,* edited by Barry Glassner and Rosanna Hertz. Thousand Oaks, CA: Sage.

Deegan, Mary Jo. 1991. *Women in Sociology: A Bio-Bibliographical Sourcebook.* New York: Greenwood Press.

Denzin, Norman. 1989. *The Research Act,* 3rd ed. Englewood Cliffs, NJ: Prentice Hall.

Denzin, Norman. 1999. "Performing Montana." Pp. 147–158 in *Qualitative Sociology as Everyday Life,* edited by Barry Glassner and Rosanna Hertz. Thousand Oaks, CA: Sage.

Denzin, Norman. 2000. "The Practices and Politics of Interpretation." Pp. 897–922 in *Handbook of Qualitative Research,* 2nd ed., edited by Norman K. Denzin and Yvonna S. Lincoln. Thousand Oaks, CA: Sage.

Denzin, Norman K., and Yvonna S. Lincoln. 1998. "Introduction: Entering the Field of Qualitative Research. Pp. 1–34 in *The Landscape of Qualitative Research: Theories and Issues,* edited by Norman K. Denzin and Yvonna S. Lincoln. Thousand Oaks, CA: Sage.

Denzin, Norman K., and Yvonna S. Lincoln (eds.). 2000. *Handbook of Qualitative Research,* 2nd ed. Thousand Oaks, CA: Sage.

Deutsch, Francine M. 1999. *Halving It All: How Equally Shared Parenting Works.* Cambridge, MA: Harvard University Press.

DeVault, Marjorie L. 1999. *Liberating Method: Feminism and Social Research.* Philadelphia: Temple University Press.

Dickson, Geraldine. 2000. "Aboriginal Grandmothers' Experience with Health Promotion and Participatory Action Research." *Qualitative Health Research* 10:188–214.

Dodson, Lisa. 1998. *Don't Call Us Out of Name: The Untold Lives of Women and Girls in Poor America.* Boston: Beacon Press.

Dohan, Daniel, and Martin Sanchez-Jankowski. 1998. "Using Computers to Analyze Ethnographic Field Data: Theoretical and Practical Considerations." *Annual Review of Sociology* 24:477–491.

Donnelly, David F., and Kristina Ross. "The Internet: Historical Media Research on the Virtual Archives." *Historical Journal of Film, Radio & Television* 17:129–137.

Ellingson, Laura. 1998. "'Then You Know How I Feel': Empathy, Identification, and Reflexivity in Fieldwork." *Qualitative Inquiry* 4:492–513.

Ellis, Carolyn. 1998. "'I Hate My Voice': Coming to Terms with Minor Bodily Stigmas." *Sociological Quarterly* 39:517–537.

Ellis, Carolyn. 1999. "Heartful Autoethnography." *Qualitative Health Research* 9:669–684.

Ellis, Carolyn, and Arthur P. Bochner. 2000. "Autoethnography, Personal Narrative, Reflexivity: Researcher as Subject." Pp. 733–768 in *Handbook of Qualitative Research*, 2nd ed., edited by Norman K. Denzin and Yvonna S. Lincoln. Thousand Oaks, CA: Sage.

Elsinger, Heidi. 1998. "Images of Women in *Sports Illustrated* and *Sports Illustrated for Kids.*" Unpublished senior thesis, University of Massachusetts–Lowell.

Emerson, Robert M.; Rachel I. Fretz; and Linda L. Shaw. 1995. *Writing Ethnographic Fieldnotes.* Chicago: University of Chicago Press.

Esterberg, Kristin. 1997. *Lesbian and Bisexual Identities: Constructing Communities, Constructing Selves.* Philadelphia: Temple University Press.

Ferrell, Jeff. 1995. "Urban Graffiti: Crime, Control, and Resistance." *Youth & Society* 27:73–93.

Fine, Michelle; Lois Weis; Susan Weseen; and Loonmun Wong. 2000. "For Whom? Qualitative Research, Representations, and Social Responsibilities." Pp. 107–131 in *Handbook of Qualitative Research*, 2nd ed., edited by Norman K. Denzin and Yvonna S. Lincoln. Thousand Oaks, CA: Sage.

Finlay, William, and James E. Coverdill. 1999. "The Search Game: Organizational Conflicts and the Use of Headhunters." *Sociological Quarterly* 40:11–30.

Fleitas, Joan. 1998. "Spinning Tales from the World Wide Web: Qualitative Research in an Electronic Environment." *Qualitative Health Research* 8:283–293.

Fontana, Andrea, and James H. Frey. 1998. "Interviewing: The Art of Science." Pp. 47–78 in *Collecting and Interpreting Qualitative Materials*, edited by Norman K. Denzin and Yvonna S. Lincoln. Thousand Oaks, CA: Sage.

Franzosi, Roberto. 1990a. "Strategies for the Prevention, Detection, and Correction of Measurement Error in Data Collected from Textual Sources." *Sociological Methods and Research* 18:442–472.

Franzosi, Roberto. 1990b. "Computer-Assisted Coding of Textual Data: An Application to Semantic Grammars." *Sociological Methods and Research* 19:225–257.

Franzosi, Roberto. 1998. "Narrative Analysis—Or Why (and How) Sociologists Should Be Interested in Narrative." *Annual Review of Sociology* 24:517–554.

Freedman, Carol. 1997. "Setting Stay-at-Home Standards: An Ethnographic Study of the Southland Mothers Association." Unpublished M.A. thesis, University of Missouri–Kansas City.

Freire, Paulo. 1970. *Pedagogy of the Oppressed.* New York: Seabury Press.

Friedman, Debra, and Michael Hechter. 1988. "The Contribution of Rational Choice Theory to Macrosociological Research." *Sociological Theory* 6:201–218.

Gamson, Joshua. 1998. *Freaks Talk Back: Tabloid Talk Shows and Sexual Nonconformity.* Chicago: University of Chicago Press.

Gans, Herbert J. 1962. *The Urban Villagers: Group and Class in the Life of Italian-Americans.* New York: Free Press.

Gans, Herbert J. 1999. "Participant Observation in the Era of 'Ethnography.'" *Journal of Contemporary Ethnography* 28:540–548.

Ganz, Marshall. 2000. "Resources and Resourcefulness: Strategic Capacity in the Unionization of California Agriculture, 1959–1966." *American Journal of Sociology* 105:1003–1062.

Garber, Marjorie. 1995. *Vice Versa: Bisexuality and the Eroticism of Everyday Life.* New York: Simon & Schuster.

Gaventa, John. 1991. "Carrying On . . ." *Social Policy* 21(3):68–70.

Gee, James. 1991. "A Linguistic Approach to Narrative." *Journal of Narrative and Life History* 1:15–39.

Geertz, Clifford. 1973. *The Interpretation of Cultures.* New York: Basic Books.

Gergen, Kenneth J. 1991. *The Saturated Self: Dilemmas of Identity in Contemporary Life.* Basic Books.

Gergen, Mary M., and Kenneth J. Gergen. 2000. "Qualitative Inquiry: Tensions and Transformations." Pp. 1025–1046 in *Handbook of Qualitative Research,* 2nd ed., edited by Norman K. Denzin and Yvonna S. Lincoln. Thousand Oaks, CA: Sage.

Gibson-Graham, J.K. 1994. "'Stuffed If I Know!': Reflections on Post-modern Feminist Social Research." *Gender Place & Culture: A Journal of Feminist Geography* 1:205–224.

Glassie, Henry. 1991. "Studying Material Culture Today." Pp. 253–266 in *Living in a Material World: Canadian and American Approaches to Material Culture,* edited by Gerald Pocius. St. John's, Newfoundland: Institute of Social and Economic Research.

Glassner, Barry, and Rosanna Hertz (eds.). 1999. *Qualitative Sociology as Everyday Life*. Thousand Oaks, CA: Sage.

Goffman, Erving. 1976. *Gender Advertisements*. London: Macmillan.

Gordon, Linda. 1988. *Heroes of Their Own Lives: The Politics and History of Family Violence*. New York: Penguin Books.

Gottlieb, Alma, and Philip Graham. 1993. *Parallel Worlds: An Anthropologist and a Writer Encounter Africa*. New York: Crown, 1993.

Greenwood, Davydd J.; William Foote Whyte; and Ira Harkavy. 1993. "Participatory Action Research as a Process and as a Goal." *Human Relations* 46:179–193.

Greer, Colin. 1991. "A Culture of Politics." *Social Policy* 21(3):53–57.

Groger, Lisa; Pamela Mayberry; and Jane Straker. 1999. "What We Didn't Learn Because of Who Would Not Talk to Us." *Qualitative Health Research* 9:829–836.

Gubrium, Jaber F., and James A. Holstein. 1997. *The New Language of Qualitative Method*. New York: Oxford University Press.

Gubrium, Jaber F., and James A. Holstein. 1998. "Narrative Practice and the Coherence of Personal Stories." *Sociological Quarterly* 39:163–187.

Harding, Sandra. 1986. *The Science Question in Feminism*. Ithaca, NY: Cornell University Press.

Harding, Sandra. 1987. "Introduction: Is There a Feminist Method?" Pp. 1–14 in *Feminism & Methodology*, edited by Sandra Harding. Bloomington: Indiana University Press.

Hartsock, Nancy. 1987. "The Feminist Standpoint: Developing the Ground for a Specifically Feminist Historical Materialism." Pp. 157–180 in *Feminism & Methodology*, edited by Sandra Harding. Bloomington: Indiana University Press.

Hays, Sharon. 1996. *The Cultural Contradictions of Motherhood*. New Haven, CT: Yale University Press.

Hodder, Ian. 1989. "Post-modernism, Post-structuralism and Post-processual Archaeology." Pp. 64–78 in *The Meanings of Things: Material Culture and Symbolic Expression*, edited by Ian Hodder. London: Unwin Hyman.

Hodder, Ian. 1998. "The Interpretation of Documents and Material Culture." Pp. 110–129 in *Collecting and Interpreting Qualitative Materials*, edited by Norman K. Denzin and Yvonna S. Lincoln. Thousand Oaks, CA: Sage.

Holstein, James A., and Jaber F. Gubrium. 1995. *The Active Interview*. Thousand Oaks, CA: Sage.

Hondagneu-Sotelo, Pierrette. 1996. "Immigrant Women and Paid Domestic Work: Research, Theory, and Activism." Pp. 105–122 in *Feminism and Social Change: Bridging Theory and Practice*, edited by Heidi Gottfried. Urbana: University of Illinois Press.

Huberman, A. Michael, and Matthew B. Miles. 1998. "Data Management and Analysis Methods." Pp. 179–210 in *Collecting and Interpreting Qualitative Materials*, edited by Norman K. Denzin and Yvonna S. Lincoln. Thousand Oaks, CA: Sage.

Humphreys, Laud. 1970. *Tearoom Trade: Impersonal Sex in Public Places.* Chicago: Aldine.

Ignacio, Emily Noelle. 2000. "'Ain't I a Filipino (Woman)?' An Analysis of Authorship/Authority Through the Construction of 'Filipina' on the Net." *Sociological Quarterly* 41:551–572.

Janesick, Valerie. 1998. *"Stretching" Exercises for Qualitative Researchers.* Thousand Oaks, CA: Sage.

Janis, Irving. 1982. *Groupthink: Psychological Studies of Policy Decisions and Fiascoes.* Boston: Houghton Mifflin.

Jayaratne, Toby Epstein, and Abigail J. Stewart. 1991. "Quantitative and Qualitative Methods in the Social Sciences: Current Feminist Issues and Practical Strategies." Pp. 85–106 in *Beyond Methodology: Feminist Scholarship as Lived Research*, edited by Mary Margaret Fonow and Judith A. Cook. Bloomington: Indiana University Press.

Karp, David A. 1999. "Social Science, Progress, and the Ethnographer's Craft." *Journal of Contemporary Ethnography* 28:597–609.

Katz, Jack. 1996. "Families and Funny Mirrors: A Study of the Social Construction and Personal Embodiment of Humor." *American Journal of Sociology* 101:1194–1237.

Kendall, Lori. 2000. "'OH NO! I'M A NERD!' Hegemonic Masculinity on an Online Forum." *Gender & Society* 14:256–274.

Keough, Noel; Emman Carmona; and Linda Grandinetti. 1995. "Tales from the Sari-Sari: In Search of Bigfoot." *Convergence* 28(4):5–16.

Kincheloe, Joe L., and Peter L. McLaren. 1998. "Rethinking Critical Theory and Qualitative Research." Pp. 260–299 in *The Landscape of Qualitative Research: Theories and Issues*, edited by Norman K. Denzin and Yvonna S. Lincoln. Thousand Oaks, CA: Sage.

Kleinman, Sherryl. 1991. "Field-Workers' Feelings: What We Feel, Who We Are, How We Analyze." Pp. 184–195 in *Experiencing Fieldwork: An Inside View of Qualitative Research*. Newbury Park, CA: Sage.

Koester, Stephen. 1994. "Copping, Running, and Paraphernalia Laws: Contextual Variables and Needle Risk Behavior Among Injection Drug Users in Denver." *Human Organization* 53:287–295.

Kondo, Dorinne K. 1990. *Crafting Selves: Power, Gender, and Discourses of Identity in a Japanese Workplace.* Chicago: University of Chicago Press.

Kotamraju, Nalini P. 1999. "The Birth of Web Site Design Skills: Making the Present History." *American Behavioral Scientist* 43:464–475.

Krieger, Susan. 1983. *The Mirror Dance: Identity in a Women's Community.* Philadelphia: Temple University Press.

Krieger, Susan. 1991. *Social Science and the Self: Personal Essays on an Art Form.* New Brunswick, NJ: Rutgers University Press.

Johnson, Timothy P.; Michael Fendrich; Chitra Shaligram; Anthony Garcy; and Samuel Gillespie. 2000. "An Evaluation of the Effects of Interviewer Characteristics in an RDD Telephone Survey of Drug Use." *Journal of Drug Issues* 30:77–102.

Labov, William. 1978. "Crossing the Gulf Between Sociology and Linguistics." *American Sociologist* 13:93–103.

Lamott, Anne. 1995. *Bird by Bird: Some Instructions on Writing and Life.* New York: Anchor.

Lareau, Annette, and Jeffrey Schultz (eds.). 1996. *Journeys Through Ethnography: Realistic Accounts of Fieldwork.* Boulder, CO: Westview Press.

LaRossa, Ralph; Charles Jaret; Malati Gadgil; and G. Robert Wynn. 2000. "The Changing Culture of Fatherhood in Comic-Strip Families: A Six-Decade Analysis." *Journal of Marriage and the Family* 62:375–388.

Laslett, Barbara, and Barrie Thorne. 1997. *Feminist Sociology: Life Histories of a Movement.* New Brunswick, NJ: Rutgers University Press.

Leblanc, Lauraine. 2000. *Pretty in Punk: Girls' Gender Resistance in a Boys' Subculture.* New Brunswick, NJ: Rutgers University Press.

LeCompte, Margaret D., and Jean J. Schensul. 1999a. *Designing and Conducting Ethnographic Research.* Walnut Creek, CA: AltaMira Press.

LeCompte, Margaret D., and Jean J. Schensul. 1999b. *Analyzing and Interpreting Ethnographic Data.* Walnut Creek, CA: AltaMira Press.

Lee, Raymond M. 2000. *Unobtrusive Methods in Social Research.* Buckingham, England: Open University Press.

Lempert, Lora Bex. 1994. "A Narrative Analysis of Abuse." *Journal of Contemporary Ethnography* 22:411–441.

Lerner, Jennifer E., and Linda Kalof. 1999. "The Animal Text: Message and Meaning in Television Advertisements." *The Sociological Quarterly* 40: 565–586.

Liebow, Elliot. 1967. *Tally's Corner: A Study of Negro Streetcorner Men.* Boston: Little, Brown.

Liebow, Elliot. 1993. *Tell Them Who I Am: The Lives of Homeless Women.* New York: Penguin Books.

Lincoln, Yvonna S., and Norman K. Denzin. 2000. "The Seventh Moment: Out of the Past." Pp. 1047–1065 in *Handbook of Qualitative Research*, 2nd ed., edited by Norman K. Denzin and Yvonna S. Lincoln. Thousand Oaks, CA: Sage.

Lincoln, Yvonna S., and Egon Guba. 1985. *Naturalistic Inquiry.* Beverly Hills, CA: Sage.

Lincoln, Yvonna S., and Egon Guba. 2000. "Paradigmatic Controversies, Contradictions, and Emerging Confluences." Pp. 163–188 in *Handbook of Qualitative Research*, 2nd ed., edited by Norman K. Denzin and Yvonna S. Lincoln. Thousand Oaks, CA: Sage

Lofland, John, and Lyn H. Lofland. 1984. *Analyzing Social Settings,* 2nd ed. Belmont, CA: Wadsworth.

Lofland, John, and Lyn Lofland. 1995. *Analyzing Social Settings,* 3rd ed. Belmont, CA: Wadsworth.

Lofland, Lyn. 1985. *A World of Strangers: Order and Action in Urban Public Space.* Prospect Heights, IL: Waveland Press.

Lykes, M. Brinton. 1997. "Activist Participatory Research Among the Maya of Guatemala: Constructing Meanings from Situated Language." *Journal of Social Issues* 53:725–747.

Macdonald, Keith, and Colin Tipton. 1993. "Using Documents." Pp. 187–200 in *Researching Social Life*, edited by Nigel Gilbert. London: Sage.

MacDougall, Colin, and Frances Baum. 1997. "The Devil's Advocate: A Strategy to Avoid Groupthink and Stimulate Discussion in Focus Groups." *Qualitative Health Research* 7:532–540.

Madriz, Esther I. 1998. "Using Focus Groups with Lower Socioeconomic Status Latina Women." *Qualitative Inquiry* 4:114–129.

Madriz, Esther. 2000. "Focus Groups in Feminist Research." Pp. 835–850 in *Handbook of Qualitative Research*, 2nd ed., edited by Norman K. Denzin and Yvonna S. Lincoln. Thousand Oaks, CA: Sage.

Manning, Peter K., and Betsy Cullum-Swan. 1998. "Narrative, Content, and Semiotic Analysis." Pp. 246–273 in *Collecting and Interpreting Qualitative Materials*, edited by Norman K. Denzin and Yvonna S. Lincoln. Thousand Oaks, CA: Sage.

Marcenko, Maureen O., and Linda Samost. 1999. "Living with HIV/AIDS: The Voices of HIV-Positive Mothers." *Social Work* 44:36–45.

Marcus, George. 1998. "What Comes (Just) After 'Post'? The Case of Ethnography." Pp. 383–406 in *The Landscape of Qualitative Research: Theories and Issues*, edited by Norman K. Denzin and Yvonna S. Lincoln. Thousand Oaks, CA: Sage.

Masuda, Kazuyo. 1998. "Cockroaches and Cops: Women Struggling in an Urban Section 8 Housing Complex." Unpublished M.A. thesis, University of Missouri–Kansas City.

McAdams, Dan P. 1993. *The Stories We Live By: Personal Myths and the Making of the Self*. New York: Guilford Press.

McNeil, Larry B. 1995. "The Soft Arts of Organizing." *Social Policy* 26:16–22.

McNicoll, Paule. 1999. "Issues in Teaching Participatory Action Research." *Journal of Social Work Education* 35:51–62.

Miles, Matthew B., and A. Michael Huberman. 1994. *Qualitative Data Analysis: An Expanded Sourcebook*. Thousand Oaks, CA: Sage.

Milgram, Stanley. 1974. *Obedience to Authority*. New York: Harper & Row.

Miller, Neil. 1995. *Out of the Past: Gay and Lesbian History from 1869 to the Present*. New York: Vintage Books.

Mishler, Elliot G. 1991. "Representing Discourse: The Rhetoric of Transcription." *Journal of Narrative and Life History* 1:255–280.

Mitchell, Richard G., Jr. 1991. "Secrecy and Disclosure in Fieldwork." Pp. 97–108 in *Experiencing Fieldwork: An Inside View of Qualitative Research*. Newbury Park, CA: Sage.

Mitchell, Richard G. 1993. *Secrecy and Fieldwork*. Newbury Park, CA: Sage.

Moen, Phyllis. 1989. *Working Parents: Transformations in Gender Roles and Public Policies in Sweden*. Madison: University of Wisconsin Press.

Montell, Frances. 1999. "Focus Group Interviews: A New Feminist Method." *NWSA Journal* 11:44–71.

Montini, Theresa. 1996. "Gender and Emotion in the Advocacy for Breast Cancer Informed Consent Legislation." *Gender & Society* 10:9–23.

Morgan, David L. 1988. *Focus Groups as Qualitative Research.* Newbury Park, CA: Sage.

Morgan, David L. 1995. "Why Things (Sometimes) Go Wrong in Focus Groups." *Qualitative Health Research* 5:516–524.

Morgan, David L. 1996. "Focus Groups." *Annual Review of Sociology* 22:129–153.

Morse, Janice M. 1998. "The Contracted Relationship: Ensuring Protection of Anonymity and Confidentiality." *Qualitative Health Research* 8:301–304.

Morse, Janice M. 1998. "Designing Funded Qualitative Research." Pp. 56–85 in *Strategies of Qualitative Inquiry*, edited by Norman K. Denzin and Yvonna S. Lincoln. Thousand Oaks, CA: Sage.

Naples, Nancy A., with Emily Clark. 1996. "Feminist Participatory Research and Empowerment: Going Public as Survivors of Childhood Sexual Abuse." Pp. 160–183 in *Feminism and Social Change: Bridging Theory and Practice*, edited by Heidi Gottfried. Urbana: University of Illinois Press.

Neuman, W. Lawrence. 1994. *Social Research Methods*, 2nd ed. Boston: Allyn & Bacon.

Neutens, James J., and Laura Rubinson. 1997. *Research Techniques for the Health Sciences*, 2nd ed. Boston: Allyn & Bacon.

Nielsen, Joyce McCarl. 1990. *Feminist Research Methods: Exemplary Readings in the Social Sciences.* Boulder, CO: Westview Press.

Oakley, Ann. 1981. "Interviewing Women: A Contradiction in Terms." Pp. 30–61 in *Doing Feminist Research*, edited by Helen Roberts. London: Routledge & Kegan Paul.

Park, Robert E. *On Social Control and Collective Behavior.* Chicago: University of Chicago Press, 1967.

Patton, Michael Quinn. 1990. *Qualitative Evaluation and Research Methods*, 2nd ed. Newbury Park, CA: Sage.

Plummer, Ken. 1995. *Telling Sexual Stories.* London: Routledge.

Plummer, Ken. 1999. "The 'Ethnographic Society' at Century's End." *Journal of Contemporary Ethnography* 28:641–649.

Posavac, Emil J., and Raymond G. Carey. 1997. *Program Evaluation: Methods and Case Studies*, 5th ed. Upper Saddle River, NJ: Prentice Hall.

Presser, Stanley, and Linda Stinson. 1998. "Data Collection Mode and Social Desirability Bias in Self-Reported Religious Attendance." *American Sociological Review* 63:137–145.

Punch, Maurice. 1998. "Politics and Ethics in Qualitative Research." Pp. 156–184 in *The Landscape of Qualitative Research*, edited by Norman K. Denzin and Yvonna S. Lincoln. Thousand Oaks, CA: Sage.

Ragin, Charles C. 1994. *Constructing Social Research*. Thousand Oaks, CA: Pine Forge Press.

Rathje, William. 1992. "How Much Alcohol Do We Drink? It's a Question . . . So to Speak." *Garbage* 4(1):18–19.

Rathje, William. 1993. "Less Fat? Aw, Baloney." *Garbage* 5(4):22–23.

Rathje, William, and Cullen Murphy. 1992. "Garbage Demographics." *American Demographics* 14:50–55.

Reinharz, Shulamit. 1992. *Feminist Methods in Social Research*. New York: Oxford University Press.

Richards, Thomas J., and Lyn Richards. 1998. "Using Computers in Qualitative Research." Pp. 211–245 in *Collecting and Interpreting Qualitative Materials*, edited by Norman K. Denzin and Yvonna S. Lincoln. Thousand Oaks, CA: Sage.

Richardson, James T. 1991. "Experiencing Research on New Religions and Cults: Practical and Ethical Considerations." Pp. 62–71 in *Experiencing Fieldwork: An Inside View of Qualitative Research*, edited by William B. Shaffir and Robert A. Stebbins. Newbury Park, CA: Sage.

Richardson, Laurel. 1992. "The Consequences of Poetic Representation: Writing the Other, Rewriting the Self." Pp. 125–140 in *Investigating Subjectivity: Research on Lived Experience*, edited by C. Ellis and M. G. Flaherty. Newbury Park, CA: Sage.

Richardson, Laurel. 2000. "Writing: A Method of Inquiry." Pp. 923–948 in *Handbook of Qualitative Research*, 2nd ed., edited by Norman K. Denzin and Yvonna S. Lincoln. Thousand Oaks, CA: Sage.

Riessman, Catherine Kohler. 1993. *Narrative Analysis*. Thousand Oaks, CA: Sage.

Ronai, Carol R. 1992. "The Reflexive Self Through Narrative: A Night in the Life of an Erotic Dancer/Researcher." Pp. 102–124 of *Investigating Subjectivity: Research on Lived Experience*, edited by C. Ellis and M. G. Flaherty. Newbury Park, CA: Sage.

Rosie, Anthony. 1993. "'He's a Liar, I'm Afraid': Truth and Lies in a Narrative Account." *Sociology* 27:144–152.

Rutter, Jason, and Greg Smith. 1999. "Presence and Absence in Virtual Ethnography." Paper presented at the annual meeting of the American Sociological Association, Chicago.

Ryan, Gery, and Thomas Weisner. 1996. "Analyzing Words in Brief Descriptions: Fathers and Mothers Describe Their Children." *Cultural Anthropology Methods* 8(3):13–16.

Sacks, Harvey. 1974. "On the Analysability of Stories by Children." Pp. 216–232 of *Ethnomethodology*, edited by Roy Turner. Baltimore: Penguin Education.

Sanders, Clinton R. 1989. "Organizational Constraints on Tattoo Images: A Sociological Analysis of Artistic Style." Pp. 232–241 in *The Meanings of Things: Material Culture and Symbolic Expression*, edited by Ian Hodder. London: Unwin Hyman.

Scarce, Rik. 1995. "Scholarly Ethics and Courtroom Antics: Where Researchers Stand in the Eyes of the Law." *American Sociologist* 95: 87–113.

Schegloff, Emmanuel. 1997. "'Narrative Analysis': Thirty Years Later." *Journal of Narrative and Life History* 7:97–106.

Schegloff, Emmanuel, and Harvey Sacks. 1974. "Opening Up Closings." Pp. 233–264 in *Ethnomethodology*, edited by Roy Turner. Middlesex, England: Penguin Books.

Schensul, Stephen L.; Jean J. Schensul; and Margaret D. LeCompte. 1999. *Essential Ethnographic Methods: Observations, Interviews, and Questionnaires.* Walnut Creek, CA: AltaMira Press.

Schiffman, Josepha. 1991. "'Fight the Power': Two Groups Mobilize for Peace." Pp. 58–79 in *Ethnography Unbound: Power and Resistance in the Modern Metropolis*, by Michael Burawoy et al. Berkeley: University of California Press.

Seidman, Irving. 1998. *Interviewing as Qualitative Research: A Guide for Researchers in Education and the Social Sciences*, 2nd ed. New York: Teachers College Press.

Shaffir, William. 1991. "Managing a Convincing Self-Presentation: Some Personal Reflections on Entering the Field." Pp. 72–81 in *Experiencing Fieldwork: An Inside View of Qualitative Research*, edited by William B. Shaffir and Robert A. Stebbins. Newbury Park, CA: Sage.

Shaffir, William, and Robert Stebbins. 1991. *Experiencing Fieldwork: An Inside View of Qualitative Research.* Newbury Park, CA: Sage.

Shuster, Evelyne. 1998. "The Nuremberg Code: Hippocratic Ethics and Human Rights." *Lancet* 351:974–978.

Sia, Ah-hiok. 2000. *A Study of International Students' Networks.* Unpublished Ph.D. dissertation, University of Missouri–Kansas City.

Small, Stephen A. 1995. "Action-Oriented Research: Models and Methods." *Journal of Marriage and the Family* 57:941–956.

Smith, Dorothy. 1987. "Women's Perspective as a Radical Critique of Sociology." Pp. 84–96 in *Feminism and Methodology*, edited by Sandra Harding. Bloomington: Indiana University Press.

Smith, Louis M. 1998. "Biographical Method." Pp. 184–224 in *Strategies of Qualitative Inquiry*, edited by Norman K. Denzin & Yvonna S. Lincoln. Thousand Oaks, CA: Sage.

Smith, Phil. 1999. "Food Truck's Party Hat." *Qualitative Inquiry* 5:244–261.

Sociology Writing Group. 1991. *A Guide to Writing Sociology Papers*, 2nd ed. New York: St. Martin's Press.

Sohrabi, Nader. "Historicizing Revolutions: Constitutional Revolutions in the Ottoman Empire, Iran, and Russia, 1905–1908." *American Journal of Sociology* 100:1383–1447.

Stacey, Judith. 1991. *Brave New Families: Stories of Domestic Upheaval in Late Twentieth Century America.* New York: Basic Books.

Stacey, Judith. 1996. "Can There Be a Feminist Ethnography?" Pp. 88–101 in *Feminism and Social Change: Bridging Theory and Practice*, edited by Heidi Gottfried. Urbana: University of Illinois Press.

Stack, Carol. 1974. *All Our Kin: Strategies for Survival in a Black Community.* New York: Harper & Row.

Stack, Carol. 1996. "Writing Ethnography: Feminist Critical Practice." Pp. 96–106 in *Feminist Dilemmas in Fieldwork,* edited by Diane L. Wolf. Boulder, CO: Westview.

Steinberg, Ronnie J. 1996. "Advocacy Research for Feminist Policy Objectives: Experiences with Comparable Worth." Pp. 225–255 in *Feminism and Social Change: Bridging Theory and Practice,* edited by Heidi Gottfried. Urbana: University of Illinois Press.

Stoecker, Randy. 1999. "Are Academics Irrelevant? Roles for Scholars in Participatory Research." *American Behavioral Scientist* 42:840–844.

Strauss, Anselm, and Juliet Corbin. 1990. *Basics of Qualitative Research: Grounded Theory Procedures and Techniques.* Newbury Park, CA: Sage.

Strauss, Anselm, and Juliet Corbin. 1998. "Grounded Theory Methodology: An Overview." Pp. 158–183 in *Strategies of Qualitative Inquiry,* edited by Norman K. Denzin and Yvonna S. Lincoln. Thousand Oaks, CA: Sage.

Stringer, Ernest T. 1996. *Action Research: A Handbook for Practitioners.* Thousand Oaks, CA: Sage.

Tewksbury, Richard, and Patricia Gagne. 1997. "Assumed and Presumed Identities: Problems of Self-Presentation in Field Research." *Sociological Spectrum* 17:127–156.

Theophano, Janet, and Karen Curtis. 1996. "Reflections on a Tale Told Twice." Pp. 151–176 in *Journeys Through Ethnography: Realistic Accounts of Fieldwork,* edited by Annette Lareau and Jeffrey Schultz. Boulder, CO: Westview Press.

Thompson, Sharon. 1995. *Going All the Way: Teenage Girls' Tales of Sex, Romance, and Pregnancy.* New York: Hill & Wang.

Thorne, Barrie. 1993. *Gender Play: Girls and Boys in School.* New Brunswick, NJ: Rutgers University Press.

Tuchman, Gaye. 1998. "Historical Social Science: Methodologies, Methods, and Meanings." Pp. 225–260 in *Strategies of Qualitative Inquiry,* edited by Norman K. Denzin and Yvonna S. Lincoln. Thousand Oaks, CA: Sage.

Viditch, Arthur J., and Stanford M. Lyman. 2000. "Qualitative Methods: Their History in Sociology and Anthropology." Pp. 37–84 in *Handbook of Qualitative Research,* 2nd ed., edited by Norman K. Denzin and Yvonna S. Lincoln. Thousand Oaks, CA: Sage.

Walters, Ian. 1997. "Vietnam Zippos." *Journal of Material Culture* 2:61–75.

Walzer, Susan. 1998. *Thinking About the Baby: Gender and Transitions into Parenthood.* Philadelphia: Temple University Press.

Webb, Eugene J.; Donald T. Campbell; Richard Schwartz; Lee Sechrest; and Janet Belew Grove. 1981. *Nonreactive Measures in the Social Sciences,* 2nd ed. Boston: Houghton Mifflin.

Werner, Oswald, and Mark G. Schoepfle. 1987. *Systematic Fieldwork: Ethnographic Analysis and Data Management,* Volume 2. Newbury Park, CA: Sage.

Whittier, Nancy. 1995. *Feminist Generations: The Persistence of the Radical Women's Movement.* Philadelphia: Temple University Press.

Whyte, William Foote. 1943. *Street Corner Society.* Chicago: University of Chicago Press.

Whyte, William Foote. 1991. "The Social Sciences in the University." *American Behavioral Scientist* 34:618–634.

Whyte, William Foote. 1995. "Learning from the Mondragon Cooperative Experience." *Studies in Comparative International Development* 30:58–68.

Whyte, William Foote. 1996. "Qualitative Sociology and Deconstructionism." *Qualitative Inquiry* 2:220–226.

Whyte, William Foote. 1999. "The Mondragon Cooperatives in 1976 and 1998." *Industrial & Labor Relations Review* 52:478–481.

Whyte, William Foote. 1993. *Street Corner Society,* 4th ed. Chicago: University of Chicago Press

Wolcott, Harry F. 1990. *Writing Up Qualitative Research.* Newbury Park, CA: Sage.

Wolcott, Harry F. 1999. *Ethnography: A Way of Seeing.* Walnut Creek, CA: AltaMira Press.

Wolf, Daniel R. 1991. "High-Risk Methodology: Reflections on Leaving an Outlaw Society." Pp. 211–223 in *Experiencing Fieldwork: An Inside View of Qualitative Research.* Newbury Park, CA: Sage.

Wolf, Diane L. (ed.). 1996. *Feminist Dilemmas in Fieldwork.* Boulder, CO: Westview Press.

Zavella, Patricia. 1987. *Women's Work and Chicano Families: Cannery Workers of the Santa Clara Valley.* Ithaca, NY: Cornell University Press.

Zavella, Patricia. 1996. "Feminist Insider Dilemmas: Constructing Ethnic Identity with Chicana Informants." Pp. 138–159 in *Feminist Dilemmas in Fieldwork,* edited by Diane L. Wolf. Boulder, CO: Westview.

Index

Abbott, Edith, 8
abstract
  in narrative analysis,
    183–184, 193
  of research report,
    207–208
access to field sites, 65–67,
  81
accretion, measures of, 116
Action Research (Stringer),
  150
Active Interview, The (Holstein and Gubrium),
  113
action research
  defined, 34
  barriers to participation
    in, 143
  defining an agenda for
    action in, 145–146
  ethical issues in, 148–149
  feminist, 139–140
  formulating a collective
    problem in, 144
  in industry, 138
  northern and southern
    traditions in, 143
  political nature of,
    137–138
  process of, 142–146
  purpose of, 135–137
  sharing power in,
    147–148
  types of, 137
  See also participatory
    action research (PAR)
Addams, Jane, 8, 19

Adler, Patricia, 61, 68, 69,
  72
Adler, Peter, 61, 68, 69, 72
Alinsky, Saul, 147
All Our Kin (Stack), 24
American Psychological
  Association, 44
American Sociological Association, 44–45, 206,
  218, 221
American Sociological Association Code of Ethics,
  221–233
analytic bracketing, 188
Analyzing Social Settings
  (Lofland and Lofland),
  82
anthropology, 8
archival materials, 130–132
Atkinson, Paul, 158, 166,
  180, 197
ATLAS.ti, 178
autoethnography, 59

*Basics of Qualitative
  Research* (Strauss and
  Corbin), 180
Becker, Bettina, 186, 197
Becker, Howard, 23, 175,
  180, 218
Berg, Bruce, 111
bias
  in research settings, 32
  in historical materials,
    132
  in interviews, 86
  in media accounts, 124

  in Web sites, 39
  social desirability, 86
Bird by Bird (Lamott), 219
Blee, Kathleen, 47
Boas, Franz, 8
body language, 103, 105.
  See also nonverbal
  communication
Boys in White (Becker et al.),
  23
Brave New Families
  (Stacey), 24
Breckenridge, Sophonisba, 8
Britton, Dana, 84
Brown, L. David, 143
Burawoy, Michael, 9, 23, 82
Buxtun, Peter, 46

Campbell, Donald, 134
Cancian, Francesca, 149
Carey, Raymond, 150
Carmona, Emman, 138
cases, comparing, 168–169
causation, 10
cautionary tales, 188,
  190–191
Census Bureau, U.S., 122
chain referral sampling,
  93–94
Chapkis, Wendy, 55
Chataway, Cynthia, 147
Chicago School, 8, 23
coda, 184, 193
code memos. *See* memos,
  procedural
codes of ethics, 44–45,
  221–233